Microsoft® 365 Word For Professionals

2nd Edition

by Dan Gookin

Microsoft® 365 Word® For Professionals For Dummies®, 2nd Edition

Published by: **John Wiley & Sons, Inc.**, 111 River Street, Hoboken, NJ 07030-5774, www.wiley.com

For general information on our other products and services, please contact our Customer Care Department within the U.S. at 877-762-2974, outside the U.S. at 317-572-3993, or fax 317-572-4002. For technical support, please visit https://hub.wiley.com/community/support/dummies.

Wiley publishes in a variety of print and electronic formats and by print-on-demand. Some material included with standard print versions of this book may not be included in e-books or in print-on-demand. If this book refers to media such as a CD or DVD that is not included in the version you purchased, you may download this material at http://booksupport.wiley.com. For more information about Wiley products, visit www.wiley.com.

Library of Congress Control Number: 2025934400

ISBN 978-1-394-32386-9 (pbk); ISBN 978-1-394-32388-3 (ebk); ISBN 978-1-394-32387-6 (ebk)

SKY10100822_032425

Contents at a Glance

Introduction 1

Part 1: Fancy Formatting and Froufrou 5

CHAPTER 1: Font Fun 7

CHAPTER 2: Paragraph and Page Preparation 25

CHAPTER 3: Terrific Tables 45

CHAPTER 4: Styles and Templates 61

Part 2: Go Graphical 75

CHAPTER 5: Text and Graphics Layout 77

CHAPTER 6: Shapes and Drawings 89

CHAPTER 7: Pretty Pictures 107

CHAPTER 8: Insert Objects Weird and Amazing 121

Part 3: Word at Work 133

CHAPTER 9: Beyond Routine Documents 135

CHAPTER 10: Document Formats and Printer Control 151

CHAPTER 11: Collaboration and Sharing 165

CHAPTER 12: Word for Lawyers 181

CHAPTER 13: Document Security 193

CHAPTER 14: Final Document Preparation and Review 207

Part 4: Word for Writers 225

CHAPTER 15: Tools for Every Author 227

CHAPTER 16: From Brainstorm to Outline 243

CHAPTER 17: Humongous Documents 257

CHAPTER 18: Document References 267

CHAPTER 19: eBook Publishing 285

Part 5: Document Automation 297

CHAPTER 20: AutoCorrect, AutoText, and AutoFormat 299

CHAPTER 21: Document Fields 311

CHAPTER 22: The Big Macro Picture 323

CHAPTER 23: Dynamic Templates with Content Controls 337

Part 6: The Part of Tens 349

CHAPTER 24: Ten Ways to Customize Word 351

CHAPTER 25: Ten Ways to Solve Word Problems 367

Index 379

Table of Contents

INTRODUCTION 1

About This Book. 1
Foolish Assumptions. 2
Icons Used in This Book 3
Beyond the Book. 3
Where to Go from Here 4

PART 1: FANCY FORMATTING AND FROUFROU 5

CHAPTER 1: **Font Fun** 7

A Knowledge of Fonts 7
Describing text. 8
Understanding text attributes 9
Choosing the best typeface 11
Dashing about 12
Typography Control 13
Changing text scale. 13
Setting character spacing. 14
Adding kerning and ligatures. 15
Adjusting text position 16
Text Effects Strange and Wonderful. 18
Accessing the Format Text Effects pane. 18
Changing text fill 19
Setting a text outline. 21
Adding a text shadow 22
Configuring text reflection and glow 23

CHAPTER 2: **Paragraph and Page Preparation** 25

To Hyphenate or Not 25
Adding a manual hyphen. 26
Automatically hyphenating text 27
Inserting an unbreakable hyphen. 28
Numbered Lists 28
Numbering paragraphs 28
Adjusting numbering indents 30
Skipping paragraph numbers 31
Restarting numbered paragraphs. 32
Numbering paragraphs starting at a specific value 32
Creating custom paragraph numbers .33

Widow and Orphan Control 34
Professional Headers and Footers 35
    Building a header 35
    Switching between the header and footer 36
    Typing text in a header 36
    Adding page numbers 37
    Placing objects in the header 39
    Resetting the header position 39
    Working with headers in sections 40
    Creating odd and even headers 41
    Removing a header 43

CHAPTER 3: Terrific Tables 45
Cobble Together a Table 45
Table Editing 46
    Working with text in a table 46
    Selecting items within a table 47
    Inserting or removing rows or columns 48
    Merging and splitting cells 49
    Setting the table size 51
    Adjusting row and column size 51
Make a Table Less Obnoxious 53
    Adding a table heading 53
    Aligning text 53
    Setting text direction 54
    Setting gridlines 55
    Applying instant table formats 55
Some Table Tricks 56
    Sorting a table 56
    Splitting a table between two pages 58
    Applying table math 59

CHAPTER 4: Styles and Templates 61
Style Management 61
    Selecting instances of a style 63
    Setting the heading style outline level 64
    Stealing a style from another document 66
Templates of Your Own 67
    Creating a custom template 68
    Building an envelope template 69
    Modifying a template 71
    Updating template documents 72
    Reassigning templates 74

PART 2: GO GRAPHICAL 75

CHAPTER 5: **Text and Graphics Layout** 77

Where Text and Graphics Meet. 77
    Finding non-text things to thrust into a document 78
    Mixing text and objects. 79

Layout Choices. 80
    Setting layout options. 80
    Using the inline option 82
    Wrapping text around an object 82
    Editing the wrap points. 83
    Setting the image's position. 85
    Floating an object in front of or behind text 86
    Aligning objects on a page 87

CHAPTER 6: **Shapes and Drawings** 89

Get Into Shapes 89
    Inserting a shape. 90
    Drawing a freeform shape 91
    Changing a shape's position 92
    Resizing a shape 93
    Rotating a shape 94
    Setting colors, line styles, and effects. 95
    Changing a shape's shape 97

Multiple Shape Mania. 99
    Arranging shapes in front or behind .99
    Aligning shapes 100
    Grouping multiple shapes 102

Text and Pictures Inside Shapes 103
    Creating a text box 103
    Linking text boxes 105
    Framing a picture in a shape 105

CHAPTER 7: **Pretty Pictures** 107

One Thousand Words. 108
    Adding an image from your computer. 108
    Copying and pasting an image 109
    Replacing an image 110

Image Adjustment. 110
    Cropping an image 110
    Removing the background. 112
    Making corrections 114
    Adjusting the image's color 115
    Adding artistic effects 115
    Restoring an image (removing effects). 116

Picture Framing 116
    Selecting a frame style 116
    Adding a border 117
    Applying a picture effect 118
Caption That Picture 118

CHAPTER 8: Insert Objects Weird and Amazing 121
More Than Plain Text 121
    Adding SmartArt 122
    Inserting a whole 'nuther Word document 123
    Summing up equations 124
Where Word Meets Excel 125
    Pasting part of an Excel worksheet into a document 125
    Copying and linking a worksheet 127
    Creating an Excel worksheet inside of Word 129
    Whipping up a chart 130

PART 3: WORD AT WORK 133

CHAPTER 9: Beyond Routine Documents 135
Cover Pages 135
    Designing a custom cover page 136
    Resetting page numbering 137
    Centering a page from top to bottom .139
    Using text boxes for titles 140
Word's Phony Watermarks 142
    Adding a preset watermark 142
    Customizing the watermark 143
    Printing background objects 144
Document Tricks 145
    Setting a page border 145
    Placing the document's filename in a header or footer 146
    Printing for three-ring binding 147
    Accessing document properties 148

CHAPTER 10: Document Formats and Printer Control 151
Documents Formats Strange and Alien 152
    Understanding document formats 152
    Saving a Word document in another format 153
    Creating a PDF 155
Open Strange Document Formats 157
    Choosing a specific document format .157
    Recovering text from any old file 158

Printer Tricks 160
    Printing multiple copies 160
    Printing on both sides of a sheet of paper 160
    Printing multiple pages per sheet. 162
    Formatting multiple pages per sheet 163

CHAPTER 11: Collaboration and Sharing 165
  Here Are My Thoughts 166
    Highlighting text. 166
    Inserting a comment. 167
    Reviewing comments 168
    Showing and hiding comments. 169
  Look What They Did! 169
    Activating the Track Changes feature. 170
    Locking the changes 171
    Showing or hiding the revision marks 171
    Accepting or rejecting changes 172
    Comparing two versions of a document 173
  Online Collaboration. 176
    Sending out invitations. 176
    Working together on a document. 178
    Ending collaboration. 179

CHAPTER 12: Word for Lawyers 181
  Line Numbers on the Page. 182
    Adding line numbers. 182
    Formatting line numbers 183
    Removing line numbers 184
  The Table of Authorities. 184
    Marking citations. 184
    Inserting the table of authorities. 186
  Other Legal Considerations. 188
    Setting a left-right block indent 188
    Redacting text 189

CHAPTER 13: Document Security 193
  Warnings Galore! 193
  The Trust Center 195
    Visiting the Trust Center. 195
    Setting trusted locations. 196
    Removing the downloaded documents restriction 197
    Controlling macro security. 198
    Unblocking certain file types 198

Document Protection 200
  Setting text-editing restrictions 200
  Marking a document as "final" 202
  Adding a password to your document 203
  Removing the password 204

CHAPTER 14: **Final Document Preparation and Review** 207
  Some AI Assistance 207
    Finding Copilot in Word 208
    Working the Copilot pane 208
    Writing that first draft 209
    Rewriting some text 211
    Adding an AI image 212
    Summarizing your document 213
  Document Inspection 214
    Finding things you forget 214
    Sizing up your writing 216
    Checking accessibility 217
    Reviewing document compatibility 219
  Document Recovery 220
    Activating automatic backup 220
    Viewing an older version of your document 221
    Searching for lost documents 222

PART 4: WORD FOR WRITERS 225

CHAPTER 15: **Tools for Every Author** 227
  Behold! The Document Window 227
    Showing or hiding the Ribbon 228
    Setting the document view 228
    Adding useful panes 229
    Controlling the status bar 230
  Count Your Words 231
    Checking the word count 232
    Inserting the current word count into your document 233
  Document Proofing 233
    Disabling on-the-fly proofing 234
    Proofing your document manually 235
    Adding a word to your personal dictionary 236
    Undoing an ignore proofing command 237
    Adjusting grammar checking sensitivity .238
  Tools for a Wordsmith 238
    Choosing a better word 239
    Translating some text 240
    Ignoring a span of foreign language text 241

CHAPTER 16: **From Brainstorm to Outline** 243

The Outline Thing 243
Word's Outline View 244
    Activating Outline view 245
    Exploring the Outlining tab 245
    Using heading styles 246
Outline Construction. 246
    Creating top-level topics. 246
    Moving topics. 247
    Demoting or promoting a topic. 248
    Moving topics and subtopics in groups .250
    Adding narrative 251
Outline Presentation. 252
    Collapsing and expanding outline topics. 252
    Printing the outline 253
    Using the navigation pane 254

CHAPTER 17: **Humongous Documents** 257

Write That Novel!. 257
    Building one long manuscript 258
    Writing one chapter per document 259
    Collecting chapters into a final document. 260
One Long Manuscript 261
    Bookmarking your text. 261
    Showing the bookmarks. 262
    Visiting a bookmark. 262
    Removing a bookmark 263
    Splitting the window 264
    Opening a second window. 265

CHAPTER 18: **Document References** 267

Table of Contents 268
    Inserting a TOC 268
    Updating the TOC 270
Footnotes and Endnotes 271
    Adding a footnote 271
    Creating an endnote 272
    Working with notes 273
    Setting note options 273
    Converting between footnotes and endnotes 274
Citations and the Bibliography 275
    Creating citations. 275
    Building the bibliography. 276

Figure Captions 277
Cross-References. 278
The Index 279
    Marking entries for the index 280
    Inserting the index 282
    Updating the index 283

CHAPTER 19: **eBook Publishing** 285
The eBook Process 285
    Writing the manuscript. 286
    Formatting your eBook document 287
    Using pictures or graphics .288
    Creating hyperlinks 289
    Adding document references 291
eBook Publishing Tips. 291
    Titling your tome 291
    Generating a cover 292
    Finding a publisher 293
    Previewing the final eBook. 294
    Setting the price. 294
    Marketing your eBook 295

PART 5: DOCUMENT AUTOMATION 297

CHAPTER 20: **AutoCorrect, AutoText, and AutoFormat** 299
Know Your Autos. 299
AutoCorrect the Boo-Boos. 301
    Working with AutoCorrect capitalization settings. 302
    Replacing typos 303
    Undoing an AutoCorrect change. 304
AutoFormat As You Type 305
    Reviewing the AutoFormat options 305
    Undoing an AutoFormat change. 307
Instant Typing with AutoText Building Blocks. 308
    Creating an AutoText building block. 309
    Reviewing your building blocks. 310

CHAPTER 21: **Document Fields** 311
Field Philosophy. 311
    Inserting a field 312
    Working with fields behind the scenes. 313
    Updating a field 314
    Finding fields in a document 314

Field Cookbook 315
    Inserting page number fields. 316
    Using date-and-time fields. 318
    Adding document info fields 319
    Echoing text in a field 321

CHAPTER 22: The Big Macro Picture. 323
Behold the Developer Tab 324
Word Macro 101 325
    Understanding macros. 325
    Recording a macro 326
    Running a macro 329
    Deleting a macro 330
Quick Macro Access 331
    Assigning a macro to a Quick Access toolbar button. 331
    Creating a macro keyboard shortcut 333
The Joys of Macro-Enabled Documents. 334
    Saving macros with the current document 335
    Creating a macro-enabled template. 335

CHAPTER 23: Dynamic Templates with Content Controls 337
The World of Content Controls 338
    Inserting a content control. 338
    Changing the content control view. 339
    Setting a content control's properties 340
    Deleting a content control 341
    Deleting a content control but not its contents 342
Useful Content Controls. 342
    Setting up a fill-in-the-blanks item 343
    Adding a multiline text field. 344
    Inserting an image. 345
    Selecting a date 346
    Building a drop-down list 347

PART 6: THE PART OF TENS. 349

CHAPTER 24: Ten Ways to Customize Word 351
Showing Special Characters. 351
Controlling Text Selection 353
Setting Text-Pasting Options 353
Disabling Annoying Features. 355
Specifying the Default Document Folder. 356

Altering Word's Appearance 356
    Showing the ruler 356
    Revealing the scrollbars 357
Customizing the Quick Access Toolbar 357
Building a Custom Tab on the Ribbon 359
Assigning a keyboard shortcut to a command 361
Setting a Symbol's Shortcut Key 363

CHAPTER 25: **Ten Ways to Solve Word Problems** 367
Your First Solution..367
Lost Documents..368
Lines You Can't Remove 369
Formatting Mysteries Revealed.............................371
An Extra, Blank Page Prints 371
The Document Needs a-Fixin' 372
The Normal Template is Broken 373
Word Startup Mode...374
Word Has a Safe Mode......................................376
The Office Repair Utility 377

INDEX...379

Introduction

Welcome to *Microsoft 365 Word For Professionals For Dummies*, a clever name given to a book that's really about oppressed workers in Asia who hand-place sesame seeds on hamburger buns. I'm not serious, of course. I'm just checking to see whether you're actually reading this introduction.

This book goes way beyond the beginner's user level when it comes to word processing with Microsoft Word. The subject matter isn't technical but rather geared toward professionals or anyone who is serious about the words they write. Microsoft Word is a powerful program, and few people venture into its more sophisticated levels. That's sad because many of Word's features can save you time and help you create a better document.

About This Book

Are you still reading the introduction? That's really weird. Most people don't even bother. In fact, they take the copy of this book that they illegally downloaded, grab the information they want, and then go on Facebook and lament how the economy is crumbling. I love that story.

Still, I'm proud of you for continuing to read this introduction. Truly, it's the best part of the book. That's because this is where I explain how this book covers a lot of material not found anywhere else. Google? Forget it. I've looked. The people (or robots) who put "help" up on Google don't know what they're talking about. If you really want to understand Word and create outstanding documents, you have the best resource in your hands right now.

This book is a reference. It's designed to cover a topic quickly and let you get back to work. Each chapter covers a topic, and major sections within the chapter go into detail. Within each section are specific activities, complete with steps or further instructions that help you accomplish a task. Sample sections in this book include

>> Adding a text shadow

>> Splitting a table between two pages

- » Wrapping text around an object

- » Opening an Excel worksheet inside of Word

- » Creating a PDF

- » Setting text-editing restrictions

- » Marketing your eBooks

- » Creating an AutoText building block

- » Recording a macro

The topics covered are vast, but you don't have anything to memorize. Information is cross-referenced. Technical tidbits are carefully shoved to the end of a section or enclosed in a box. Though it would be great to master all that Word offers, my sense is that you prefer to find out only what you need to know and then get back to your work.

Foolish Assumptions

This book assumes that you have a basic knowledge of Word. You know how the program works, and you've created crude and ugly documents. Perhaps you didn't believe them to be crude and ugly, but they are. And that's why you purchased this book, because you want to create more professional, respectable documents.

You are using Microsoft 365, which is an online subscription service that includes the Microsoft Word application. The text also applies to older versions of Word, though some of the command names and icons have changed. In fact, as Microsoft 365 is continuously updated, some of the material in this book may not match exactly what you see on the screen.

This book mentions the Copilot artificial intelligence (AI) tool that adds certain features to Word. Obtaining Copilot requires an additional subscription. Where Copilot affects Word and can improve your writing is covered throughout this book.

This book does not cover Word for the Macintosh. If you see an Apple logo on your computer, I can't promise that anything in this text applies to your computer setup.

If you need more basic information on Word, I can recommend *Microsoft Word For Dummies* (Wiley). That book covers material deemed too basic or common for this book, though it's still good material. For example, that book covers mail merge, which this book shuns like that steaming pan of gray goo at the back of an all-you-can-eat five-dollar buffet.

Icons Used in This Book

Festooning this book's pages are icons. These consist of the traditional four *For Dummies* margin icons. They are:

TIP

This icon flags a useful suggestion or kindhearted tip. I'd like to think of all text in this book as a tip, but my editor dislikes it when I overuse the Tip icon. So only the very bestest tips are flagged.

REMEMBER

This icon appears by text that gives you a friendly reminder to do something, to not forget something, or to do something else, which I don't recall at the moment.

WARNING

This icon highlights things you're not supposed to do, like try to put sheet metal into a computer printer. That sounds cool, but if you really want a document to shine, I have better advice.

TECHNICAL STUFF

This icon alerts you to information you can happily avoid reading. I use it to flag parts of the text where I get technical, go off on a tangent, or mention material that's not really necessary to the topic, but my inner nerd just can't control himself. Feel free to avoid anything flagged with the Technical Stuff icon.

Along with the icons, you'll find margin art. These marginal masterpieces represent various items you see on the screen while using Word. They might be command buttons, doodads, controls, gizmos, or flecks of paint that look interesting. These micons (margin icons) help you navigate through steps in the text.

Beyond the Book

My email address is dgookin@wambooli.com. Yes, that's my real address. I reply to all email I receive regarding this book, and you get a quick reply if you keep your question short and specific. Although I enjoy saying Hi, I cannot answer technical support questions or help you troubleshoot your computer. Thanks for understanding.

You can also visit my web page for more information or as a diversion:

wambooli.com

I also have a vast collection of videos on YouTube that cover using Microsoft Word and that offer various tricks and tips. Check them out at:

```
youtube.com/@dangookin
```

As part of my contractual obligation, I'm required to mention the publisher's page, where you can find more information including this book's secret "Cheat Sheet":

```
dummies.com
```

Search for this book's title (*Microsoft 365 Word For Professionals For Dummies*) on that site to locate the Cheat Sheet. (They keep moving it, so searching is your best bet.)

Where to Go from Here

The first thing you need to do is stop reading the introduction. I'm serious: It's over. The book's vast pages await a bright reading light and your eager gaze.

Check out the table of contents and see what interests you. Peruse the index and look up a special topic. Or just flip to a page and become enlightened. Word does so much and offers so many tools to help you make better documents that you can truly start anywhere.

Enjoy this book. And enjoy Word as much as you can stand it.

1

Fancy Formatting and Froufrou

IN THIS PART . . .

Discover how to best use fonts.

Get to know about page formatting.

Work with tables and information in a grid.

Apply informative headers and footers to a document.

Use styles to quickly format text.

Get familiar with templates, and start creating documents quickly.

IN THIS CHAPTER

» **Understanding fonts**

» **Using typefaces appropriately**

» **Setting text scale and spacing**

» **Raising or lowering text**

» **Applying fun text effects**

» **Filling a font with color**

» **Enhancing headings with shadows**

Chapter **1**

Font Fun

blame the Macintosh for computer users' infatuation with fonts. The Font menu appeared in the early MacPaint and MacWrite programs. It listed a variety of what are more properly termed *typefaces*. But a *font* is really a combination of typeface, size, style, and other attributes. Regardless, the term *font* has stuck. In Word, plenty of options are available to manipulate and preset a font on the page.

A Knowledge of Fonts

Font selection may seem to be secondary to the contents of the document's text. Even so, selecting a proper font is important for readability and presentation. Here are a few general items to understand about fonts before digging into the dirty details.

>> Fonts are installed into Windows, not Word. In Windows 11, use the Settings app, Personalization screen, to find and manage fonts. In Windows 10,

you use the Control Panel and choose the Appearance and Personalization category. Click the Fonts heading to view installed fonts.

» Many fonts are shown as available in Word but must be downloaded to be used. Downloading takes place automatically when you apply the font.

Describing text

Do you remember when you learned to write? Your teacher handed out *ruled* paper. You copied letters and words and used the rules (lines) as a guide. These rules come from the history of printed text, where everything has a name and a purpose, as shown in Figure 1-1.

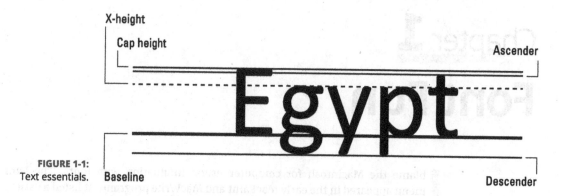

FIGURE 1-1:
Text essentials.

As you progress through school and into the workplace, only the baseline remains as a guide, though the other lines still exist in the world of fonts. They're relevant in typesetting — and in Word. Here are descriptions of the text measurements illustrated in Figure 1-1:

Baseline: Text is written on the baseline.

Cap height: Capital letters extend from the baseline to the cap height.

X-height: Most lowercase letters rise to the x-height, which is named after the lowercase letter *x* and not anything mysterious.

Ascender: Taller lowercase letters extend to the ascender line, such as the *t* shown in Figure 1-1.

Descender: Lowercase letters that dip below the baseline drop to the descender line.

The purpose of these lines is consistency. Though fonts have different character shapes and sizes, these rules help the reader absorb the text. When fonts disobey the rules, the text becomes more difficult to read.

>> In the typesetting community, uppercase letters are known as *majuscule*. Lowercase letters are *miniscule*.

>> The reason uppercase and lowercase letters are given these names dates to the printing press. Majuscule letters were kept in the top or upper part of a case; miniscule letters were kept in the lower part.

Understanding text attributes

A font has many attributes to define the way the font looks and how it can be best put to use. Many of the font attributes are related to Word's text formatting commands. Here's the Big Picture:

Typeface: The font name is called the *typeface*. In Word, the font "Times New Roman" is really a typeface. Only when coupled with other attributes does it officially become a font.

Serif/sans serif: These are the two styles of typeface. A *serif* is a decoration added to each character, a small line or embellishment. Serifs make text easier to read, so serif typefaces are preferred for body text. *Sans serif* typefaces lack the decorations and are preferred for document titles and headings. Figure 1-2 illustrates serif and sans serif typefaces.

Times New Roman
Serif typeface, proportional

Helvetica Neue
Sans serif typeface, proportional

Courier New
Serif typeface, monospaced

FIGURE 1-2:
Typefaces of
differing styles.

Proportional/monospaced: A proportionally spaced typeface uses different sized letters, so a little *I* and a big *M* are different widths. A monospaced typeface features letters all the same width, as you'd find on a typewriter. Figure 1-2 illustrates both proportional and monospace typefaces.

Size: Typeface size is measured in *points*, or units equal to $\frac{1}{72}$ of an inch. So, a typeface 72 points tall is 1 inch tall. The measurement is made from the typeface's descender line to its cap height (refer to Figure 1-1).

Weight: The weight value is either part of the typeface itself or added as an effect, such as the bold text attribute. But for many fonts, the weight is selected with the typeface, as shown in Figure 1-3.

Myriad Pro Light

Myriad Pro Regular

Myriad Pro Semibold

Myriad Pro Bold

Myriad Pro Black

Myriad Pro Light Italic

Myriad Pro Italic

Myriad Pro Semibold Italic

Myriad Pro Bold Italic

Myriad Pro Black Italic

FIGURE 1-3:
Typefaces of
differing weights
and slants.

Typeface weights

Typeface weights & slants

Slant or slope: A typeface's slope refers to how the text is angled. The most common slope is italic. Oblique text is similar to italic, but subtler. The slant can also tilt to the left, which is more of a text effect than anything you'll commonly see associated with a typeface.

Width: Many typefaces feature condensed or narrow variations. These fonts include the same basic design, but the text looks thin or skinny.

Effects: Effects have little to do with the typeface. They are applied by Word to add emphasis or just to look cool. See the later section "Text Effects Strange and Wonderful."

Text on a line can be manipulated to change the way it looks. For example, tracking can be adjusted to scrunch up characters on a line of text. Kerning can be applied to bring letters closer together. Later sections in this chapter describe the details.

REMEMBER

>> A font is a collection of text attributes. What the computer industry calls a "font" is really a typeface.

>> Text is also measured from side to side. The yardstick that's used is the width of the big *M*. That measurement is called an *em*. In digital typefaces, the *em square* is a box used for designing typefaces.

>> Font width varies depending on the font's design, whether the font is heavily weighted, and whether the font is proportionally spaced or monospaced. See the next section for details on these terms.

>> Proportionally spaced typefaces are easier to read than monospace.

TIP

>> Select a heavy typeface over applying the bold text format. Word may select the heavy typeface automatically when you set the bold attribute. The result is that the heavy typeface looks better than when Word attempts to make text look bold.

>> Other typeface weights, not shown in Figure 1-3, include Book, Roman, and Heavy. Still other variations might be available, depending on how the font is designed and named.

>> Just as you should choose a heavy typeface instead of applying the bold text format, if an italic or oblique typeface is available, use it instead of applying the italic text format. See the next section.

Choosing the best typeface

The general rule for text design is to use sans serif fonts for titles and headings and use serif fonts for document text. Like all rules, this one is broken frequently and deliberately. Even in Word, the default document theme uses sans serif Calibri as both the body text and headings typeface.

If you have trouble choosing fonts, take advantage of the Design tab's document themes in Word. Follow these steps:

1. **Click the Design tab.**

2. **In the Document Formatting group, select a theme.**

   Each theme combines typeface elements with colors and other tidbits to help your document maintain its overall appearance.

As you point the mouse at various themes, the document's text updates to reflect the theme's attributes.

>> Choosing a new document theme is optional. You can always create your own document styles to set heading and body typefaces.

COMPUTER FONT STANDARDS

Beyond typeface and other typographical nonsense, a few digital standards rule the world of computer fonts. These standards are TrueType and OpenType.

TrueType is a digital font standard created by Apple and Microsoft. It was designed to compete with Adobe's PostScript fonts, which rendered better on the computer screen back in the early 1990s. OpenType is the successor to TrueType, which was developed in the late 1990s.

To determine which font is which, open the Font dialog box by pressing the Ctrl+D keyboard shortcut. Choose a font, and its type is confirmed below the Preview window.

Other fonts are stirred into the mix and flagged as non-TrueType in Word. These fonts may not look as good as TrueType/OpenType fonts. You may also find that some of Word's advanced text-effect commands don't apply to non-TrueType/OpenType fonts.

WARNING

>> Avoid using decorative or ornamental typefaces as your document's text. They look nifty but make reading difficult.

>> A *scripted* typeface looks handwritten, and you might feel it adds a personal touch. For a short note, an invitation, or a thank-you card, that typeface works well. For a long document, however, a scripted typeface hinders readability.

Dashing about

One character on the keyboard specifically has a role when it comes to understanding fonts. It's the lowly hyphen. This character is used to hyphenate words, to set a range (as in pages 15–16), and stands in for the minus sign in mathematical equations. The hyphen has two siblings that are based on the font size.

The em dash. A dash equal in width to the *M* character is called an *em dash*. In Word, the keyboard shortcut Ctrl+Alt+(hyphen) produces an em-dash character, where the hyphen key is on the numeric keypad.

The en dash. A dash equal in width to the letter *N* is an *en dash*. Its keyboard shortcut is Alt+Shift+(hyphen), where the hyphen key is on the numeric keypad.

The *hyphen* character itself is shorter than the en dash, but sharp–eyed typesetters (and editors) spy the difference. In modern typefaces, the em dash is the width of the uppercase M character. The en is equal in width to the uppercase *N*.

>> The em dash is used to create a parenthetical clause or as a replacement for the colon. En dashes are preferred by editors to set a range or use connections, as in topsy-turvy.

>> Word automatically converts a hyphen separated by spaces into an en dash. This change is part of Word's AutoCorrect feature.

>> The AutoFormat feature converts two hyphens together -- into an em dash.

>> Violent clashes erupt between copy editors over whether to add spaces to either side of the em dash. The current victors believe no spaces should cushion the ends of the em dash. These people are incorrect and will eventually be punished.

Typography Control

Word offers some typeface options that let you manipulate the typeface in degrees beyond standard text attributes. These modifications reset text size, spacing, and position — options not normally available in a standard word processor.

Changing text scale

The Scale command changes the text size in a horizontal direction. This increase is different from the *point size*, which sets the typeface's overall size. Use the Scale command to fatten or thin your text, making it wider or narrower, say for a heading or other text decoration that draws attention.

To adjust the width of a chunk of text, obey these directions:

1. **Select the chunk of text to modify.**

2. **Press Ctrl+D.**

3. **Click the Advanced tab in the Font dialog box.**

4. **From the Scale menu, choose a percentage or type a specific value.**

   The larger the percentage, the wider each character becomes.

   Use the Preview box in the Font dialog box to get a sense of how the command affects the selected text (from Step 1).

   TIP

5. **Click OK.**

   The new width is applied to your text.

Figure 1-4 illustrates the effect of changing the text scale. For each scale percentage, note that the text *height* (size in points) remains the same. Only the text width changes.

Take in that view!
Scale 66%

Take in that view!
Scale 100%

FIGURE 1-4:
Examples of
text scale.

Take in that view!
Scale 150%

REMEMBER

>> If the typeface offers a Narrow or Wide variation, use it rather than the Scale command.

>> Some typefaces don't scale well at the larger end of the spectrum. You must decide whether a scaled typeface is worth any ugliness generated by the effect.

Setting character spacing

You probably don't think about the spacing between characters, which is exactly what a typeface designer wants. Despite all their talent and effort, Word lets you override the decisions of a typeface designer and reset the amount of space between characters. Obey these steps:

1. Select the text you want to expand or condense.

2. Press Ctrl+D to bring up the Font dialog box.

3. Click the Advanced tab.

4. From the Spacing menu, choose Expanded or Condensed to increase or reduce the space between letters in the selected text.

5. Manipulate the By gizmo to set how wide or narrow to set the spaces between letters.

   Use the Preview box to see how the settings affect the selected text.

6. Click OK to set the character spacing.

As with changing the text scale (refer to the preceding section), I recommend manipulating character spacing only for document titles, headings, or other text you want to draw attention to.

Adding kerning and ligatures

To adjust the spaces between specific letters in a typeface, you can apply kerning to the text or use special character combinations known as ligatures.

Kerning is a character-spacing command that involves only specific letters. It scrunches together those characters, such as the *A* and *V*, to make the text more readable, as shown on the left in Figure 1-5. To kern text in your document, heed these directions:

1. **Press Ctrl+D.**

   The Font dialog box appears.

2. **Click the Advanced tab.**

3. **Place a check mark by the setting Kerning for Fonts.**

4. **Set a text size value in the Points and Above box.**

5. **Click OK.**

Unlike other items in the Font dialog box, kerning is applied to all text throughout the document, though the text's point size must be larger than what's set in Step 4.

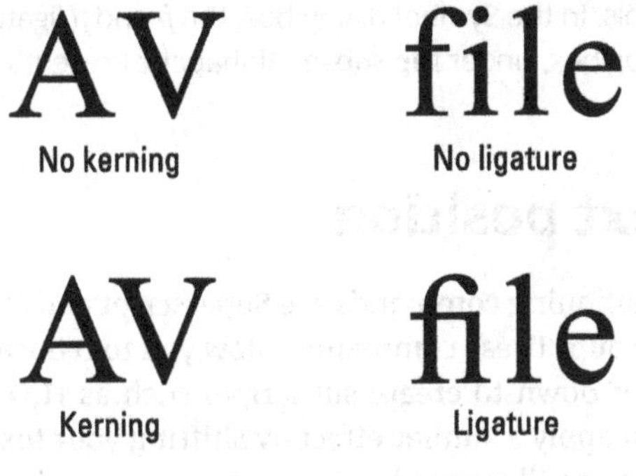

AV
No kerning

file
No ligature

FIGURE 1-5: Examples of kerning and ligatures.

AV
Kerning

file
Ligature

Another way to make text more readable and decrease the space between certain letters is to apply ligatures. A *ligature* connects two or more letters, such as the *F* and *I* in the word *file*, as shown on the right in Figure 1-5. Converting text in this manner is a feature of the OpenType font, so it's not available to all typefaces. If you want to try it, follow these steps:

1. **Select the chunk of text to which you want to apply a ligature.**

2. **Press Ctrl+D.**

3. **In the File dialog box, click the Advanced tab.**

4. **From the Ligatures menu, choose Standard Only.**

   If this choice has no effect on the text, choose All.

5. **Click OK.**

The All setting (refer to Step 4) adds just about every ligature possible, which may produce some funky results in the text. If so, consider scaling back your choice to Standard and Contextual.

TECHNICAL
STUFF

REMEMBER

>> Without kerning, some words appear to have extra space in them. Kerning addresses this issue.

>> Technically, kerning intrudes upon the integrity of the virtual em square around each character in a digital font. Because kerning is applied only to specific letters, the effect improves readability.

>> If you desire to kern all letters on a line of text, adjust the character spacing instead. Refer to the preceding section.

>> Not every font (typeface) sports ligatures.

>> You can also insert ligatures directly. On the Insert tab, choose Symbol and select More Symbols. In the Symbol dialog box, the *fi* and *fl* ligatures are found in the Symbol dialog box, under the subset Alphabetic Presentation Forms.

Adjusting text position

The two basic text-positioning commands are Superscript and Subscript, found in the Home tab's Font group. These commands allow you to reduce the text size and shift the baseline up or down to create subscripts such as H_2O and superscripts such as $E=mc^2$. You can apply a similar effect by shifting your text's distance from the baseline up or down, as illustrated in Figure 1-6.

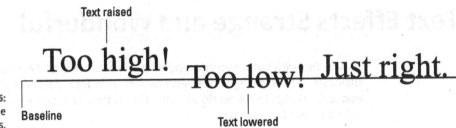

Text raised

Too high! Too low! Just right.

FIGURE 1-6:
Text baseline
adjustments.

Baseline

Text lowered

To adjust text position above or below the baseline, heed these directions:

1. **Select the text you want raised or lowered.**

   Ensure that it's a small chunk of text. Raising an entire line of text would be impractical.

2. **Press Ctrl+D to bring forth the Font dialog box.**

3. **Click the Advanced tab.**

4. **From the Position menu, choose Raised or Lowered.**

5. **Select a point value from the By gizmo.**

   For example, to raise a word 3 points from the baseline, choose Raised and then 3 pt from the box.

6. **Click OK to apply the new text position.**

To remove raised or lowered text, repeat these steps and choose Normal in Step 4, and then click OK.

>> Raising or lowering text affects line spacing within a paragraph as well as spacing between paragraphs. If you have paragraph line spacing at the Exactly setting, the text may bump the line above or below.

X_2

>> The Subscript command button is shown in the margin. Its keyboard equivalent is Ctrl+=. Use this command to subscript a single character of text.

X^2

>> The Superscript command button is shown in the margin. Its keyboard equivalent is Ctrl+Shift+=. This command is preferred when you want to superscript a single character.

Text Effects Strange and Wonderful

To have fun with fonts, consider applying some text effects. These aren't typeface attributes, but rather special effects applied to a font. And like all strange and wonderful things in the world of fonts, these effects are best suited for headings and titles, not for body text.

Accessing the Format Text Effects pane

To apply text effects, summon the Format Text Effects pane, illustrated in Figure 1-7.

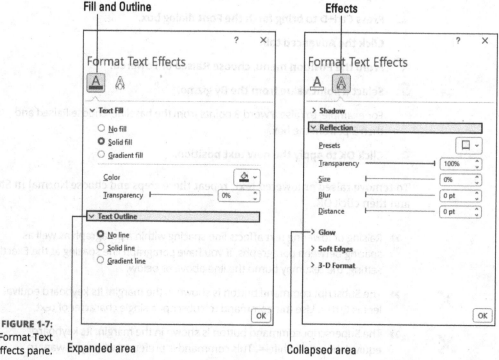

FIGURE 1-7:
The Format Text
Effects pane.

To display this pane, follow these steps:

1. **Press Ctrl+D to bring forth the Font dialog box.**

2. **Click the Text Effects button.**

   If this button is disabled, the current typeface cannot be manipulated.

The Format Text Effects pane features two tabs, illustrated in Figure 1-7. The left tab handles text fill and outline options. The right tab lists a host of effects.

Each item in the Format Text Effects pane is collapsible. Click the chevron to expand the item; click again to collapse, as illustrated in Figure 1-7.

To make adjustments, select the text you want to format. Work in the pane to apply the effects, which, sadly, cannot be previewed. After making adjustments, click the OK button to apply, and then click OK again to close the Font dialog box.

Changing text fill

Coloring text in a document is a standard Word command. To apply more than a solid color, however, use the Text Fill area of the Format Text Effects pane, as shown back in Figure 1-7.

Three options are available for Text Fill in the Format Text Effects pane:

» No Fill removes any previously applied fill effects.

» Solid Fill works just like the Font Color command, though you can use the Transparency slider to add a transparent, "ghost" effect to the text.

» Gradient Fill presents multiple controls for applying a rainbow of colors to the text.

Figure 1-8 illustrates the controls available to apply different colors or shades that fade into each other as applied to the text. A sample of the specific gradient settings is shown on the right in the figure.

The key to creating the gradient is to use the Gradient Stops bar. Each stop represents a different color set at a specific position with a given transparency and brightness. These colors blend in a pattern, set by the Type and Direction options, to build the gradient.

Follow these steps to create a gradient fill pattern:

1. **Select the text.**

   Gradient fill works best on titles or other decorative text element.

2. **Press Ctrl+D.**

REMEMBER

3. **Click the Text Effects button in the Font dialog box.**

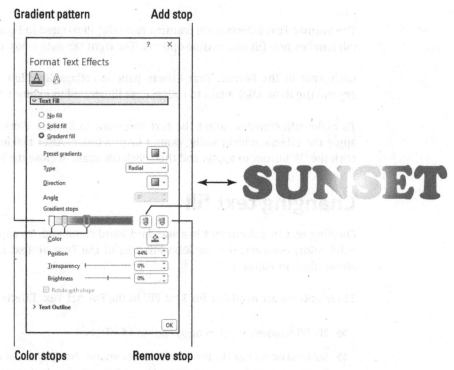

Gradient pattern   **Add stop**

SUNSET

FIGURE 1-8:
Gradient fill.

Color stops   **Remove stop**

4. **Click the Fill and Outline tab on the Format Text Effects pane.**

    Refer to Figure 1-7 for the tab's location.

5. **Expand the Text Fill area.**

6. **Choose Gradient Fill.**

    Use the Preset Gradients button to apply one of Word's automatic gradients to the text. If you find one you like, you're done! Merrily skip to Step 9.

7. **Select the gradient Type.**

    Use the Type menu to choose one of four gradient types. In Figure 1-8 you see a Radial gradient, which fans out from a center point. The Position box sets the center point. Use the Direction button to see how the gradient is applied to the text.

8. **Adjust the gradient's colors.**

    Click the Add Stop button to add a color on the Gradient Stops bar. Set the stop's color and other options. Use the Remove Stop button to remove a stop.

9. **Click OK to apply the fill, and then click OK again to close the Font dialog box.**

TIP

Unfortunately, the Gradient settings changes aren't previewed live in your document. The best way to see the effect is to click OK. Use the Preview portion of the Font dialog box to check your work.

Setting a text outline

A text outline is applied as an effect; it's not a standard font attribute. To add a decorative outline to your document's text, obey these steps:

1. **Select the text.**

   The text should be a title, heading, or other decorative text element.

2. **Press Ctrl+D and click the Text Effects button in the Font dialog box.**

3. **Ensure that the Fill and Outline tab is chosen in the Format Text Effects pane.**

4. **Expand the Text Outline area.**

5. **Choose Solid Line or Gradient Line to set the type of outline.**

   For Gradient Line, you can configure the gradient color stops and other options, as discussed in the preceding section.

6. **Use the Width gizmo to set the outline width.**

   Width is measured in points. Larger values show a heavier outline.

7. **Set other options to customize how the line looks.**

   Several options set how the line looks:

   Compound Type: Use the Compound Type menu to choose line styles, such as a double line, thick and thin lines, and more.

   Dash Type: The Dash Type menu sets whether the line is solid or composed of dashes or dots in various patterns and lengths.

   Cap Type: Items on the Cap Type menu set how the border goes around a curve. The options are Square, Round, and Flat. This effect doesn't really show up unless the text is quite large or the outline is thick.

   Join Type: The Join Type menu determines what happens when lines meet. As with the cap type, this effect requires large text or thick lines to show up.

8. **Click OK, and then click OK again to view the outline effect.**

The text modifications may not show up in the Font dialog box's Preview window, so you must return to the document to witness your efforts.

To remove the text outline, choose the option No Line in Step 5.

Adding a text shadow

The Shadow effects can help a title or graphical element stand out, almost as if it's hovering on the page, as illustrated in Figure 1-9. This effect is applied from a gallery of preset options, or you can toil creating your own by manipulating the various settings in the Format Text Effects pane. Follow these directions apply this effect:

1. **Select the text.**

The Shadow effect works best on titles and other decorative text elements.

2. **Press Ctrl+D to bring up the Font dialog box.**

3. **Click the Text Effects button.**

4. **Click the Text Effects tab (the second letter "A") in the Format Text Effects pane.**

Refer to Figure 1-7 for the tab's appearance and location.

5. **Expand the Shadow area.**

Preset shadow effects

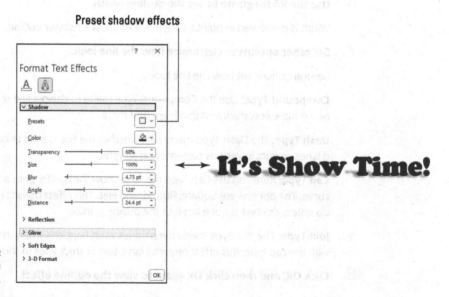

FIGURE 1-9:
Text with a
shadow attached.

6. Choose an item from the Presets menu button.

TIP

The best way to apply a text shadow is to choose an item from the Presets menu, shown on the right in Figure 1-9.

7. Use the remaining items in the Shadow portion of the Format Text Effects pane to make fine adjustments to the preset options.

8. Click OK, and then click OK again to view the shadow effect.

You may have to repeat these steps a few times to get the effect just right, but choosing a preset shadow (refer to Step 6) really helps to expedite the process.

Configuring text reflection and glow

The Reflection and Glow text effects work similarly to the Shadow effect, covered in the preceding section. These effects and their settings are illustrated in Figure 1-10.

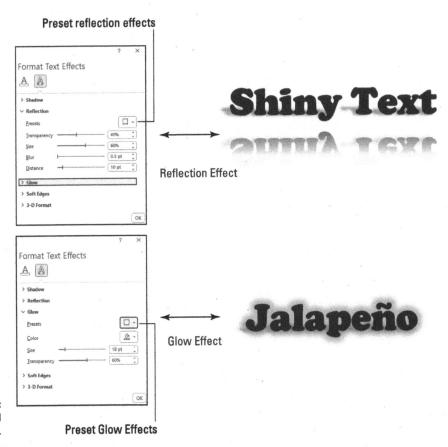

FIGURE 1-10:
Reflection and
Glow text effects.

To best apply text Reflection and Glow effects, first select text and then choose a preset from the Presets button. (Refer to Figure 1-10.) You can make further adjustments to the effects, which requires that you click OK (twice) to view the text and then return to the Format Text Effects pane to jiggle the various controls.

>> The Reflection effect increases the text's line height. Again, this type of effect works best on a chapter title or other graphical element, not on body text.

>> The Soft Edges effect doesn't apply to most text (if any). It's an echo of the Soft Edges effect applied to other graphics in a document. See Chapter 7.

IN THIS CHAPTER

» **Inserting hyphens**

» **Numbering lists**

» **Changing list numbering**

» **Saving widows and orphans**

» **Creating headers and footers**

» **Making a header stand out**

» **Alternating headers**

Chapter **2**

Paragraph and Page Preparation

ormatting a paragraph or page is basic stuff in Word. To go beyond it, you must know which standard formatting commands offer more features. The goal is customization, which helps make your document stand out. Nothing is better than the feeling you get when someone else looks at your document and wonders, "How did you do that?" This chapter provides a few paragraph and page preparation tips and tricks.

To Hyphenate or Not

Hyphenation was more of a big deal back when typewriters were the office tool of choice. When you reached the end of a line, but not the end of a word, you could hyphenate it. Cleaving a word by syllables was one way to keep the paragraph's right margin from appearing too ragged.

Thanks to proportional typefaces, and Word's capability to adjust spacing between words, rarely do you think about hyphenation when word processing. You can still hyphenate a long word, splitting it between two lines, which readers understand and accept. Word offers some hyphenation features to keep that right margin neat and tidy.

>> Hyphenation is used primarily when paragraphs are formatted at full justification.

>> The best time to hyphenate is when text is formatted for short lines or multiple columns on a page. It's also good to hyphenate longer words where not doing so makes the paragraph formatting look ugly.

>> Hyphenation is an optional thing. I recommend using it only when the hyphenated word improves a paragraph's visual presentation. For example, when Word spaces out a line of text to the point where it looks like a picket fence. In such instances, hyphenation is necessary.

Adding a manual hyphen

Word's Hyphenation feature can check a document and automatically apply hyphens where needed. If you prefer to apply your own hyphenation, I recommend that you use the hyphen character (–) instead. Also called the *minus sign*, this character splits words at the end of a line, such as the one illustrated in Figure 2-1. See the ugly gap?

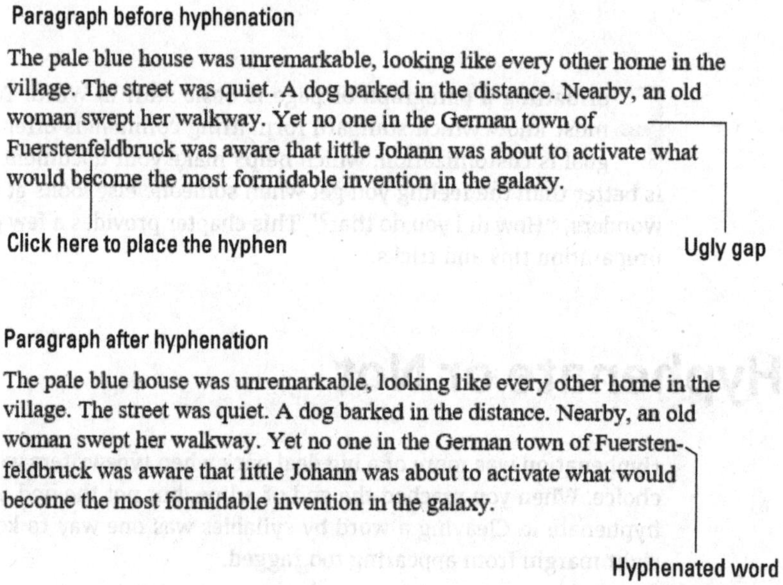

Paragraph before hyphenation

The pale blue house was unremarkable, looking like every other home in the village. The street was quiet. A dog barked in the distance. Nearby, an old woman swept her walkway. Yet no one in the German town of Fuerstenfeldbruck was aware that little Johann was about to activate what would become the most formidable invention in the galaxy.

Click here to place the hyphen   Ugly gap

Paragraph after hyphenation

The pale blue house was unremarkable, looking like every other home in the village. The street was quiet. A dog barked in the distance. Nearby, an old woman swept her walkway. Yet no one in the German town of Fuersten-feldbruck was aware that little Johann was about to activate what would become the most formidable invention in the galaxy.

FIGURE 2-1:
Hyphenating a
long word.

Hyphenated word

To hyphenate the word, follow these steps:

1. **Click the mouse to place the insertion pointer at the appropriate spot.**

2. **Press the – (hyphen) key.**

    The word is split betwixt two lines, as illustrated in Figure 2-1.

For better results, in Step 2 press Ctrl+(hyphen), which inserts the optional hyphen character. Unlike the standard hyphen character, the optional hyphen character vanishes from view should the word not need to be hyphenated. For example, if you re-edit the paragraph and the hyphen is no longer necessary. But it appears again, should the need arise.

TIP

>> You hyphenate a word between two syllables or double letters. If you don't know the exact position, consider activating manual hyphenation as covered in the next section.

>> To view optional, hidden hyphens, use the Show/Hide command, shown in the margin. This command is found on the Ribbon's Home tab in the Paragraph group. The optional hyphen character appears as the ¬ symbol when Show/Hide is active.

Automatically hyphenating text

When hyphenating words isn't something you do often, or you're frightened to do it wrong, you can take advantage of Word's Hyphenation feature. In this mode, Word automatically inserts the optional hyphen characters in your text as needed. Obey these directions:

1. **Click the Layout tab.**

2. **In the Page Setup group, click the Hyphenation button.**

3. **From the menu, choose Automatic.**

When this feature is active, Word hyphenates text as necessary. You may see hyphens added and removed quickly as you work on the text.

TIP

If you prefer to review Word's hyphenation choices, choose Manual in Step 3. You see the Manual Hyphenation dialog box, shown in Figure 2-2. Click to place the hyphen and then click Yes to hyphenate the word. Click No to leave the word unhyphenated.

FIGURE 2-2:
The Manual
Hyphenation
dialog box.

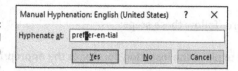

Manual Hyphenation: English (United States)   ?   ✕

Hyphenate at: prefer-en-tial

Yes   No   Cancel

Continue working the Manual Hyphenation dialog box to hyphenate (or not) words throughout the document. When hyphenation is complete, click OK.

REMEMBER

Manual hyphenation isn't interactive; it's done all at once. So, after choosing Manual, select the None option from the Hyphenation menu to disable automatic hyphenation.

Inserting an unbreakable hyphen

An unbreakable hyphen prevents Word from splitting text you don't want split, such as a phone number, mathematical equation, or other text that looks odd when hyphenated.

To insert the unbreakable hyphen character, press Ctrl+Shift+(hyphen). The unbreakable hyphen looks like a regular hyphen, though Word won't split its text between two lines.

TIP

Just as you can insert an unbreakable hyphen, you can also insert a nonbreaking space when you don't want related words split between two lines. The nonbreaking space character keyboard shortcut is Ctrl+Shift+spacebar.

Numbered Lists

Many Word users express frustration over its automatic paragraph numbering command. The problem is customization. Word can number paragraphs automatically while reducing your workload and making the text look great. But when you need to go beyond this feature's basics, you can employ some advanced but not obvious text numbering options.

Numbering paragraphs

Word's Numbering command not only supplies automatic numbers to sequential paragraphs, it updates the numbering for you. They remain in order when you edit or add paragraphs. Follow these steps:

1. **Type the paragraphs.**

   Don't type the numbers. If you do, you'll engage Word's AutoFormat As You Type feature, which you might find annoying. Therefore, just type out the list one line (or paragraph) at a time.

2. **Select the paragraphs.**

3. **Click the Home tab.**

4. **In the Paragraph group, click the Numbering button.**

   If you click the button itself, the paragraphs are formatted with sequential numbers, 1 through *n*. Otherwise, you can click the menu button and choose a number format from the list, as shown in Figure 2-3.

Menu

FIGURE 2-3:
The Numbering menu.

If you apply numbering to text as you type, press the Enter key twice to stop numbering. Or you can click the Numbering button again or choose the None option (refer to Figure 2-3) to remove the number from a paragraph.

>> To change the numbering style for a group of numbered paragraphs, select the lot of them and choose a new format from the Numbering button menu.

>> Don't edit the paragraph numbers! If you need to renumber the paragraphs, see the later section "Skipping paragraph numbers."

Adjusting numbering indents

Word formats its numbered paragraphs with a hanging indent. A tab character is automatically inserted after the number. You can use the Ruler to adjust the indent, but the process may frustrate you. Instead, you can use the Adjust List Indents dialog box. Heed these directions:

1. **Select all numbered paragraphs.**

2. **Right-click the selection.**

3. **Choose the command Adjust List Indents.**

   The Adjust List Indents dialog box appears, illustrated in Figure 2-4.

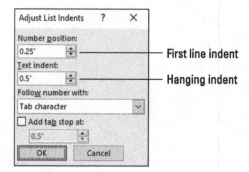

FIGURE 2-4: The Adjust List Indents dialog box.

4. **Use the gizmos in the box to set the number and text-indent positions.**

   These two items control both the first line and hanging indents, as illustrated in Figure 2-4.

5. **Select the character to follow the number.**

   Options are a tab, a space, or nothing.

6. **Click OK.**

If you choose a tab to follow the number (refer to Step 5), the Text Indent item and Tab Stop settings (on the Ruler) are affected. If the text indent is too close to the number position, text slides over to the next tab stop position. This effect might not be what you want; click OK to confirm. Otherwise, use the Adjust List Indents dialog box to set a new tab stop to line up text.

Skipping paragraph numbers

Not every paragraph must be numbered. Sometimes, a numbered paragraph is followed by plain paragraphs, and then the numbering picks up again later. Word performs this trick for you automatically, though you may find its behavior to be inconsistent.

An approach I can recommend is to number all paragraphs in the list. Then go back and remove numbering for certain paragraphs. Heed these steps:

1. **Apply numbering to the original set of paragraphs.**

   For example, in Figure 2-5, all paragraphs were originally numbered, 1 through 6. The numbering on paragraph 3 was removed and the remaining paragraphs are automatically renumbered.

Left Indent gizmo

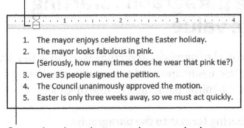

1. The mayor enjoys celebrating the Easter holiday.
2. The mayor looks fabulous in pink.
   (Seriously, how many times does he wear that pink tie?)
3. Over 35 people signed the petition.
4. The Council unanimously approved the motion.
5. Easter is only three weeks away, so we must act quickly.

FIGURE 2-5: Turning numbers on and off.

Currently selected paragraph, no numbering

2. **Click in the paragraph you do not want numbered, assuming the numbering has already been applied.**

3. **On the Home tab, in the Paragraph group, click the Numbering icon.**

   The number is removed from the single paragraph, but the paragraph loses its indentation formatting.

4. **Adjust the Left Indent gizmo on the Ruler to line up the paragraph's text with the rest of the numbered paragraphs.**

   Refer to Figure 2-5: The Left Indent gizmo (the square box) is adjusted to line up the unnumbered paragraph with the rest of the paragraphs.

If you need to remove numbering from more than one paragraph, select all the paragraphs in Step 2. You need to reapply formatting to the group, as described in Step 4.

Restarting numbered paragraphs

Suppose that you need to start a new set of numbered paragraphs, yet Word stubbornly insists on continuing numbers from the previous series. For example, you type 1, but Word keeps slapping 6 onto the paragraph. To address this issue, follow these steps:

1. **Right-click the mouse on the paragraph where you want to start renumbering.**

2. **Choose the command Restart at 1.**

The paragraphs start numbering all over again at 1.

Conversely, if you want Word to continue the previous set of numbers but it won't, choose the Continue Numbering command from the right-click shortcut menu (Step 2). This command works no matter how distant the current paragraph is from the last range of numbered paragraphs.

Numbering paragraphs starting at a specific value

Word doesn't always need to number paragraphs starting with 1. For example, when you're starting a new document and need to continue numbering from another document, you can reset the initial paragraph numbering value. Obey these steps:

1. **Apply the numbering format to the paragraphs.**

Use the Numbering command button as described elsewhere in this section.

2. **Right-click the paragraph where you want the new numbering series to begin.**

3. **Choose the command Set Numbering Value.**

The Set Numbering Value dialog box appears.

4. **Ensure that the option Start New List is selected.**

5. **Use the Set Value To gizmo to specify the starting number value.**

6. **Click OK.**

Paragraphs are renumbered starting with the value you choose in Step 5.

Creating custom paragraph numbers

The Define New Number Format dialog box is used to specify numbering schemes not available on the Numbering menu. You can even craft your own numbering style, such as the colon format, shown in Figure 2-6. To mess with the number formats, follow these directions:

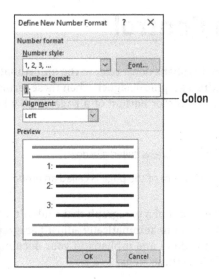

— Colon

FIGURE 2-6:
The Define New
Number Format
dialog box.

1. **Click the Home tab.**

2. **Click the Numbering button's menu.**

3. **Choose the command Define New Number Format.**

   The Define New Number Format dialog box appears.

4. **Choose a style from the Number Style menu.**

   Only a given list of styles is presented; you cannot create a new number style.

   Not all styles shown on the Number Style menu are available on the Numbering button's menu, such as the cardinal and ordinal options.

5. **Edit the number format.**

   You don't want to change the number, but you can add text after the number, such as the colon shown in Figure 2-6.

6. **Select a new alignment for the number and its format.**

   Use the Preview window to examine how the settings will appear.

7. **Click OK to confirm the custom number settings.**

The advantage of Word's Numbering command is that it applies the numbers automatically. If the numbering schemes or methods don't meet with your approval, you can manually number and format the paragraphs. The only drawback is that the numbers aren't automatically updated as you edit or add to your text.

Widow and Orphan Control

With text layout, widows and orphans don't refer to the unfortunate. Well, they're not unfortunate unless you're a graphic designer. Then these terms refer to single lines of text that appear at the top or bottom of a page. Here's how the experts define them:

>> A single line lingering atop the page is called a *widow*.

>> A single line lagging at the bottom of the page is called an *orphan*.

In both cases, the single line is part of a paragraph that couldn't all fit on the previous or next page. Word is preset to automatically adjust paragraphs so that you don't unintentionally create widows and orphans in your document. To confirm that this setting is active, follow these steps:

1. **Click the Home tab.**

2. **In the Paragraph group, click the Launcher.**

   The Paragraph dialog box appears.

3. **Click the Line and Page Breaks tab.**

4. **Ensure that a check mark is set by the Widow/Orphan Control option.**

5. **Click OK.**

Three other options that lurk in the Paragraph dialog box, on the Line and Page Breaks tab, also control paragraphs and how they flow on a page. Choose one of these options in Step 4 to create the desired effect:

Keep with Next: This setting keeps a group of paragraphs on the same page, no matter how the document is formatted.

Keep Lines Together: This option prevents a single paragraph from splitting between two pages.

Page Break Before: This setting starts a paragraph at the top of a page, regardless of how text lays out on the preceding page.

The mnemonic for widows and orphans is, "An orphan has no past; a widow has no future." An orphan is "born" at the bottom of a page. A widow is "left behind" at the top of a page.

WARNING

Don't try to fix the widow/orphan problem by inserting empty paragraphs into your document! Sure, press the Enter key a few times, and the paragraph pops up on the next page. The problem is that as you edit and reformat your document, these empty paragraphs cause undue formatting woe.

Professional Headers and Footers

Quality documents and self-published e-books all feature headers and footers. These text tidbits dwell atop or below a page and provide consistent, helpful information to your reader. Word comes with preset headers and footers that may do the job, but to give your documents a more professional edge, consider crafting your own unique and expressive headers and footers.

Building a header

The header is nothing more than an extension of your document. The big difference is that its text is echoed over every page. Therefore, the information you set in a header can be whatever is required for consistency, such as your name, the document title, the date, page numbers, your blood type, and so on.

To build your own header, or to edit the current header, follow these steps:

1. **Click the Insert tab.**

2. **In the Header & Footer group, click the Header button.**

3. **Choose Edit Header.**

   The document's text goes dim, the Header & Footer tab appears, and the insertion pointer blinks inside the Header area, illustrated in Figure 2-7.

The sections that follow detail what you can do in the header as well as the document footer. (I use the term *header* to describe both.) Beyond text, the tools you need to work with the header or footer are found on the Header & Footer tab on the Ribbon.

When you finish editing the header, click the Close Header and Footer button, illustrated in Figure 2-7.

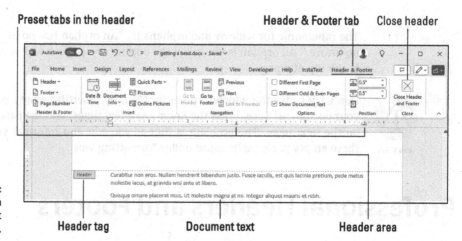

Preset tabs in the header · Header & Footer tab · Close header

FIGURE 2-7:
Creating a document header.

Header tag · Document text · Header area

TIP

To quickly access the document header, double-click the mouse at the top of the page. Similarly, to exit the header, double-click the mouse in the document's text.

Switching between the header and footer

You don't need to exit the Header & Footer tab to switch between the document's header and footer. Instead, use the Navigation group's Go To buttons:

To switch from the header to the footer, click the Go to Footer button.

To switch from the footer to the header, click the Go to Header button.

Available commands on the Ribbon don't change whether you're working on the header or footer. Also, the paragraph format is the same in both header and footer, with a center tab stop and right tab stop, as illustrated in Figure 2-7. The tag says *Header* or *Footer*, depending on which one you're editing; in Figure 2-7, the Header tag is shown.

Typing text in a header

Anything you can place into a document can go into a header. This list includes text, pictures, and graphic elements. Any formatting that's set in a document can also be set in a header. To add your own text to a header, heed these steps:

1. **Edit the header.**

If the header exists, double-click its text. Otherwise, follow the steps from the preceding section to access the document's header.

2. **Type the text.**

   Be brief. Headers are not wordy.

3. **Close the header when you're done adding the text.**

Examples of great header text include your name, the document's title, the chapter number, the course name, your evil corporation's name, and so on.

TIP

The header is preformatted with two tab stops: a center tab stop in the middle of the page and a right tab stop at the right paragraph indent. (Refer to Figure 2-7.) Use these tab stops!

In Figure 2-8, you see my name, the document title, and the page number set in the header. Tabs separate each element, which align at the tab stops, as shown in the figure.

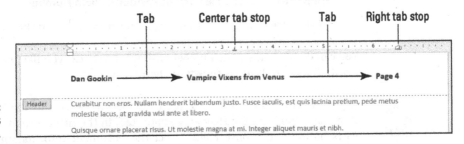

FIGURE 2-8:
Using tab stops in a header.

You don't have to use the preset tab stops. In fact, you can remove or replace them with other tab stops more suitable to the header you need.

REMEMBER

» Headers appear on every page in the document. Avoid the temptation to burden the header with obnoxious quantities of information. A single line of text in the header is ideal.

» If you need text at the bottom of the page, use a footnote. See Chapter 18.

» Word comes with a preset header style, though you can create your own. Header text is smaller than body text, often in the same typeface as the document's headings.

Adding page numbers

The most popular thing to stick into a header (or footer) is the page number. It's not just any old page number, either: What you insert into the header is a page number field. The goal is to have each page's header shows the current page number.

To place the current page number in a header, obey these steps:

1. **Edit the header.**

Refer to the section "Building a header," earlier in this chapter.

2. **Place the insertion pointer at the position where you desire the page number to roost.**

You can keep the insertion pointer at the left margin, press Tab once to center it, or press Tab twice to right-align the page number, similar to what's shown in Figure 2-8.

3. **In the Header & Footer tab on the Ribbon, click the Page Number button.**

4. **From the menu, choose Current Position ⇨ Plain Number.**

A field representing the current page number appears in the header.

You can decorate the page number with whatever text you like, such as prefixing it with the word Page, as shown in Figure 2-8.

TIP

If you also desire to insert the total number of pages into the header, use the NumPages field. On the Header & Footer tab, in the Insert group, click the Quick Parts button and choose Field. Select the Document Information category, and then choose the NumPages field. Click OK to insert the field.

The total number of pages is often used in a header to display page numbers, as in

Page 1/32

where 1 is the current page and 32 is the total number of pages reported by the NumPage field.

See Chapter 21 for additional information on fields.

>> Other document properties you can include in the header are the current date, the date and time, the document filename, your name, the document title, chapter numbers, and so on. Some of these items are fields, which are covered in Chapter 21. The document filename field is demonstrated in Chapter 9.

>> If you've configured the document to sport different headers for odd- and even-numbered pages, you might want to set the page number on the left for

an even page and on the right for an odd page. See the later section "Creating odd and even headers."

>> There is no need to duplicate information in a header or footer. For example, if your name or the page number is in the header, don't put identical information in the footer.

Placing objects in the header

As the header can contain any item that otherwise goes into a document's text, you can add pictures and graphics to a header. My only advice is to keep these items small enough so as not to crowd the document's text. Large objects can be placed with the Behind Text layout option, which might alleviate overcrowding.

>> The preset header and footer examples shown on the Header and Footer menus give you an idea of what kind of graphics can be set in a header or footer. These menus are found on the Header & Footer tab, as well as the Insert tab.

>> See Chapter 5 for layout options, such as Behind Text.

>> Shapes are covered in Chapter 6.

Resetting the header position

Word positions the header half an inch from the top of the page. For most margin settings, this location is well within the page margin and above where the text starts. If you've set custom margins, or you desire a different page look, you can adjust the header position relative to the top of the page. Heed these directions:

1. **Click the Insert tab.**

2. **In the Header & Footer tab, Position group, use the Header Position From Top gizmo to adjust the distance.**

    The button's icon is shown in the margin. The distance is measured from the top of the header to the top edge of the page.

    Use the Footer from Bottom gizmo to adjust the document's footer spacing. Its icon is shown in the margin. This distance is measured from the bottom of the footer to the bottom of the page.

>> You don't want to get the header too close to the top of the page or it may not print on some printers.

>> The further you move the header from the top of the page, the more it encroaches onto the document's text.

Working with headers in sections

A header is a page-level format. As such, it's affected by section breaks within a document. Unless you direct otherwise, the header extends, or links, between all sections in a document. By breaking the link, however, you can set different headers for different sections. For example, to set different headers for different chapters in a manuscript.

In Figure 2-9, you see headers from a document with two sections. Each section is referenced in the header tag: Section 1 and then Section 2.

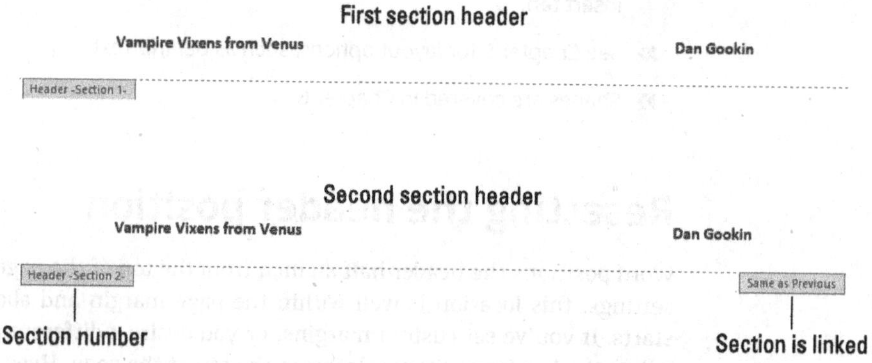

First section header

Vampire Vixens from Venus   Dan Gookin

Header -Section 1-

Second section header

Vampire Vixens from Venus   Dan Gookin

Header -Section 2-   Same as Previous

FIGURE 2-9: Headers, linked across two sections.

Section number   Section is linked

The headers in Section 1 and Section 2 are identical in Figure 2-9 because they're *linked:* If you change one header, both are updated.

To separate the headers, and make them differ between sections, you must break the link. Follow these steps:

1. **Edit the header.**

Double-click at the top of the page, in the header's text.

2. **On the Header & Footer tab, in the Navigation group, click the Next button.**

You must be in the second header, or any header that follows another section's header.

3. **In the Navigation group, click the Link to Previous button.**

The Same As Previous tag disappears from the header. (Refer to Figure 2-9.) The header's text isn't removed, though you're free to change it for a separate header in the current section.

If you change your mind and desire to keep the links between section headers, click the Link to Previous button in Step 3 to assert this setting. Click Yes in the confirmation dialog box, and the previous section's header is restored. The Same As Previous tag reappears, as shown in Figure 2-9.

>> If your document has additional sections, you can link or unlink each one. Use the Next button to page through the sections, hopping from header to header.

>> Use the Previous button, also found in the Navigation group, to hop to the previous section's header. Use the Next and Previous buttons to review headers in the document's different sections.

>> It's possible to have one header in Section 1, and then no header in Section 2, and then the same header from Section 1 in Section 3. To do so, unlink all sections as described in this book. Next, copy the header from Section 1 and paste it into Section 3.

>> One of the ways section links can vex you is when you try to edit a second section's header and the changes don't stick. The reason is that the headers are linked. Unlink them as described in this section.

Creating odd and even headers

Another way your document can sport different headers is to set one for the odd pages and another for the even. This book uses that configuration, with the even page footers showing the page number and part title and the odd page footers showing the chapter title and page number.

To set different headers (or footers) on odd and even pages, obey these steps:

1. **Edit or create the header.**

Double-click the mouse at the top of the page, in the header's text.

2. **On the Header & Footer tab, in the Options group, place a check mark by the option Different Odd & Even Pages.**

The header tag changes to reflect whether it's on an odd or even page, as illustrated in Figure 2-10.

Odd page header

Vampire Vixens from Venus   Page 1

Odd Page Header

- -

Even page header

FIGURE 2-10:   Page 2   Dan Gookin
Odd and even
page headers.

Even Page Header

- -

3. Edit the odd page header.

Click the Previous button to ensure that you see the odd page header, identified by its tag in the lower left corner. (Refer to Figure 2-10.)

4. Edit the even page header.

Click the Next button to hop over to the even page header.

When you break up your document into sections, they also hold the odd/even format, with each section having its own set of odd/even headers. The links between sections are as a unit, with both odd and even headers linked between sections.

REMEMBER

>> The odd page header comes first because Page 1 is the first page of your document.

>> When the document contains multiple sections, the section name and number follow the odd or even header tag, as in "Odd Page Header –Section 2–."

>> Odd and even headers are affected when you reset the page numbering. For example, your introduction uses Roman Numerals and then you switch to a new numbering scheme for the main document, the page numbers change values. The header that's used always reflects the odd or even page number, regardless of how many physical pages the document has at that point.

>> The Next and Previous buttons hop between odd and even headers and then to the next or previous section's odd or even header.

TECHNICAL
STUFF

>> In a bound book, odd pages are always on the right, even pages on the left. The reason is that the first page is presented on the right side of the binding.

Removing a header

The complicated way to remove a header is to edit away all its text. A better way is to follow these steps:

1. **Click the Insert tab.**

2. **In the Header & Footer group, click the Header button to view its menu.**

3. **Choose Remove Header.**

   And it's gone.

If the document is split into sections, these steps affect only the current section. See the earlier section "Working with headers in sections."

If you're using different odd/even headers, these steps remove both odd and even headers.

IN THIS CHAPTER

» **Placing text in a table**

» **Adding rows and columns**

» **Adjusting the table size**

» **Setting text alignment and direction**

» **Formatting a table**

» **Sorting table rows**

» **Performing table math**

Chapter **3**

Terrific Tables

To best organize information in a grid, shove a table into your document. Word's table creation cup overflows with options, formatting choices, and superpowers you probably weren't aware of or just didn't care about — until now.

» Word's table commands are not a substitute for using a spreadsheet like Excel. Truly, if you need information organized into a grid, use Excel and not Word.

» See Chapter 8 for information on the frightening prospect of inserting an Excel worksheet into a Word document.

Cobble Together a Table

Basic information on creating a table is found in my book *Word For Dummies* (Wiley). As a quick review, and to prime you for being overwhelmed, Word offers five ways to create a table. Table creation commands are found on the Ribbon's Insert tab, in the Tables group. Here's a summary:

Use the Insert Table dialog box. Choose Table ➪ Insert Table. Use the Insert Table dialog box to set the number of rows and columns. Click OK. Ta-da!

Use the Table menu grid. From the Table button menu, drag the mouse over the grid presented to set the number of rows and columns for the table, which is instantly plopped into your document at the insertion pointer's position.

Draw a table. From the Table button menu, choose the Draw Table command. Drag the mouse to create a rectangle in your document — the table. Continue using the mouse to draw rows and columns. Choose the Draw Table menu command again to exit table-drawing mode.

Convert a tabbed list into a table. Select the paragraphs containing the tabbed list. From the Table button menu, choose the command Convert Text to Table. Correct the Convert Text to Table dialog box, though its guesses are probably accurate. Click OK to convert the text.

Use a preset table. From the Table button menu, choose the Quick Tables command, then select one of Word's predesigned tables from the list.

Table Editing

Tables dance the line between what Microsoft Word does and what Excel can do. Both deal with information held in a grid, rows and columns. Excel is built upon the grid and has mathematical genius and database powers. Word is built upon the page and offers better text formatting and document preparation. Although working with a table in Word can be frustrating due to this limitation, this section contains a few tricks to make table editing tolerable.

Working with text in a table

Text is typed into a table's cells just as it's typed elsewhere in a document. A cell can contain a character, word, or paragraph or multiple paragraphs. You don't want to get wacky in a table with too much text, which can destroy the table's uniformity.

>> Word automatically adjusts a table's cell size to accommodate the text — unless you've set specific cell widths. See the later section "Adjusting row and column size."

>> To move from one cell to the next, tap the Tab key.

>> To move backward through the cells, press Shift+Tab.

>> If you press the Tab key in the far-right column's cell, the insertion pointer moves to the first cell in the next row.

>> If you press the Tab key in the bottom right cell in the table, Word adds a new row to the table.

>> On the off chance that you need to type a tab character in a cell, press Ctrl+Tab. Keep in mind, however, that tabs in table cells are ugly. Even so, use the Ruler to set tab stops and indents for a cell just as these items are set for any paragraph.

TIP

>> You can click the mouse in any cell to begin typing in that cell.

>> Pressing the Enter key in a cell starts a new paragraph inside the cell.

>> All text and formatting commands apply to a cell. If you need to center a cell's contents, apply the center-justification attribute to the paragraph: Press Ctrl+E. Also see the section "Aligning text," later in this chapter.

When you work inside a table, two new tabs appear on the Ribbon: Table Design and Table Layout. Using commands on these tabs is covered throughout this chapter.

Selecting items within a table

Tables add an extra layer of frustration to the selection process. You can select text within the table, or you can select parts of the table itself. To best describe how these techniques work, I've placed them into . . . a table! Refer to Table 3-1 for the details.

TABLE 3-1   **Table Selection**

Object	Mouse Pointer	What You Do
Cell	➚	Point the mouse at the lower left corner of the cell. Click to select.
Row	⟋	Point the mouse at the left side of the row.
Column	⬇	Point the mouse at the top of the column, above the table.
Table	✛	Click the mouse on the table's handle, located in the upper left corner of the table. If you don't see the handle, click the mouse in the table.

If you find any of the techniques listed in Table 3-1 to be awkward, follow these steps to select items in the table:

1. **Click the mouse inside the table.**

   If you need to select a cell, column, or row, click inside that object.

2. **On the Table Layout tab, in the Table group, use the Select menu to select a specific part of the table.**

To deselect any part of the table, tap any of the cursor keys (such as the left-arrow key) or click elsewhere in the text.

Inserting or removing rows or columns

No table is born perfect. Adding or removing rows or columns is something you may frequently do, especially when Bill in Finance discovers a new month between October and November, or the CEO doesn't like those January numbers.

To add a new row or column to a table, follow these steps:

1. **Click the mouse in a cell above or below or to the left or right of the new row or column you want to add.**

   For example, if you need a new column between existing columns 2 and 3, click the mouse in a cell somewhere in Column 2.

   You don't need to select an entire row or column to insert a new row or column.

2. **On the Table Layout tab, in the Rows & Columns group, click the proper command button.**

   Your choices:

   Insert Row Above

   Insert Row Below

   Insert Column Left

   Insert Column Right

3. **Repeat the command to add more rows or columns.**

All new rows and columns are inserted empty. Existing columns may be resized to accommodate the addition.

These steps are also used to purge rows and columns, though in Step 2 choose a command from the Delete button menu: Delete Cells, Delete Columns, Delete

Rows, or Delete Table. The Delete Cells command further prompts you as to how to fill the "hole" created by the deleted cell.

TIP

>> To add a new row to the bottom of a table, click the mouse in the far-right cell in the last row and press the Tab key.

>> If you find accessing Ribbon commands tedious, point the mouse to the left of the table between the rows you want to add. When the Add Row gizmo appears, as shown in the margin, click the plus sign icon to insert a new row at that spot.

>> Likewise, when you want to add a new column, point the mouse above the column gridline where you want the new column to appear. Click the plus in the gizmo (shown in the margin) to insert a new column at that spot.

Merging and splitting cells

A table grid need not hold the same number of cells in each row or column. Word lets you split and merge cells. It's not something you do for every table, but it does address some unique situations.

To combine two cells, follow these steps:

1. **Select the cells.**

These can be left-right or top-bottom to each other. You can select two or more cells, but they must all be in the same row or column, as illustrated in Figure 3-1.

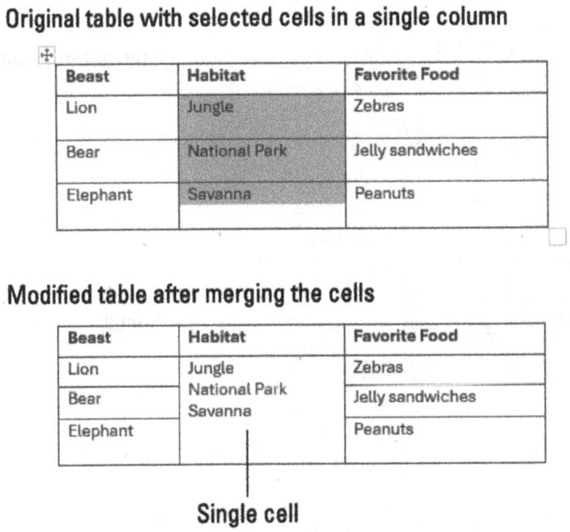

Original table with selected cells in a single column

Beast	Habitat	Favorite Food
Lion	Jungle	Zebras
Bear	National Park	Jelly sandwiches
Elephant	Savanna	Peanuts

Modified table after merging the cells

Beast	Habitat	Favorite Food
Lion	Jungle	Zebras
Bear	National Park Savanna	Jelly sandwiches
Elephant		Peanuts

Single cell

FIGURE 3-1:
Merging cells
in a table.

2. On the Table Layout tab, in the Merge group, click the Merge Cells button.

The two cells are combined.

The text from the right or lower cell is placed in a new paragraph in the combined cell.

To split a cell, follow these steps:

1. Click the mouse in the cell you want riven.

2. On the Table Layout tab, in the Merge group, click the Split Cells button.

The Split Cells dialog box appears. It gives you control over how the cells are split, setting the rows and columns so that the new cells fan out in the proper direction(s).

3. Set the number of rows or columns for the split.

4. Click the OK button.

The single cell is split into multiple cells, as illustrated in Figure 3-2.

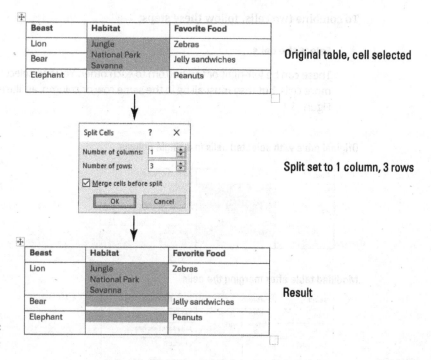

FIGURE 3-2:
Splitting a cell.

Original table, cell selected

Split set to 1 column, 3 rows

Result

And now . . . a shortcut!

The quickest way to edit cells in a table is to use the Draw Table command and use the mouse to add or remove rows and columns. On the Table Layout tab, in the Draw group you find two commands to help you use the mouse to modify the table:

 Click the Draw Table button and use the mouse pointer drawing tool (shown in the margin) to draw a line in a cell, effectively splitting the cell.

 Click the Eraser button and use the Eraser mouse pointer (shown in the margin) to remove lines in a table; click on a line to erase it.

Setting the table size

For a quick adjustment to the table's width in your document, follow these steps:

1. Click the mouse inside the table.

 2. On the Table Layout tab, in the Cell Size group, click the AutoFit button.

3. Choose AutoFit Window.

The table instantly expands to fill the paragraph's margins.

If you want to tighten up the table, choose the AutoFit Contents command in Step 3.

You can also adjust the table size by dragging the box located in the table's lower right corner, though this method isn't as precise as using the AutoFit commands.

Adjusting row and column size

Word accommodates both your left- and right-brain abilities to mess with a table's inner arrangement.

For the left brain, you can use the mouse to adjust rows and columns. In fact, Word features a quick shortcut to adjust the column width to match the widest line of text in the column. Heed these steps:

1. Point the mouse at a column separator.

When you get to the sweet spot, the mouse changes to the left-right pointer, illustrated in the margin.

2. Double-click the mouse.

Instantly, the column is resized to reflect the widest cell to the left of the separator line.

Rather than double-click, you can drag the mouse to resize the cells. Point the mouse at the line between cells and the pointer changes as shown in the margin. Drag up or down to resize.

The mouse-pointing method can be imprecise, so Word offers a solution for your right brain: With the insertion pointer thumping away inside the table, click the Table Layout tab. In the Cell Size group, four gizmos are available to precisely set cell height and column width, as illustrated in Figure 3-3.

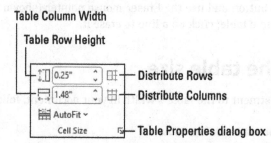

FIGURE 3-3:
The Table Layout tab's Cell Size group.

Use the Table Row Height and Table Column Width gizmos to set the specific height or width for the selected row(s) or column(s).

The Distribute Rows and Distribute Columns buttons split the table evenly, allocating dimensions to rows or columns without regard to the contents.

WARNING

>> I recommend that you select multiple rows and columns if you want to effectively use the gizmos in the Cell Size group. (Refer to Figure 3-3.) Otherwise, you may screw up the table's presentation.

>> Click the Launcher icon in the lower right corner of the Table Layout tab's Cell Size group to behold the Table Properties dialog box. Use the Row and Column tabs in this dialog box to make more specific adjustments across the table.

>> On the Table Layout tab, in the Alignment group, click the Cell Margins button to view the Table Options dialog box, which contains controls to set interior cell margins.

TIP

>> Adjusting row width and column height affects the table's size. This effect can't be avoided, so you may end up adjusting the overall table size after resetting the row or column size. Refer to the preceding section.

Make a Table Less Obnoxious

Word really crammed a whole truckload of table commands onto the Ribbon. Your goal isn't to use all of them when you craft a table for your document. Instead, you just want to make the table look presentable. It must convey information in an organized manner without detracting from its own content or other items on the page.

Adding a table heading

Tables often contain a header row. Most of the time, the header row is the top row, though some tables feature the header on the left side. Some tables feature both top row and left column as headers.

No secret exists to create a table heading. What I do is select the entire row and press Ctrl+B to make it bold. You could apply a style to the table heading, or you could use a preset style, as covered in the later section "Applying instant table formats."

One question to ask is whether you plan to manipulate the table's contents — for example, to sort the rows. If so, you must tell Word that the table contains a header row. Obey these directions:

1. **Click the mouse in the table.**

2. **In the Table Design tab's Table Style Options group, place a check mark by the item Header Row.**

   The item might already be selected: Word is smart, and it may set this item whenever it sees bold text applied to the table's top row.

See Chapter 7 for information on adding a caption to the table. The caption techniques presented in that chapter also apply to tables.

Aligning text

Paragraph formatting commands can align text within a table's cell, just as they align any paragraph in Word: Left, Right, Centered, Justified. Although you can use these commands within a table's cell, better and more sophisticated alignment options are found on the Table Layout tab. Follow these steps:

1. **Select the cells you want to align.**

   Drag to select individual cells or rows or columns or the entire table.

2. **On the Table Layout tab, in the Alignment group, click the appropriate Align button.**

Nine buttons are available, as illustrated in Figure 3-4. Each one sets the text's position according to the icon's graphic.

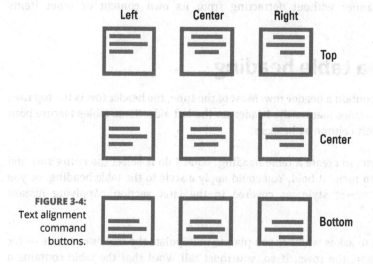

FIGURE 3-4:
Text alignment
command
buttons.

The top three buttons align text the same as the paragraph formatting commands: Left, Center, and Right. The rows set the text's vertical alignment.

Setting text direction

Text in a table need not flow from left to right. When you prefer another direction, or you simply enjoy watching your readers turn their heads, reset the text direction. Heed these instructions:

1. **Click the cell containing the text you want to reorient.**

Or select a group of cells.

2. **On the Table Layout tab, in the Alignment group, click the Text Direction button.**

Every time you click the button, the text changes direction by 90 degrees clockwise.

3. **Keep clicking the button until the text is properly oriented.**

Flinging around the text direction adjusts the cell size to accommodate your text. You may have to resize rows and columns afterward to make the table more presentable. Refer to the earlier section "Adjusting row and column size."

Setting gridlines

When you add a table to your document, it's set with a border style applied to the table grid. That style applies color and thickness to the table's grid. You can remove the grid's border style or selectively apply it. Follow these steps:

1. **Select the entire table.**

   Click the table's handle in the upper left corner.

2. **On the Table Design tab, in the Borders group, click the Borders button.**

   The Borders menu appears.

3. **To remove the grid, choose No Border.**

   The table border vanishes, but you probably would appreciate still viewing gridlines while you work on the table, so:

4. **Click the Borders button again and choose the View Gridlines command.**

   A faint, dashed line appears to delineate the table's presence in your document. This gridline does not print.

The Borders group on the Table Design tab features a host of controls to set border styles, line types, thicknesses, and colors.

If you want more control over border formatting, click the Borders button and choose the Borders and Shading command. You can use the Borders and Shading dialog box to set how lines are applied to various elements within the table.

Also on the Table Design tab, in the Table Styles group, you can use the Shading button to apply background color to selected portions of a table.

Applying instant table formats

If you want to get wacky with a table's design, skip over all the details and use one of Word's preset table styles. Follow these steps to best apply a table style:

1. **Create the table.**

   Fill in the cells' contents, adjust the table's presentation, and get everything *just so*. Using a table style works best when you have some semblance of a table to work with.

2. **On the Table Design tab's Table Styles group, hover the mouse over one of the styles.**

   The style is previewed on the selected table.

3. **Click a style to apply its attributes — color, shading, line styles, typeface — to your table.**

 To view more styles, Click the More button in the lower right corner of the Gallery. The expanded list displayed is quite extensive.

To remove the attributes applied with a table style, follow Steps 1 and 2, and then click the More button to display all the styles. Choose the Clear option.

> **TIP**
>
> ➤ Word's Table Styles gallery contains options to allow for every-other-row shading. It's much easier to select a preset style to apply that format than to apply shading manually. Ditto for other presentations, such as header rows and columns, which can be applied from the same Table Styles gallery menu.
>
> ➤ The instant preview capability (Step 2) is available only for current Word document versions. If it doesn't work, convert the document: Click the File tab, choose Info, and click the Convert button.

Some Table Tricks

The only table trick I knew as a kid is the old Up Table game. I could never figure out whether Uncle Ed kept rulers up his sleeves to make the thing work. Word's table tricks aren't as sneaky, but they aren't that obvious, either.

Sorting a table

One example of Word borrowing heavily from its spreadsheet sibling is the capability to sort contents in a table. This command is also used to sort boring old paragraphs, though it adds more horsepower when used in a table.

 The best way to sort a table is to ensure that it has a header row. Refer to the earlier section "Adding a table heading."

TIP

When you're certain that the table features a header, obey these directions to start sorting:

1. **Click to select the table.**

2. **On the Table Layout tab, in the Data group, click the Sort button.**

   The Sort dialog box appears. When a header row is defined in the column, the header's column text appears in the dialog box. For example, the table back in Figure 3-2 had Beast as its first column heading. The Sort dialog box shown in Figure 3-5 uses this heading text, which is the advantage of setting a header row in your table.

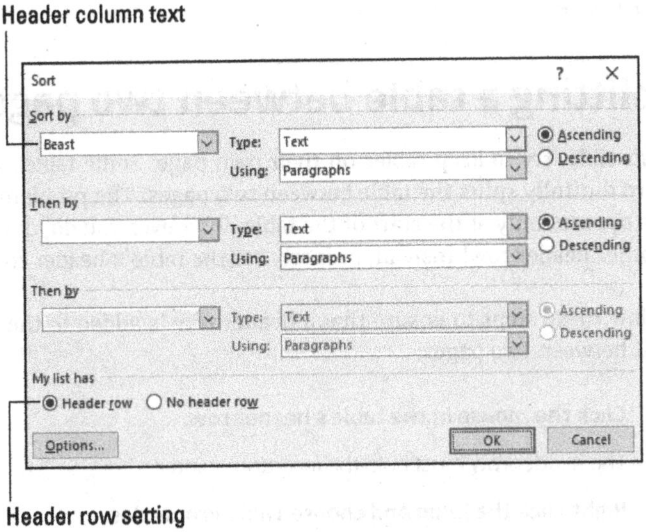

Header column text

FIGURE 3-5:
The Sort
dialog box.

Header row setting

3. **Choose a column heading from the Sort By list.**

4. **Choose how to sort from the Type list.**

   Choose Text for an alphabetic sort, Number for a numeric sort, or Date for a time sort.

5. **Set Ascending or Descending to determine the sort order.**

   For example, A-to-Z is an ascending text sort.

6. **If you want to sort by a second column, choose a column heading from the Then By menu.**

   For example, you could sort first by the Date column and then by the Amount column. These values, Date and Amount, would be the column headings in the table.

7. **Confirm that the Header Row option is set, as illustrated in Figure 3-5.**

   This setting confirms to Word that the table features a header row, which is not included in the sort.

8. **Click the OK button.**

   The table is sorted.

The Sort command button is also found on the Home tab, in the Paragraph group. It's used to sort lines of text, which don't necessarily need to be organized into a table.

Splitting a table between two pages

If possible, try to keep tables on their own page. Some tables get rather long, so Word dutifully splits the table between two pages. The problem is that the header row appears only at the start of the table. Whatever you do, don't manually insert another header row! Instead, properly set the table's header row property.

Follow these steps to ensure that a header row is added to the table, should it be split between two pages:

1. **Click the mouse in the table's header row.**

   The header row must hold the insertion pointer.

2. **Right-click the table and choose Table Properties.**

3. **In the Table Properties dialog box, click the Row tab.**

4. **Place a check mark by the option Allow Row to Break Across Pages.**

5. **Place a check mark by the option Repeat As Header Row at the Top of Each Page.**

6. **Click OK.**

The table is now configured so that, should it split across a page break, the first row — the *header* row — is echoed on that second page.

WARNING

>> Some of Word's preset tables automatically split across two pages.

>> Don't manually insert header rows. When you do, you run the risk that the table split may move as you edit and update your document.

>> I recommend placing a large table in its own section. The goal is to keep the table on its own page or, if required, create a special page format for this section.

- » Instead of starting a table's section at the start of the page, you could reset the page orientation to horizontal for the table. This trick works only when you split your document into sections.

- » On the Table Layout tab, in the Merge group, you'll find the Split Table button. Use this command to break a table into two separate tables. The split is made above the current row, and it doesn't reproduce the header in the second table.

- » You can also use the Split Table button to insert a paragraph before a table at the tippy-top of a document.

Applying table math

One area where Word's tables horn into Excel's spreadsheet turf is table math. It's possible in Word to add formulas to a table. These formulas provide for simple calculations and other operations within a table's cells.

In Figure 3-6, you see a table filled with boring numbers. A formula, inserted into the bottom row, tallies the total of the items above it. The Formula dialog box is shown, which is how the formula is inserted into the table.

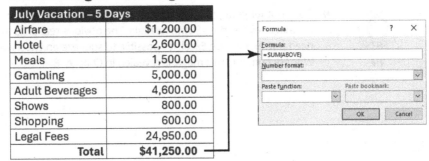

Travel Budget – Las Vegas

July Vacation – 5 Days	
Airfare	$1,200.00
Hotel	2,600.00
Meals	1,500.00
Gambling	5,000.00
Adult Beverages	4,600.00
Shows	800.00
Shopping	600.00
Legal Fees	24,950.00
Total	**$41,250.00**

FIGURE 3-6: Formulas in a table.

To stick a formula into a table, heed these directions:

1. Click in the cell.

For example, click in the cell at the bottom of a column into which you want to place the total (sum) of the values in the cells above it.

2. **On the Table Layout tab, in the Data group, click the Formula button.**

The Formula dialog box shows up. Word is clever at this point: The formula you most likely need is presented in the dialog box. If not, delete the formula and choose a new one from the Paste Function menu.

3. **Click OK.**

The formula is inserted into the cell, reflecting the proper result.

The formula is secretly a field. If you modify the table, you need to refresh the field: Right-click on the cell and choose the Update Field command. See Chapter 21 for more information on fields.

>> Word features a variety of functions that you can paste into the Formula field in the Formula dialog box. The list is shown on the Paste Function menu.

>> The four major table references are ABOVE, BELOW, LEFT, and RIGHT, which refer to cells above or below or to the left or right of the current cell.

>> You can combine two references, such as =SUM(ABOVE,LEFT), to get the sum of a row and column's values.

>> You can also refer to specific cell numbers using the common Excel format C*n*, R*n*, or R*n*C*n*. C is the column containing the formula's cell; R is the row. The value *n* represents a specific cell in the column or row where 1 is the first cell.

TIP

>> Don't bother getting fancy with the formulas in a table. I've never used anything beyond the =SUM() formula. The obvious reason is that when you need power, just use Excel. It's possible to squeeze an Excel worksheet into a Word document. This magic is revealed in Chapter 8.

IN THIS CHAPTER

» Finding styles in a document

» Creating heading levels

» Borrowing styles

» Building a custom template

» Updating templates and their documents

» Changing a document's template

Chapter **4**

Styles and Templates

A budding cook isn't content with putting a premade box of food in a microwave. No, the desire is to craft good victuals from scratch, adding flavor and flair along the way. It also helps to know that *victuals* is pronounced "vittles," and it refers to food.

Like that budding chef, you may suspect that Word comes with plenty of advanced, "professional" options for styles and templates, stuff beyond the basic "microwave" variety text formatting. You can use these tips and tricks presented in this chapter to go beyond what mere mortal Word users know about styles and templates.

Style Management

As a style maniac, I prefer to have all my styles visible and available for use. Although a handful of styles appear on the Home tab's Styles group, the best way to view and access the lot is to summon the Styles pane.

1. **On the Home tab, in the Styles group, click the Launcher icon.**

   The launcher icon appears in the lower-right corner of the group and is shown in the margin, shown in the margin and illustrated Figure 4-1. Lo, the Styles pane appears.

Styles gallery   Launcher icon   Styles pane (docked)

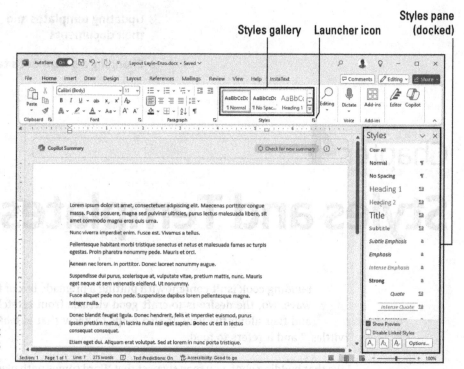

FIGURE 4-1:
A document with the Styles pane docked.

2. **If the Styles pane is "floating" over the document window, drag it to the right side of the window to "dock" it.**

   I prefer the Styles pane docked to the right side of the window, where the styles are easily accessible, as shown in Figure 4-1.

3. **For extra help in locating styles, check the Show Preview button.**

   This button is found below the scrolling list of styles in the Styles pane.

TIP

4. **In the Styles pane, click the Options button.**

   Because styles can be numerous and are affected by any attributes you apply to your text, I limit their display in the Styles pane. The Style Pane Options dialog box helps keep the style list brief so that I don't need to scroll.

5. In the Styles Pane Options dialog box, place a check mark by the item **Paragraph Level Formatting.**

Setting this option removes some of the more obscure styles from the Styles Pane.

6. Click OK to dismiss the Styles Pane Options dialog box.

As I work on a document, I like to limit the number of styles shown in the Styles pane. To do so, summon the Styles Pane Options dialog box again (Step 5) and from the Select Styles to Show menu, choose the In Use option. This choice is preferred especially when editing a document.

Selecting instances of a style

When you modify a style, you change all text in a document to which the style is applied. Where is it applied? To discover how often a style is used, display its menu. This menu is best accessed from the Styles pane, which is covered in the preceding section.

To the right of each style listed on the pane is a secret menu button. Point the mouse at the style in the Styles pane, then click the menu button to view the menu, as illustrated in Figure 4-2.

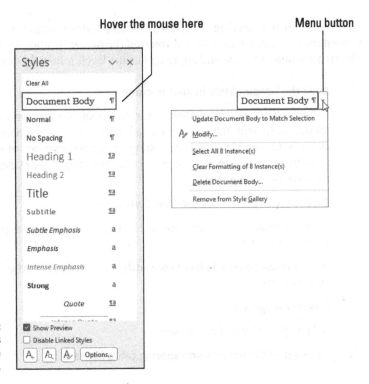

FIGURE 4-2:
The Styles
pane shows a
modified style.

In Figure 4-2, you see that the Document Body style is applied eight times in the document. If this style were altered, say the margins were changed, a second entry for Document Body appears. Choose the second entry, and then select the option to Select All Instances to quickly modify the style, perhaps restoring it back to its original format.

TIP

>> When a style is unused, the Select All Instances menu item says No Data.

>> Your clue that a style has been modified in a document is the plus sign (+) in the Styles pane. The plus sign indicates that the base style has the addition of another element, such as modified text or paragraph formatting.

>> To re-apply the original style to a modified (+) style, select all instances of the modified style and then choose the original style from the Styles pane.

Setting the heading style outline level

Word comes with preset heading styles, named Heading 1, Heading 2, and so on. These styles represent heading levels within a document, but they also carry an outline level paragraph attribute. This attribute is used in Word's Outline mode, plus it comes in handy when creating a Table of Contents as well as setting Bookmarks and when using other useful features.

Setting an outline-level for your own heading styles is important if you want to ease document automation — and you find the preset Heading styles to be boring. To create a heading style and apply an outline level, follow these steps:

1. **Build the heading style in your document.**

   It's best to format the paragraph first. In fact, create the top-level heading style for your document. This text isn't the title, but rather a section heading. For example, the title of this section, "Setting the heading style outline level," is formatted at outline level 2. The main section heading, "Style Management," is formatted at outline level 1.

2. **On the Styles pane, click the New Style button.**

   If the Styles pane isn't visible, click the Home tab and in the Styles group click the Launcher icon.

3. **In the Create New Style from Formatting dialog box, click the Format button.**

4. **Choose Paragraph.**

   The Paragraph dialog box appears.

5. **Ensure that the Indents and Spacing tab is forward.**

6. **Click the Outline Level menu.**

7. **Choose Level 1.**

Level 1 is the top level for the document's primary heading style.

8. **Click OK.**

9. **Make any additional changes in the Create New Style from Formatting dialog box.**

For example, you may want to choose a style for the next paragraph from the Style for Following Paragraph menu. I chose the Body Text style to follow my document's headings.

10. **Continue creating the style.**

Add whatever other formatting the style needs.

11. **Type the style's name.**

12. **Click OK.**

The heading style is created with the proper outline-level attribute set.

When you create the next level heading in your document, for example heading 2, base it on the top-level heading format: Use the Style Based On menu in the Create New Style from Formatting dialog box. Also, repeat Steps 3 through 7 to set the outline level, but set it at the next level, such as Level 2.

REMEMBER

>> When you ensure that all headings in your document support an outline-level attribute, other Word tools recognize and use the headings as described elsewhere in this book.

>> The top-level heading style generally uses the largest point size. The heading styles decrease in size with each level.

>> Graphic designers prefer sans serif fonts in boldface type for document headings. Refer to Chapter 1.

>> For plain text, you choose the Body Text outline level. This option is the default for new styles based on the Normal style.

>> I use the style name *A Head* for my document's top-level heading. The next level is *B Head*, and then *C Head*, and so on. This is the nomenclature used in the publishing industry to refer to document heading levels.

>> Word's default heading styles are used when creating an outline. See Chapter 16.

>> See Chapter 18 for more information on creating an automatic table of contents in a document.

Stealing a style from another document

Styles are held in templates, but any Word document you create also holds styles. Rather than recreating these styles, or resorting to copy-and-paste, you can take advantage of a hidden Word tool to purloin styles directly from any document. The secret is to summon the Organizer dialog box, shown in Figure 4-3.

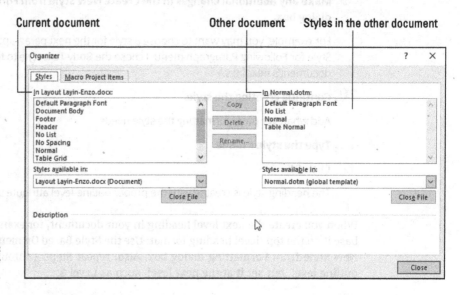

FIGURE 4-3:
The Organizer dialog box.

To access the Organizer dialog box and steal styles, follow these perfectly legal steps:

1. **In the Styles pane, click the Manage Styles button.**

   If the Styles pane isn't visible, refer to the earlier section, "Selecting instances of a style."

   The Manage Styles dialog box appears.

2. **Click the Import/Export button, located at the bottom left of the Manage Styles dialog box.**

   The Manage Style dialog box vanishes, and the Organizer dialog box takes its place, as shown in Figure 4-3. The current document appears on the left, and the Normal template is shown on the right.

3. **Click the Close File button on the right side of the dialog box.**

4. Click the Open File button.

It replaces the Close File button from Step 3.

You see an Open dialog box. Your job is to find the document file that contains the style(s) you want to pilfer. Word automatically chooses the current location for any document templates.

5. Work the controls in the Open dialog box to locate the document that contains the style you want to copy.

If the document isn't a template, change the file type from All Word Templates to All Word Documents. Navigate to the folder that contains the document you need.

6. Select the Word document, and then click the Open button.

The document isn't opened. Instead, you see a list of its styles shown in the Organizer dialog box, as illustrated in Figure 4-3.

7. Click to select the style you want to copy.

Press and hold the Ctrl key to select multiple styles.

8. Click the Copy button.

The selected styles are copied to the current document.

9. Click the Close button when you're done copying the styles.

10. Save the current document.

Styles copied or imported from another document remain in the current document, even when a style isn't applied in the text.

Templates of Your Own

When you create the same type of document over and over, or you work on a project that involves many similar documents, you need to build your own document template. Doing so saves oodles of time.

>> Templates offer document consistency. They also provide standard elements, such as a letterhead or company logo.

>> The most common feature in a template is a collection of styles. The styles guarantee that the template's documents all feature the same text formats.

>> If you're writing a novel, ensure that all chapters use the same template. See Chapter 17 for details.

>> Not every document needs a custom template. For a one-off document, it's perfectly okay to use the Normal template: Press Ctrl+N to start a new, blank document.

Creating a custom template

As with creating styles, it's easier to base a template on something existing than it is to create one from scratch. I recommend you write that first document, experiment with styles, layout, and other common elements, and then build a template based on that prototype.

Here are the steps I take to create a custom template:

1. Create the prototype document.

Build styles, set graphics, design the layout, program macros, apply page formatting. Not all these tasks are necessary for every document, but the point is to have a foundation upon which to build a document.

2. Remove the document's specific text.

A template can contain text, but this text is useful only when it applies to *all* documents the template creates; for example, your name and address for a letter template or a header/footer for a manuscript.

3. Add content controls.

If your template is used by others, content controls can help direct them where and how to type text. See Chapter 24.

4. Save the template as a template.

When using the Save As dialog box, choose Word Template as the file type. When you do, Word automatically chooses the Custom Office Templates folder as the file's location.

5. Close the template document.

You don't want to further edit the document, because it's now a template. Any changes that are made affect the template itself.

The template is now available on the File tab's New menu. Click the Personal tab when searching for templates to access your creation.

Building an envelope template

Perhaps one of the most useful templates you can create is a personal envelope. It comes preset with your return address plus a text box where you can set the recipient's address. Follow these steps to build your own custom envelope template:

1. **Start off with a new document.**

    Press Ctrl+N. As with all new documents, this one is based on the Normal template.

    Your first task is to set the paper size to an envelope.

2. **On the Layout tab, in the Page Setup group, click the Size button and choose Envelope #10.**

    The document's dimension changes to reflect a common envelope, but the orientation is wrong, as are the margins.

3. **Click the Orientation button and choose Landscape.**

4. **Click the Margins button and choose Narrow.**

    The page's margins are set to a half inch around the envelope.

    Your next task is to apply the template's consistent text, which is your return address.

5. **Type your return address.**

    Press Shift+Enter to end each line with a line break as opposed to a paragraph break, which keeps the address text tight.

6. **Format the return address text.**

    Apply formatting as desired, setting font, size, and so on.

TIP

    After formatting the return address, consider creating a new style to represent this next text format.

    The next task is to add a text box for the recipient's address.

7. **On the Insert tab, in the Text group, click the Text Box button and choose Simple Text Box.**

    Don't worry about the text box's current position.

8. **Set the text box's layout to In Front Of Text.**

    Click the mouse on the text box's border to view the Layout Options button, illustrated in Figure 4-4. Click the Layout Options button and choose In Front Of Text as the text box's layout.

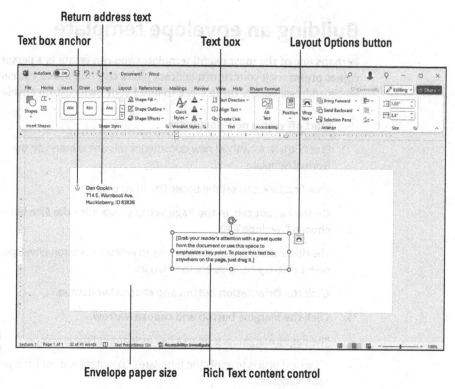

Return address text

Text box anchor

Text box

Layout Options button

Dan Gookin
714 E. Wambooli Ave.
Huckleberry, ID 83836

[Grab your reader's attention with a great quote from the document or use this space to emphasize a key point. To place this text box anywhere on the page, just drag it.]

FIGURE 4-4:
An envelope template in the making.

Envelope paper size

Rich Text content control

9. **Drag the text box to the approximate location of the recipient's address on the envelope.**

10. **On the Shape Format tab, in the Shape Styles group, click the Shape Outline button and choose No Outline.**

11. **Format the placeholder text inside the text box.**

If you created a style for the return address, you can apply it here — or create a new style for the recipient's address.

12. **Delete the placeholder text in the text box.**

You can leave the text if you like, but I prefer to add my own Rich Text content control for the recipient's address. See Chapter 24 for information on creating this content control.

The final task is to save the envelope template.

13. **Press the F12 key.**

This keyboard shortcut summons the traditional Save As dialog box, which is quicker for saving a document template than using the default Word Save screen.

14. **From the Save As Type menu, choose Word Template (*.dotx).**

The Save As dialog box automatically shows the location of all your personal Office templates.

15. **Type a name for the template, such as My Envelope.**

16. **Click OK.**

The template is saved.

17. **Press Ctrl+W to close the document window.**

You don't want the template to linger on the screen because it's now a template and not a document you want to edit.

To confirm that the template operation was successful, click the File tab and choose New. Click the Personal heading to locate your envelope template, or whichever template you just created. You don't see a preview, as you do with Word's own templates, but the template is available. Choose it to create a new envelope document.

REMEMBER

The only text you want to keep in a template is text that's needed for every document the template creates. If your template document contains any surplus text, remove it before you save the template.

Modifying a template

You can't just open a template file to make changes. When you do, you create a new document based on that template. To modify a template, you must be specific. Follow these steps:

1. **Press Ctrl+F12 to summon the traditional Open dialog box.**

2. **From the file type menu, choose All Word Templates (*.dotx, *.dotm, *.dot).**

3. **Delete the text in the address bar and type** %USERPROFILE%\Documents\ Custom Office Templates.

Click once in the address bar to select its text, then press the Delete key. After you type **%USERPROFILE%** and press the backslash key, Windows autocompletes text for you, ensuring that you properly type the folder name as presented.

4. **Select the template file you want to edit.**

5. **Click the Open button.**

6. **Edit the template.**

REMEMBER

You're editing a template — not a document. A good clue is that the template filename, not the generic "Document *n*," appears on the window's title bar.

Modify styles, add or remove text, create other elements, and do whatever is necessary to update the template.

7. **Press Ctrl+S to save the template.**

Because you're editing the template directly, the changes you save are made to the template, not to a new document.

8. **Press Ctrl+W to close the template document window.**

A logical question at this point is, "Are all my documents updated?" The answer is a vague, "They could be!" Whether existing documents change depends on the settings you make when you create a new style. See the next section.

>> Generally speaking, changing a template affects only new documents created with the template as a base.

>> Anything beyond a style, such as text and graphics, appears only in new documents created by selecting the template.

Updating template documents

When you change a template, you affect only new documents created with that template. Any older documents associated with the template remain unchanged — unless you alter how template updates affect a document.

To update an existing document's styles to reflect any changes made to its template, follow these steps:

1. **On the File tab, choose Options.**

The Word Options dialog box appears.

2. **Choose Add-Ins from the left side of the Word Options dialog box.**

3. **At the bottom of the dialog box, from the Manage menu choose Templates and click the Go button.**

The Templates and Add-Ins dialog box appears, illustrated in Figure 4-5.

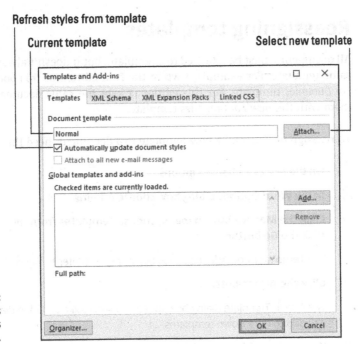

Refresh styles from template

Current template

Select new template

Templates and Add-ins

Templates | XML Schema | XML Expansion Packs | Linked CSS

Document template

Normal   Attach...

☑ Automatically update document styles
☐ Attach to all new e-mail messages

Global templates and add-ins

Checked items are currently loaded.

Add...
Remove

Full path:

Organizer...   OK   Cancel

FIGURE 4-5:
The Templates
and Add-Ins
dialog box.

4. **Click to place a check mark by the item Automatically Update Document Styles.**

5. **Click OK.**

The template's documents are now updated whenever the template is edited with changes made to its styles.

TIP

If you've activated the Ribbon's Developer tab, click it. In the Templates group, click the Document Template button. This shortcut saves you from going through Steps 1 through 3 in this section. See Chapter 22 for information on showing the Ribbon's Developer tab.

» If a document doesn't reflect changes made to the template, close it and then open it again.

» Only changes to the template's styles are reflected in the document. Any other changes or additions, including text or graphics, are reflected only in new documents created.

Reassigning templates

All documents must be attached to a template, but it doesn't always need to be the same template. For example, I wrote the first edition of this book with an older *For Dummies* template. For this edition, I kept the same documents but updated them with the new *For Dummies* template.

To reassign or "attach" a new template to a document, heed these directions:

1. **On the File tab, choose Options.**

2. **In the Word Options dialog box, choose Add-Ins.**

3. **Click the Manage button menu, choose Templates from the menu, and click the Go button.**

The Templates and Add-Ins dialog box appears. (Refer to Figure 4-5.)

4. **Click the Attach button.**

The Attach Template dialog box appears. It works like an Open dialog box, but it's used to hunt down templates.

5. **If you're attaching one of your own templates, click in the dialog box's address bar and type the location for your personal templates.**

This location is **%USERPROFILE%\Documents\Custom Office Templates**

Press Enter after typing the address to view your templates.

6. **Select the template you want to attach to the document.**

7. **Click the Open button.**

The Document Template item is updated in the Templates and Add-Ins dialog box.

8. **Ensure that a check mark is placed by the item Automatically Update Document Styles.**

You want the styles imported from the new template, replacing the old styles.

9. **Click OK to assign the new template.**

Reassigning a template doesn't remove text or graphics associated with the original template. Styles from the new template are available to the document and updated if they have the same names.

If you want to remove a template, or apply the Normal template to any document, in Step 6 click in the Document Template text box and type **Normal**. Click OK.

TIP

2

Go Graphical

Learn about page layout techniques.

Add shapes and create line art in your documents.

Discover how to add pictures, illustrations, and captions to a document.

Create interesting items inside your text, and work with Excel in Word.

IN THIS CHAPTER

» **Exploring graphical options**

» **Understanding graphics on a page**

» **Changing the layout**

» **Controlling text flow**

» **Positioning graphics**

» **Setting an object away from text**

» **Lining up objects**

Chapter **5**

Text and Graphics Layout

Let boring people use only words in their documents. To improve upon a dreary, text-filled manuscript, Word lets you toss graphics into the mix. It features the capability to insert pictures, shapes, and other items smack dab onto the digital page. These graphical goobers can help illustrate a point or just make the result look extra fancy.

Mixing text and graphics is fun, but it presents a curious problem: How do text and graphics mix on a page? The solution is something called *layout*. This topic is something you should know about to best present that graphical whatzit in a document.

Where Text and Graphics Meet

Early word processors had no more power than today's meager text editors. The notion of inserting an image into a document was considered blasphemy. But during the Great Feature Wars of the 1990s, software developers kept thinking of ways to improve their products — and to outdo their competition. The result is a profane mixture of text and graphics.

Finding non-text things to thrust into a document

Non-text elements on a page aren't limited to pictures. True, pictures were first in line. But Word also allows you to insert a host of other items, which I call *objects*, into a document. For mixing text and graphics, each of these items is considered the same. Here's the short list:

Pictures: The traditional graphical item, a picture can be an image, some clip art, a photograph, an illustration, or one of a host of other graphical goodies you can insert into your document.

Shapes: A shape is a drawing object, what the graphic designers call *line art*. Shapes can be applied as decorative elements, combined into complex structures, converted into text or picture boxes, and manipulated by a host of interesting commands.

SmartArt: Word's SmartArt gallery presents a selection of prebuilt shapes (drawing objects) with fill-in-the-blanks placeholders. This feature allows you to quickly add artwork to a document.

Charts: Rather than cobble together a pie chart or line graph, Word hosts a gallery of charts and graphs you can add as graphical elements to your document.

Text boxes: Word features a specific text box command. It lists various text boxes, all designed and made to look pretty. This feature is truly a shortcut because you can convert any shape (drawing object) into a text box.

These items are all located on the Insert tab. Most are found in the Illustrations group. The text box appears in the Text group, though you can convert most drawing objects (shapes) into a text box. Figure 5-1 illustrates the locations on the Insert tab.

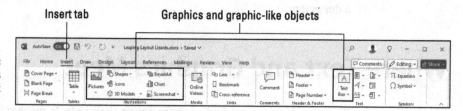

FIGURE 5-1:
Graphical objects you can insert into a document.

Other items are treated like graphics as well. The difference between these objects and items such as tables, is that these elements feature the Layout Options button, shown in the margin. See the later section "Setting layout options."

>> It's also possible to paste graphics in from another program. Providing that the image is in a format Word recognizes, the process works like pasting in text, but the result is an image in your document.

>> See Chapter 6 for specifics on shapes and text boxes.

>> Chapter 7 covers pictures and other graphics.

>> SmartArt and charts are covered in Chapter 8, along with other, non-traditional document objects.

Mixing text and objects

When word processors first allowed graphics and text to mingle, images were set at the same level as text; a picture acted like a large, single character. You could set it on a line by itself, center it as a paragraph, and call it all good. That trick worked for a while, but eventually word processing users demanded more.

Graphics can still exist in-line with text. This option is what Word chooses when you first insert a picture, text box, or drawing object into your document. You can then free the object from the text, set it at a specific position, or wrap text around the object. These topics are covered elsewhere in this chapter, but before you dive into these settings, it helps to understand how Word structures elements on a page.

Figure 5-2 illustrates a page in a Word document. The base layer is the page itself, which could be the paper upon which a document is printed. Above the base layer comes any watermark, background color, or image. The next layer consists of any graphical object set to float behind the text. The text itself exists at the next layer, along with any in-line graphics or graphics set with a wrapping option. Finally, the top level, the one "closest" to you, contains graphical objects floating in front of the text.

The layers illustrated in Figure 5-2 are relevant to layout options. You can position items in different layers to adjust appearances. Beyond these layers, when you apply drawing objects, they can be set in front of or behind each other — like layers within layers. But in the big picture, layout options are set as illustrated in Figure 5-2.

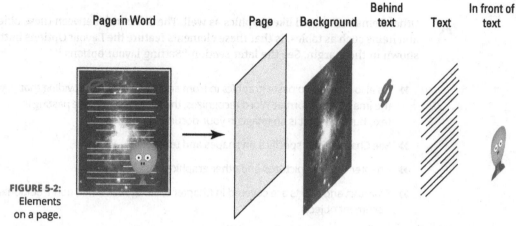

| Page in Word | Page | Background | Behind text | Text | In front of text |

FIGURE 5-2: Elements on a page.

Image by ESO/J. Emerson/VISTA

Layout Choices

When graphics and text became a thing in word processing, users had to discover how to mix the two. The solution is to choose a layout option. The term comes from graphic design, where underpaid and underappreciated artists organize and present text and graphics on a page.

Layout options can be freely ignored. Doing so harkens to an early age when graphics existed along with text as just another character. But Word offers more, depending on how professionally you want to present the information in your document.

Setting layout options

The general method of inserting a graphic or other object in your text works like this:

1. **Position the insertion pointer at the location where you want the image to appear.**

   It doesn't matter if you're precise at this point. Graphics can be moved and arranged later, but first you must get the thing into the text.

2. **Click the Insert tab.**

3. **Choose the item to insert, such as Picture or Shape.**

   Details for selecting items are found in Chapters 6, 7, and 8. When it's in your document, the graphical gewgaw is selected and appears as illustrated in Figure 5-3.

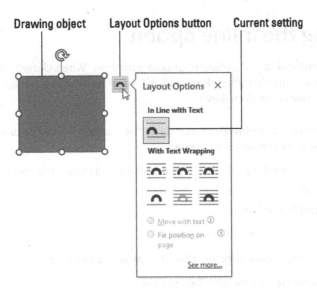

Drawing object   Layout Options button   Current setting

FIGURE 5-3:
A drawing object,
in line with text.

4. **Click the Layout Options button.**

The button appears when a graphical object is selected. If you don't see the button, click the object.

The Layout Options pop-up menu lists the seven layout options available.

5. **Choose another layout option from the pop-up menu.**

These options are described throughout this chapter.

Beyond the layout options, you have the choice of how to position an object on the page. You can set an object at an absolute position or position it relative to a certain paragraph. See the section "Setting the image's position."

TIP

>> If the Layout Options button doesn't appear, the object you've selected can't be repositioned on the page.

>> Some objects, such as tables, can be inserted into a text box. In this configuration, you can apply layout options to the object.

>> Layout options are also available on the Ribbon. After selecting an object, click the Format tab (Shape Format, Picture Format, and so on). In the Arrange group, click the Wrap Text button and choose a layout option from the menu.

>> The same layout options are found on a right-click shortcut menu: Right-click the object and choose Wrap Text from the pop-up menu. Layout options are shown on the Wrap Text submenu.

Using the inline option

The traditional layout option is In Line with Text. When chosen, the object works just like a giant character along with all the other text in a paragraph. To set this option, obey these directions:

1. **Click to set the insertion pointer at the location in your document where you want the object to appear.**

   I recommend creating an empty paragraph and placing the object in that paragraph.

2. **Insert the object.**

   Chapters 6, 7, and 8 offer specifics.

3. **With the object selected, click the Layout Options button.**

4. **Choose the In Line with Text option.**

   This layout setting directs Word to place the object in the text, just like other characters and words.

The object now moves with the rest of the text. To free it from the text, choose another layout option.

Wrapping text around an object

Four layout options allow you to wrap text around an object. Unlike the In Line with Text option, the object's position isn't locked into a paragraph's text. These four options are:

Square: The object sits inside a rectangle, no matter what the object's shape. Text flows around the rectangle, keeping equidistance from the object.

Tight: This setting is similar to Square, though the text is closer to the object and matches its shape. So, if the object is a triangle, the "hole" in the text is shaped like a triangle.

Through: If the image's shape allows, text flows through the image, perhaps filling an interior space or a space between separate sides of the same object. When you choose this setting, you may have to edit the object's bounding box and position its wrap points to make the effect work. See the next section.

Top and Bottom: The image is held in a box with the top and bottom extending to the page margins.

The effect for each of these settings is illustrated in Figure 5-4. In each instance, the object was selected, and the indicated wrapping option was chosen from the Layout Options menu.

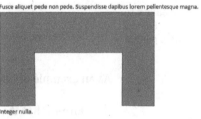

FIGURE 5-4: Layout options with text wrapping.

» The Tight option works best when the image is of an irregular shape, like a drawing object or a picture with a transparent background. The triangle shown in Figure 5-4 (bottom left) was saved with its background set to transparent, which is why the Tight layout option looks good.

» The Through example in Figure 5-4 works because the wrap points are edited to allow text to flow below the object. See the next section.

Editing the wrap points

Both the Tight and Through layout options allow you to add more integrity to the polygon separating the object from the text, what I call the bounding box. To hone this shape, you can edit the wrap points that define the polygon. This trick works only for the Tight and Through layout options.

Figure 5-5 illustrates an example of wrap points around a crescent shape, though any irregularly shaped object works.

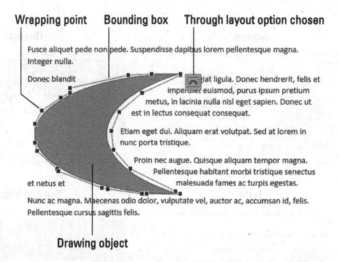

FIGURE 5-5:
Editing
wrap points.

As an example of how to edit wrap points, follow these steps:

1. Ensure that the document contains text so that you can play with the wrap.

If you're just goofing around, type **=lorem(10)** on a line by itself and press the Enter key to generate ten paragraphs of standard *Lorem Ipsum* placeholder text.

2. On the Insert tab, in the Illustrations area, click the Shapes menu to locate and insert an object, such as the crescent shown in Figure 5-5.

Drag the mouse over the document's text to create the shape. After releasing the mouse, you see size handles appear, as well as the Layout Options button. The Shape Format tab appears on the Ribbon.

 3. Click the Layout Options button and choose the Tight option.

The option is shown in the margin. After choosing this option, the text lines up very close with the shape, which is the Tight layout option's default operation.

 4. On the Shape Format tab, in the Arrange area, click the Wrap Text button to show its menu.

5. Choose the command Edit Wrap Points.

A red line envelops the shape. Black squares on the line represent handles. At this point you can move the handles to reshape the bounding box, you can add a wrap point, you can remove a wrap point.

Move a wrap point. Point the mouse at a wrap point. The mouse pointer changes, as shown in the margin. Drag the point to a new position to adjust the distance between the text and the object.

 Add a wrap point. To create a new wrap point, press the Ctrl key on the keyboard. The mouse pointer changes, as shown in the margin. Click on the bounding box (the red line) to drop a new wrap point. You can then drag that point to adjust the bounding box and set the distance between the text and the object.

 Remove a wrap point. To get rid of a wrap point, press the Ctrl key and point the mouse at a wrap point. The mouse pointer changes, as shown in the margin. Click the mouse to remove the wrap point.

6. **When you're done editing the wrap points, click the mouse in the document's text.**

The object is deselected, and you can return to editing text.

It's easy to get carried away with wrap points and editing the bounding box, but the results can look pretty sharp, especially when you have an object that Word doesn't wrap properly.

Setting the image's position

Pictures, illustrations, and other objects are commonly related to the surrounding text. For example, that image of a cake best sits on a page with its recipe. To help you make an association between an image and the text that describes it, Word anchors objects to a paragraph. As you work on the document, the image shifts along with its anchored text. The goal is to prevent having an image on one page and its text reference on another.

To confirm that an image is anchored to a paragraph, obey these directions:

1. **Click to select the image.**

 2. **Look for the Anchor icon in the page's left margin.**

The Anchor icon, shown here in the margin, is positioned next to the start of a paragraph to which the object is attached. It appears only when the object is selected.

3. **Click the Layout Options button.**

4. **Ensure that the option Move with Text is selected.**

When the Move with Text item is chosen, the graphic moves with the paragraph as you edit or add text to the rest of the document.

The other option on the Layout Options button menu is Fix Position on Page. This option frees the image's position from the text. When it's chosen (in Step 4), the object stays at the same location on the page regardless of how text flows around it.

If you want to be precise about where an object appears on a page, click the See More link in Step 4. The Layout dialog box appears. On the Position tab, you can set the Absolute Position options for the object's Horizontal and Vertical locations. In Figure 5-6, I've set the object's location at a specific location from the page's top and left edges.

Absolution position set   **Relative to the page**

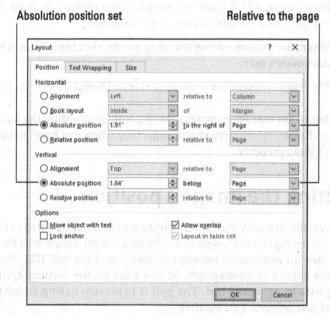

FIGURE 5-6: Setting absolute page position.

The page position setting affects all layout options except for In Line with Text.

» The In Line with Text option is automatically anchored to the paragraph in which it sits.

» The floating options, Behind Text and In Front of Text, can also be anchored to text or set to a specific position on the page. See the next section.

Floating an object in front of or behind text

Two layout options free the graphical object from the confines of your document's text. The object can float in front of the text or behind the text, and rest at any absolute position on the page. Earlier, in Figure 5-2, you see two such objects, one floating in front of text and the other behind the text.

To set an item's layout in front of or behind text, click the object and choose either item from the Layout Options pop-up menu.

>> Of the two choices, I prefer to float objects in front of text. For example, if I'm creating a cover page with a text box for the title, I release the text box and set its layout to float in front of the text. That way, I can position the object exactly on the page.

>> It can be difficult to select and move an object placed behind text. You must keep pointing the mouse at the object until the mouse pointer changes to the four-way arrow thing, shown in the margin. Then you can click to select the object or drag it to a new position.

>> If you have trouble selecting an object floating behind the text, on the Shape Format (or Picture Format) tab, in the Arrange group, choose Selection Pane. Click to select the object in the Selection pane, after which you can use the arrow keys on the keyboard to move the object.

TIP

>> Solid objects behind the text look best when their transparency level is set. For example, a setting of 80 or 90 percent transparency ensures that the image is visible, but doesn't distract from the text in front of it.

>> Objects in front of or behind text can still be anchored to a paragraph or the page. Refer to the preceding section for directions on how to set these options.

Aligning objects on a page

Word helps you to line up and arrange objects by showing alignment guides. These lines appear as you drag around an object. They represent the page's top, bottom, left, and right margins, plus a centerline down the middle of the page and at the top of each paragraph.

To see the alignment guides, drag around a graphical object. As the object nears one of the margins, a green guideline appears, as illustrated in Figure 5-7. Use the guides to position the object's center or its edges with the page or paragraph elements.

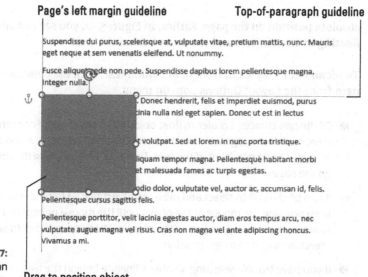

Page's left margin guideline

Top-of-paragraph guideline

Suspendisse dui purus, scelerisque at, vulputate vitae, pretium mattis, nunc. Mauris eget neque at sem venenatis eleifend. Ut nonummy.

Fusce aliquet pede non pede. Suspendisse dapibus lorem pellentesque magna. Integer nulla.

. Donec hendrerit, felis et imperdiet euismod, purus cinia nulla nisl eget sapien. Donec ut est in lectus

volutpat. Sed at lorem in nunc porta tristique.

liquam tempor magna. Pellentesque habitant morbi et malesuada fames ac turpis egestas.

odio dolor, vulputate vel, auctor ac, accumsan id, felis. Pellentesque cursus sagittis felis.

Pellentesque porttitor, velit lacinia egestas auctor, diam eros tempus arcu, nec vulputate augue magna vel risus. Cras non magna vel ante adipiscing rhoncus. Vivamus a mi.

Drag to position object

FIGURE 5-7:
Setting an object's position.

The page's centerline appears whenever an object nears the center of the page. Use the center handles on the object to position it centered left-to-right on the page.

>> If the alignment guides fail to appear, on the Shape Format tab, in the Arrange Group, click the Align Object menu. Choose the command Use Alignment Guides to view them.

>> Page layout artists are persnickety about text and graphics lining up on a page. Setting the image aligned with a page margin, or just the top of a paragraph, helps give the document a professional look, even though few readers notice the effort put into this task.

TIP

Chapter **6**

Shapes and Drawings

urther proving that a document contains more than just text, Word sports a handy Shape menu. Use it to plop down a shape or two into your document, clearly in defiance of the "documents are all about text" mandate that I made up in my earlier book, *Word Processing Is All About Text and Not Graphics For Dummies* (Wiley).

Mandates and fictitious titles aside, Word lets you festoon your document with all sorts of interesting shapes and drawings. These shapes can be used in a document for decorative purposes, to add graphical elements, or just because you're bored.

Get Into Shapes

Word has a shape for just about every need in your document, all ready and available for a quick thrust into the text. Choose a preset shape or draw your own. The journey starts on the Insert tab, in the Illustrations group. There lurks the Shapes button. Its menu bursts with a delightful assortment of interesting *line art*, like a box of lights and ornaments ready to decorate otherwise dreary text.

Inserting a shape

Sticking a shape into your document requires less effort and fewer words than it does to write about how you insert a shape into a document. Here are the general steps:

1. **Scroll to the part of your document where you want to set the shape.**

You don't need to position the insertion pointer specifically; just have the page upon which you want the shape set visible on the screen.

2. **On the Insert tab, in the Illustrations area, click the Shapes button.**

A long menu unfurls, listing a smorgasbord of shapes.

3. **Click on the shape you desire.**

The mouse pointer changes to the Plus icon, indicating that drawing mode is active.

4. **Drag the mouse down and to the right to create the shape.**

Or you can just click in the document to plop down the shape. The location and size are approximate at this point; you can adjust everything later.

When you release the mouse button, the shape appears in your document, as shown in Figure 6-1. The Shape Format tab appears on the Ribbon, which helps you further modify or mangle the shape.

>> Just as you can copy and paste text, you can copy and paste shapes: Click to select the shape, and then press Ctrl+C to copy. Press Ctrl+V to paste the shape.

>> The shape's color reflects the document's current theme. Or, if you've previously set a shape's color and line style in the document, new shapes use those attributes.

>> Shapes are given the default layout In Front of Text. Refer to Chapter 5 for information on graphics layout.

>> The shape's layout also includes an anchor to a paragraph of text. Chapter 5 describes how the anchor works to keep the shape with a specific paragraph.

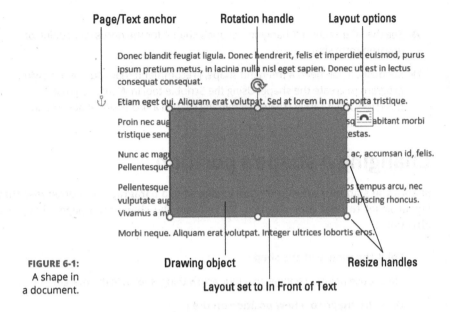

Page/Text anchor   **Rotation handle**   **Layout options**

FIGURE 6-1:
A shape in
a document.

Drawing object   **Resize handles**

Layout set to In Front of Text

Drawing a freeform shape

Every item on the Shapes menu represents some type of polygon or other inter-esting graphic — all but one. When you feel compelled to Picasso your own shape, use the Scribble tool. Heed these directions:

1. **On the Insert tab, in the Illustrations group, click the Shapes button.**

2. **Choose the Scribble tool.**

The tool is found on the far right in the Lines area.

3. **Drag the mouse to draw a free-form shape in your document.**

The mouse pointer changes to the Pencil icon as you drag and draw.

4. **Close the shape.**

Ensure that you drag the mouse over the shape's starting position.

Step 4 is most important! When you're done doodling, loop around to the shape's starting point, like tying a knot in a string. If you don't close the shape, it will be ugly and I shall frown upon you incessantly.

>> If you screw up, try again: Delete the shape (press the Delete key or Ctrl+Z to undo).

>> When you fail to close the shape, Word refuses to apply a fill color or style. The uncompleted shape is still valid but limited in its application.

TIP

>> See the later section "Changing a shape's shape" for the necessary editing of any free-form shape.

>> Seriously, if you need a freehand shape, I recommend that you use a drawing program to create the shape. Using the Scribble tool in Word is a great diversion, but it rarely creates something seen in a professional document.

Changing a shape's position

Shapes you slap into a document are anchored to a paragraph, but otherwise their layout is set to float atop the text. To relocate the shape on a page, obey these directions:

1. **Point the mouse at the shape.**

The mouse pointer changes to a four-arrow thing, shown in the margin.

2. **Drag the shape to a new position on the page.**

As you drag, you may discover green guidelines that appear over the text. These lines help to position the shape relative to the page's margins, the tops of paragraphs, and the centerline down the middle of the page.

For precise relocation of a shape, you can use the Position button. Follow these steps:

1. **Click to select the shape.**

2. **On the Shape Format tab, in the Arrange group, click the Position button.**

A menu appears showing various positions for the shape relative to the page, as illustrated in Figure 6-2.

3. **Choose a position from the menu.**

As you point the mouse at each item, the shape relocates to give you a preview of what its new arrangement looks like. Click an item to select that position.

If you don't like the shape's new location, repeat the steps in this section. If you want the shape to float in front of the text, in Step 2 choose the Wrap Text button instead of Position. From the Wrap Text menu, choose the command In Front of Text.

TIP

>> If it helps, use the Zoom tool on the status bar to resize the page in the document window. When you can see the full page, you can better judge how the shape appears.

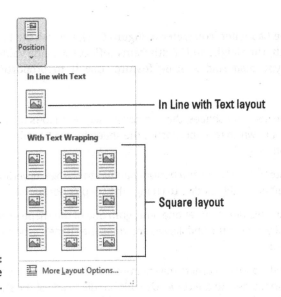

In Line with Text layout

Square layout

FIGURE 6-2:
Selecting the
shape's position.

>> Refer to Chapter 5 for more information on the green guidelines you see
when moving a shape on a page, as well as graphics layout options.

**TECHNICAL
STUFF**

>> Even more precise positioning of the shape is possible if you use the Layout
dialog box. Repeat the steps in this section, but in Step 3 choose More Layout
Options. In the Layout dialog box, use the Position tab to set the shape's exact
location on the page.

Resizing a shape

The simplest way to change a shape's size is to use the mouse to drag one of its
eight handles in or out, as shown in Figure 6-1. To change the shape's size precisely, select the shape and on the Shape Format tab, in the Size group, use the
Shape Height and Shape Width gizmos to specify an exact size for the shape. These
gizmos are shown in Figure 6-3.

Shape Height

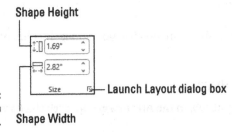

Launch Layout dialog box

FIGURE 6-3:
Setting a
shape's size.

Shape Width

If you click the Launcher icon (refer to Figure 6-3), you see the Layout dialog box. On the Size tab, the Height and Width items reflect the same values shown on the Ribbon. But you also find a Scale feature. Use it to proportionally alter the shape's size.

>> For non-rectangular shapes, the size gizmos set the shape's bounding box, or the limit to which text approaches the shape for the Square and Tight layout options.

>> Manipulate a shape's top and bottom handles to change its vertical size; use the left and right handles to change the shape's horizontal size.

>> To resize in two directions at one time, grab one of the shape's corner handles. If you hold the Shift key as you drag, the shape's aspect ratio is maintained.

>> Shapes with rounded corners may feature an additional handle, a yellow one positioned next to the curve. Use this handle to adjust the shape's curved edge.

TIP

>> In the Layout dialog box, on the Size tab, you can select the Lock Aspect Ratio option to ensure that the percentage-size changes you make are equal for the shape's height and width.

Rotating a shape

To spin a shape around, follow these steps:

1. Point the mouse at the shape's Rotation handle.

The Rotation handle is found at the shape's top center. (Refer to Figure 6-1.) When you find the sweet spot, the mouse pointer changes, as shown in the margin.

2. Drag the mouse to spin the shape around.

If you press and hold the Shift key as you drag the mouse, the shape rotates in 15-degree increments.

If you want to rotate a shape in precise 90-degree increments, follow these precise steps:

1. Click to select the shape.

2. On the Shape Format tab, in the Arrange group, click the Rotate Objects button.

3. **Choose Rotate Right 90° or Rotate Left 90° to rotate the shape in that given increment.**

You can repeat this step to continue to rotate the shape.

For additional rotation control, choose the command More Rotation Options in Step 3. You see the Layout dialog box with the Size tab forward. Use the Rotation gizmo in the Rotate area to set a specific rotation amount. Click OK.

>> Also available on the Rotate Objects menu are options to flip the shape along the vertical (up-down) and horizontal (left-right) axis.

>> In the Layout dialog box, a value of 0° sets the shape "upright," or in its original orientation when you first drew the shape. Setting the value to 0° effectively undoes any weird rotation angle you've applied.

TIP

Setting colors, line styles, and effects

Word uses the current document theme to apply color, line weight, and effects to any shape spawned in your document. You're not stuck with these options, as you can also set the shape's fill color, line color, line weight and style, as well as apply any effects to the shape. These items are controlled from the Shape Format tab, in the Shape Styles group, as shown in Figure 6-4.

Also appearing in Figure 6-4 is the Shape Styles gallery. You can use that list to select a shape design that includes preset colors, designs, and effects.

Setting the fill color. Click the Shape Fill button (refer to Figure 6-4) and choose one of the Theme colors, a Standard color, or No Fill. See the nearby sidebar, Creating a New Color for information on how to use the More Fill Colors option. Other options include setting gradients and textures. Inserting a picture into the shape is covered in the later section, "Adding a picture to a shape."

Setting the outline. Outlines also have colors, which are selected from the Shape Outline menu. Additionally, you can set the line thickness from the Weight submenu. Other options shown in Figure 6-4 include sketched lines, dashed lines, and adding arrows (to lines, not outlines).

Applying effects. Click the Shape Effects menu to view a selection of shadows, reflections, bevels, and other effects that you can apply to the shape.

Colors are removed by setting the No Fill or No Outline option. No Fill leaves a shape hollow or see-through. No Outline removes the outline. To remove an effect, choose Preset ⇨ No Presets from the menu.

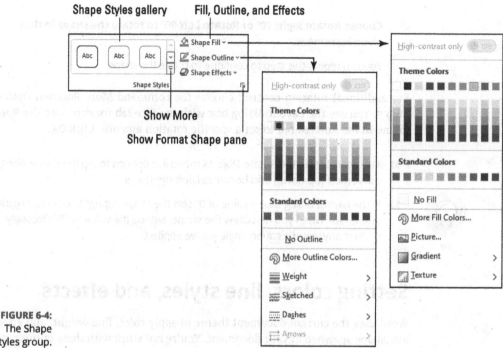

Shape Styles gallery   Fill, Outline, and Effects

Show More

Show Format Shape pane

FIGURE 6-4:
The Shape
Styles group.

TIP

>> Because many of the outline elements exist on the same menu, it often takes a few clicks to set the best shape outline, thickness, and style.

>> The easiest way to style a shape is to select a preset option from the Shape Style gallery.

>> The color pallets shown on the Shape Fill and Shape Outline menus are related to the document theme. You see the theme colors first and then a palette of standard colors.

>> The Gradient item on the Shape Fill menu lets you choose more than one color for the fill. The colors blend to form a gradient pattern. You can choose a preset gradient from the submenu or select the More Gradients item to build your own gradient fill.

>> In addition to fill colors, you can set a fill pattern: On the Shape fill menu, choose Texture. Select a pattern from the Texture submenu.

>> To change the document theme colors, click the Design tab and choose a new theme from the Colors menu.

WARNING

>> Be careful when selecting a preset shape from the Shape Styles gallery. Those thumbnails featuring *Abc* indicate that the format that's applied also transforms the shape into a text box.

CREATING A NEW COLOR

When you're displeased with the preset choice of colors, you can craft your own. To do so, choose the More Colors command from any color palette menu. You see the Colors dialog box with two tabs: Standard and Custom.

Use the Standard tab to choose a color from a matrix. You can also set transparency values.

Use the Custom tab to set a specific color. Choose a color from the grid, or set individual Red, Green, and Blue values. Set the darkness slider. Set the transparency. You can use the model to create over 16 million different colors. Try them all!

The color you create is applied to the currently selected shape.

Changing a shape's shape

If you're unhappy with a shape, don't delete it! Word allows you to reset a shape without the bother of deleting and replacing. This trick maintains the shape's color, line, effects, size, and position.

To swap one shape for another, follow these directions:

1. **Click to select the shape.**

 2. **On the Shape Format tab, in the Insert Shapes group, click the Edit Shape button.**

    The button's icon is shown in the margin.

3. **Choose Change Shape.**

    A submenu of shapes appears.

4. **Select the new shape from the list.**

    The new shape replaces the old shape without altering the shape's style or position on the page.

When the new shape you desire doesn't exist, you can edit the shape — just as if Word is a graphics program. It isn't, of course. But don't let that stop you from altering a preset shape into something you want. Follow these steps:

1. **Click to select an existing shape.**

2. **On the Shape Format tab, in the Insert Shapes group, click the Edit Shape button and choose Edit Points.**

Black squares appear on the shape's line, or *path*, indicating where an anchor point is set. You can move those points, add new points, or remove points.

 Move an anchor. To move an anchor, point the mouse at the black square and drag it elsewhere. When you find the sweet spot, the mouse pointer changes as shown in the margin.

 Add an anchor. To add a new anchor point, press the Ctrl key and click on the line (path) that defines the shape. The mouse pointer changes as shown in the margin when you're able to click and create a new point. You can then drag the point to a new location to build the shape.

 Remove an anchor. To remove an anchor point, press the Ctrl key and click on the black square. 1The mouse cursor changes, as shown in the margin, when you can click to remove a point. Doing so drastically alters the shape.

Some shapes feature handles on their anchor points, as illustrated in Figure 6-5. When you click on the anchor point, you can adjust each of the handles to reshape the path's curve. These handles appear only when the shape's path has a curve.

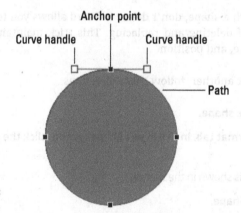

Anchor point

Curve handle   Curve handle

Path

FIGURE 6-5:
Editing a curve.

 WARNING

>> If you remove too many points, you may "undefine" the shape; its size grows immeasurably small or large. When this change happens, try to undo your edits, or delete the shape and start over.

>> The techniques for setting and moving anchor points are similar to the techniques for setting and moving the text-wrapping bounding box for the Tight and Through layout settings. Refer to Chapter 5.

 TECHNICAL STUFF

>> The line creating a shape is known as a *path*. The handles that create a curved point on the path are known as *Bézier* curve handles. Adjusting the curve handles is a visual thing, but what you're affecting is far more technical and dictates how the path is drawn.

Multiple Shape Mania

When a single shape doesn't create the art you want, you can work with shapes in groups. Available commands help resolve interesting problems, such as which shapes appear in front of or behind others and how the shapes are aligned. Word also lets you set shapes into a single drawing canvas, which transforms several shapes into a single piece of artwork — though probably nothing the local museum would desire to hang in its gallery.

Arranging shapes in front or behind

As far as layout is concerned, shapes can float behind text, mix with text, or float in front of text. Within these layers, however, the shapes stack up one atop the other.

The first shape you stick into a document is on the bottom of the stack. The next shape that you draw is in front of the previous shape. The more shapes you draw, the deeper the stack. Some shapes can obscure others.

To reorder the shape stack, follow these steps:

1. **On the Shape Format tab, in the Arrange group, choose Selection Pane.**

The Selection pane appears. It lists all shapes on the page, in order from visible (top) to behind other shapes (bottom), as illustrated in Figure 6-6.

2. **In the Selection pane, click the shape you want to reorder.**

The names shown relate to the order in which you added the shape. In Figure 6-6, say I want to move Group 19 behind the larger rectangle, Rounded Rectangle 17.

3. **Click in the Selection pane to select the group you want to reorder.**

4. **Use the chevron buttons — Bring Forward and Send Backward — to reorder the selected shape or group.**

Continuing with the example in Figure 6-6, click the Send Backward button to send the group behind Rounded Rectangle 17.

5. **Close the Selection Pane when you're done.**

The Selection Pane is ideal for working with multiple shapes, including some behind others that you can't otherwise access by using the mouse. When you can see the shapes, you can use the Bring Forward and Send Backward buttons on the Shape Format tab to manipulate the shapes' order.

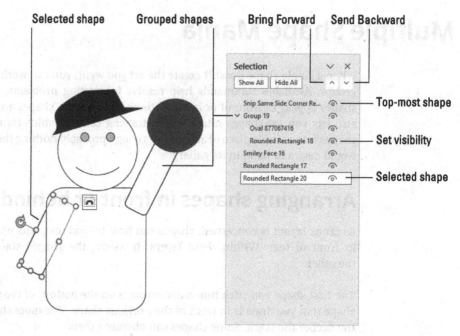

Selected shape   Grouped shapes   Bring Forward   Send Backward

Top-most shape

Set visibility

Selected shape

FIGURE 6-6:
The Selection
Pane and its list
of shapes.

>> Changing the order of any shape doesn't alter its applied layout. See Chapter 5 for details.

>> The Bring Forward and Send Backward buttons have menus that let you shove a shape all the way forward or backward, respectively.

>> Arranging shapes works best when they sport the same layout, such as In Front of Text.

Aligning shapes

Eyeball all you want and drag shapes around with the mouse, but when you really need shapes to line up perfectly, you must surrender to Word's alignment commands. These commands can help you arrange a single shape or a series of shapes in a neat and clean manner.

The key to aligning shapes is to use the Align button menu, illustrated in Figure 6-7. This button is found on the Shape Format tab, in the Arrange group.

 Use the Align button menu (icon shown in the margin) to align single shapes on a page. First, choose the Align To Page option from the menu (refer to Figure 6-7). Then set the alignment from the menu, such as Align Center. The image is perfectly centered on the page.

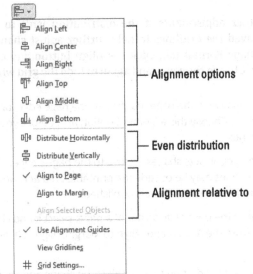

Alignment options

Even distribution

Alignment relative to

FIGURE 6-7:
The Align
button menu.

For multiple shapes, select each one: Press the Ctrl key as you click to select them. From the Align menu, choose Align Selected Objects. Then choose an alignment option from the menu to arrange the shapes by their centers, middles, tops, bottoms, and so on.

When more than two shapes are selected, you can distribute them in an even manner. The goal is to ensure that the shape's positions are evenly set, as shown in Figure 6-8.

Page edge   Shapes distributed horizontally   Page margin

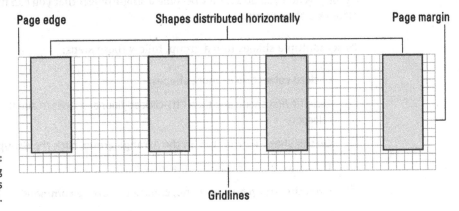

Gridlines

FIGURE 6-8:
Distributing
shapes
across a page.

With the multiple shapes selected, choose a distribution option from the Align button's menu, either Distribute Horizontally or Distribute Vertically, depending on how the shapes are arranged. (In Figure 6-8, they're arranged horizontally.)

You can make further adjustments if the distribution isn't to your liking. In Figure 6-8, I displayed the gridlines to help further adjust shapes. To view the gridlines, on the Shape Format tab, click the Align button and choose the View Gridlines command. Choose the command again to hide the grid when you're done.

» Alignment is set relative to the page margins, to the page edge, or to the shapes themselves. Choose this alignment option *first*, before you align one or more shapes.

» The Align to Page option sets shapes relative to the page's edge. This choice means that the shapes may be outside the printable area and won't completely show up when the document is published.

» To place a shape in the upper left corner of a page, select it and choose these items (in order) from the Align menu: Align to Margin, Align Left, and then Align Top.

» To place a shape dead-center on a page, select the shape and choose from the Align menu: Align to Page, Align Center, and then Align Middle.

» The Use Alignment Guides option (refer to Figure 6-7) is what sets those green lines you see when you drag a shape around on a page. They represent the page's margins, tops of paragraphs, as well as the page's centerline.

Grouping multiple shapes

After you have shapes arranged and aligned, my advice is to lock them together as a group. When you do so, they become a single object that you can move or manipulate as a single unit.

To set multiple shapes into a group, follow these steps:

1. Click to select two or more shapes.

Click the first shape and then Ctrl+click additional shapes to add them to the selection.

2. On the Shape Format tab, in the Arrange group, click the Group button.

The button's icon is shown in the margin.

3. From the Group button menu, choose the Group command.

The selected shapes from Step 1 are corralled into a single unit.

When you select any shape in the group, you select the entire group. You can still select individual shapes and adjust them: First click to select the group, and then click again to select and manipulate an individual shape.

To ungroup the shapes, repeat the steps in this section, but in Step 4 choose the Ungroup command.

TIP

>> After shapes are grouped, you can apply the same color and style to all shapes in the group.

>> Layout options chosen for a group affect all shapes within the group as a unit.

>> The group can be moved forward or back in the stack of shapes on a page. Refer to the earlier section "Arranging shapes in front or behind."

>> An alternative to grouping shapes is to set them on a drawing canvas. On the Insert tab, in the Illustrations group, click the Shapes button and choose New Drawing Canvas from the menu. You can set shapes into the canvas, which automatically groups them as a unit.

Text and Pictures Inside Shapes

Beyond filling a shape with color, you can also use a shape as a frame. Inside this frame you can set text or an image. In fact, the text box is a common tool that Word uses to help you arrange text on a cover page or create a callout to otherwise break up a page full of boring text.

Creating a text box

Word features a Text Box command, which directly sets a rectangle shape into a document, already decorated and eager for text. This command is found on the Insert tab in the Text group. The Text box button (icon shown in the margin) displays a menu from which you can pluck a preformatted text box.

The text box works like a shape and can be formatted as such, with fill colors and styles. It can be aligned, grouped, changed in size, and rotated. It has layout options. Effectively, it *is* a shape. In fact, any shape other than a line can be a text box.

To change a shape into a text box, follow these steps:

1. **Insert a shape into the document.**

   Refer elsewhere in this chapter for details.

2. **Right-click the shape and choose the Add Text command.**

   The insertion pointer blinks in the middle of the shape, indicating that you can type. The text format is paragraph-centered and aligned with the middle of the shape.

3. **On the Shape Format tab, in the Text group, click the Align Text button.**

4. **Choose a vertical alignment for the text: Top, Middle or Bottom.**

5. **Use the standard paragraph alignment commands to set horizontal alignment.**

   These are Left (Ctrl+L), Center (Ctrl+E), Right (Ctrl+L), and Justified (Ctrl+J).

6. **Type the text that goes into the box.**

   The text's color depends on the document's theme. You can click the Home tab and set a new text color so that the results meet with your approval.

7. **Click outside the box when you're done typing text.**

If the Add Text command doesn't appear on the shortcut menu (refer to Step 2), the shape cannot accommodate text. Try resizing the shape.

TIP

>> Text boxes can be linked so that text from one shape can flow into another. See the next section.

>> Text inside a shape is formatted just like text anywhere else in Word. You can even use the Ruler to set indents and tabs, though doing so is a bit extreme.

>> When a shape features text, you must click the mouse on the shape's edge to select the shape or to drag it around. If you click inside the shape, you're clicking inside its text.

TIP

>> If you have trouble accessing the text in a shape, right-click inside the shape and choose the Edit Text command.

>> You cannot reverse the shape-to-text-box transformation, but you can delete all the text inside a shape.

Linking text boxes

When you have more text than can fit into a shape, you can flow text into an additional shape. This linking process prevents you from having overly large text boxes in a document, but it also helps continue text between shapes without a lot of copy-and-paste on your part.

To link text between two shapes, obey these steps:

1. Create both shapes, ensure that they can both accept text.

If necessary, convert the shapes into text boxes as described in the previous section.

Not every shape accepts the text conversion.

2. Fill the first shape with text.

3. Click to select the first shape, the one that contains the overflow text.

4. On the Shape Format tab, in the Text group, click the Create Link button.

The mouse pointer changes to something that looks like a bucket spilling out letters, as shown in the margin.

5. Click on the second shape.

Text flows from the first shape into the second shape.

You can repeat these steps to make overflow text from the second shape flow into a third shape, and so on. Avoid being silly.

>> The surefire way to screw up text links is to delete a shape. When you do, you essentially need to start over again: Delete all linked shapes.

>> To unlink shapes, click on the original (or previous) shape. On the Shape Format tab, in the Text group, click the Break Link button. This button replaces the Create Link button. After clicking the button, the text no longer flows into the second shape.

Framing a picture in a shape

One of the options for setting a shape's fill color is to use a picture. The effect is that the shape becomes a picture frame. To use a shape as a picture frame, follow these steps:

1. Add a shape to your document.

It must be a shape suitable for framing a picture, though it's surprising into which shapes you can set a picture.

2. **Select the shape.**

3. **On the Shape Format tab, in the Shape Styles group, click the Shape Fill button.**

4. **From the Shape File menu, choose the Picture command.**

   The Insert Pictures dialog box appears.

5. **Choose From a File.**

   Other options on the menu use different tools to set a picture, but I'm guessing that the image you want is already stored on your computer.

6. **Use the Insert Picture dialog box to hunt down an image.**

7. **Click to select the image, and then click the Insert button.**

   The image is placed in the shape.

You can modify the shape — for example, choose a new border. Or you can change the shape, as described in the earlier section, "Changing a shape's shape."

TIP

To adjust the picture, right-click inside the shape and choose the Format Shape command. Use the Format Picture pane to modify the picture. For example, you can adjust the picture's position within the shape by using the Picture Position controls found beneath the Crop heading in the Format Picture pane.

See Chapter 7 for information on cropping an image inside a shape.

IN THIS CHAPTER

» **Sticking a picture into your document**

» **Stealing images from the web**

» **Swapping pictures**

» **Trimming an image**

» **Adjusting and modifying the picture**

» **Framing a picture**

» **Using various frame effects**

» **Adding a caption**

Chapter **7**

Pretty Pictures

Word makes it cinchy to stick a picture, an illustration, or another type of graphic into your document. It's almost *too* easy. To thwart you, Microsoft added an armada of picture-editing tools, commands, features, and options. So, even though sticking a photo of Uncle Earl into your essay on the "olden days" isn't just a three-click operation, you're also faced with dozens of options and diversions that can transform a rudimentary operation into a complex ordeal that you might eventually enjoy more than actually writing text.

» All of Word's layout options apply to images you insert into your document. Refer to Chapter 5 for details.

» Many of the arranging and ordering commands for drawing objects (shapes) also apply to pictures in a document. See Chapter 6.

TECHNICAL STUFF

» If you get serious about mixing text and pictures, I recommend obtaining a desktop publishing (DTP) program. This software is designed specifically to manage text and graphics across large documents. Word can do the job in a pinch, but professionals use DTP software.

One Thousand Words

Nothing brings up the level of sophistication in a document like a well-placed photograph, piece of art, or scribble that you just made in the Paint program while you were yammering on the phone. Providing that the image complements your text, insert it.

Adding an image from your computer

To shove a picture into your document, gently follow these steps:

1. **Set the insertion pointer to the spot where you want the image to appear.**

   Pictures are inserted with the In Line with Text layout option selected. You can change this option, as described in Chapter 5.

2. **On the Insert tab, in the Illustrations group, click the Pictures button and choose This Device.**

   The Insert Picture dialog box appears. It works like an Open dialog box, though it's configured to show only pictures and images compatible with Word documents.

3. **Work the dialog box to locate the image file.**

   Use the controls to navigate to the proper folder on your PC's storage system where the image is buried.

4. **Select the image and click the Insert button.**

   The image appears in the document's text, at the spot where you set the insertion pointer in Step 1.

After the image sits in your document, you might want to adjust it and perhaps apply layout, formatting, or a caption. To assist you, the Picture Format tab appears on the Ribbon. Other sections in this chapter describe how to use this tab's commands.

>> To remove an image, click to select it and then press the Delete key on the keyboard.

>> If you choose Stock Images in Step 2, you see a gallery of photos categorized by topic. You can search this list for something specific or waste office hours browsing. These images are free to use but carry the stigma of being stock images.

>> Choosing Online Pictures in Step 2 opens an Online Pictures window. It shows a Bing image search, which you can browse or refine.

>> Word recognizes and consumes common graphics file formats. These include the PNG, JPEG, and GIF file formats popular on the Internet, as well as Windows BMP files and TIF files.

>> The Picture Format tab appears only when a picture is selected.

>> A picture can be also applied to the page background or watermark. See Chapter 9.

Copying and pasting an image

One of the easiest ways to get an image into a document is to copy and paste. It's such a simple operation that people forget this trick. Heed these kindergarten steps:

1. **From any other program, select and copy an image.**

   Click to select an image. On a web page, you can right-click and choose the Copy Image (or similar) command.

2. **In Word, set the insertion pointer to the location where you want the image pasted.**

3. **Press Ctrl+V.**

   The image appears in the document — unless it's of an incompatible file format. If so, select another image and try again.

TIP

It's also possible to drag an image from another program or from a File Explorer window into a Word document. This method may not be completely successful due to overlapping windows and incompatible file formats.

WARNING

>> Just because you find an image on the Internet doesn't mean that you have the right to use it. The image must be flagged as public domain, free to use, "copyleft," or otherwise specifically made available for anyone to use. Always assume that *all* Internet images are copyrighted.

>> The copyright laws allow what's called *fair use* for educational, research, and other purposes. This exception doesn't grant you immunity. If you are preparing a document for any professional purposes, for profit, for marketing, or to promote services, then standard copyright law applies.

Replacing an image

If you have an image positioned, formatted, and captioned but find a better image later, please don't start over! You can swap out the image while retaining its location and layout. Follow these thrilling steps:

1. **Select the image.**

2. **On the Picture Format tab, in the Adjust group, click the Change Picture button.**

3. **Choose a source from the Insert Picture dialog box, such as This Device.**

   At this point, the picture is selected and inserted into the document as described in the earlier section "Adding an image from your computer," though it retains the same position and size as the original.

Any image effects or styles that applied to the original image are not applied to the replacement.

Image Adjustment

Thanks to a selection of interesting and useful tools, Word does well at pretending to be a graphics manipulation program. You can add some fine-tuning to an image, apply special effects, and perform basic operations such as cropping, resizing, and rotating. The goal is to make the image look good so that people pay less attention to your horrible writing.

>> Ideally, the image should be perfect when you insert it. When it's not, Word offers tools necessary to help you finish the job.

>> Information on resizing and rotating shapes is found in Chapter 6. This information also applies to pictures.

>> The commands in this section affect an image directly. See the later section "Picture Framing" for information on how to control the appearance of an image's frame in a document.

Cropping an image

Cropping isn't the same thing as resizing. When you resize an image, you change its dimensions, but not its content. Cropping is like taking a pair of scissors to an image and slicing away a chunk, though in Word the sliced-away chunk is merely hidden. Follow these steps to crop an image:

1. **Click to select the image with an unwanted chunk.**

Refer to Figure 7-1 for an example of how cropping works.

Original picture

Crop bars

Cropped image

FIGURE 7-1:
The cropping process. Crop rectangle set

2. **On the Picture Format tab, in the Size group, click the top part of the Crop button.**

The image changes to grow cropping bars in its corners, replacing the re-sizing handles.

3. **Adjust the cropping bars to slice out part of the image.**

Drag the bars inward to slice out a portion of the image. As you drag, the portion to be removed is shaded in dark gray, shown in the lower left in Figure 7-1.

4. **Press the Enter key to lock in the changes.**

The image is cropped, which reduces its overall size.

Besides the Crop command (Step 2), two other options are available on the Crop menu are:

Crop to Shape: Choose a shape from the submenu to instantly crop the image to that given shape. For example, to place the picture into an oval, choose the Oval shape from the Crop to Shape submenu.

Aspect Ratio: Select an aspect ratio from the submenu to resize and crop the image to match the horizontal-to-vertical ratio. Keep in mind that the ratios are organized in portrait and landscape orientations. Press Enter after choosing the ratio to complete the crop.

The final two items on the Crop menu affect pictures placed into shapes. Refer to Chapter 6 for information.

TIP

>> You can press Ctrl+Z to undo a crop immediately after completing Step 4. If you want too long, however, Ctrl+Z doesn't work. Instead, select the cropped image and from the Crop button menu choose the Fit command to restore the image.

>> The Crop to Shape command is just a handy shortcut for inserting a shape and adding a picture as the background. Refer to Chapter 6.

Removing the background

Erasing the background from a picture is a feature you might expect from a sophisticated photo-editing app. But no! These apps have nothing on Word, which features a Remove Background button on the Picture Format tab. To put this tool to work, follow these steps:

1. **Select the picture.**

2. **On the Picture Format tab, in the Adjust group, click the Remove Background button.**

   Word examines the image. It sets a color highlight to areas that it believes to be the background, shown in Figure 7-2. If you're good with Word's choices, skip to Step 5.

3. **Click the Mark Areas to Keep button and use the mouse to scribble out portions of the image to keep.**

   Click the button (refer to Figure 7-2) and draw on the image to "erase" the shaded portion of the image. Your goal is to mark portions of the image mistakenly flagged as background.

Drag over the image to mark areas to keep

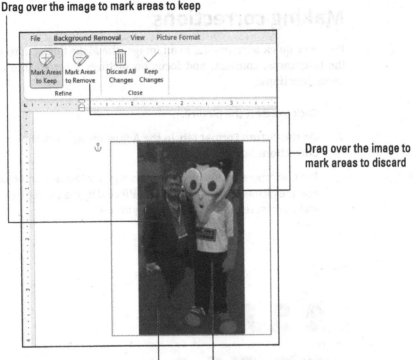

Drag over the image to mark areas to discard

FIGURE 7-2:
Removing a picture's background.

Portion of the image that
Word has marked for removal

Portion of the image that
Word has marked to retain

4. **Click the Mark Areas to Remove button and use the mouse to draw out portions of the background.**

   After clicking the button, drag the mouse over a portion of the image that should be in the background, or removed from the image.

5. **Click the Keep Changes button.**

   Word replaces the picture background with a transparent layer.

At this point, you might want to crop the image and adjust the layout to account for the new shape. Use the Fit command on the Crop button's menu; refer to the preceding section.

The Remove Background tool works best on pictures with a solid or consistent background.

REMEMBER

Making corrections

For some quick adjustments to an image, the Make Corrections command adjusts the brightness, contrast, and focus on pictures inserted into a document. Obey these directions:

1. **Click to select the picture.**

2. **On the Picture Format tab, in the Adjust group, click the Corrections button.**

The Corrections button menu displays a grid of image thumbnails showing how the picture (chosen in Step 1) is affected by the various focus, brightness, and contrast settings, as shown in Figure 7-3.

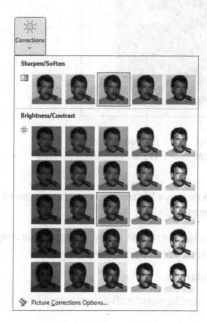

FIGURE 7-3: Correcting an image's sharpness, brightness, and contrast.

3. **Choose a thumbnail from the menu.**

The effect is applied to the image.

You may need to repeat these steps a few times to get both sharpness and brightness/contrast settings correct. If not, in Step 2, choose the command Picture Correction Options. You see the Format Picture pane with specific controls presented to adjust the sharpen/soften settings, brightness, and contrast.

If somewhere down the road you don't like the changes you've made and you want to restore the image, see the later section "Restoring an image (removing effects)."

Adjusting the image's color

Don't tell anyone, but many photographers subtly adjust the colors in their pictures. They desire to bring out the best colors and highlight certain parts of the image. They claim that it's to make the picture look its best, but it's all lies! You can practice the same type of deception for photos in Word.

To adjust color in a picture, heed these devious directions:

1. **Click to select the picture.**

2. **On the Picture Format tab, in the Adjust group, click the Color button.**

   A menu of color choices appears as thumbnails, detailing how each option affects the selected image.

3. **Choose a thumbnail from the gallery to apply its effect to the image.**

As an example, you need to make a color image monochrome. If so, select the Grayscale effect. It's located in the Recolor area — first row, second column.

TIP

If you point the mouse at one of the Color gallery's thumbnails, you see a preview of the effect applied to the image in your document. It may take a moment for that effect to preview, so wait for it. The color isn't set until you click the mouse.

To remove any color effects, see the later section "Restoring an image (removing effects)."

Adding artistic effects

If you want to get all fancy with your images, you can add some cheesy artistic effects. No, these aren't special effects, like you'd see in a movie. They're image effects, and they're cheesy because people use them not to add anything but because they're fun to apply. Follow these fun steps:

1. **Click to select the picture.**

   The nifty thing about the cheesy artistic effects is that the worse the picture, the more effective these augmentations. So don't be shy with that cheese.

2. **On the Picture Format tab, in the Adjust group, click the Artistic Effects button.**

   Behold a palette of thumbnails detailing how the various effects apply to the selected image.

3. **Click to select a thumbnail and apply that effect to the image.**

These effects cannot be adjusted. The command at the bottom of the menu, Artistic Effects Options, does offer more detailed control over the effects as they're applied.

Restoring an image (removing effects)

The Undo command, Ctrl+Z, is your first recourse when you mess up image adjustment. After a while, however, whacking Ctrl+Z repeatedly is counter productive. A better solution is to reset the image, converting it back to its original state before you went nuts.

To peel away image modifications, heed these steps:

1. Select the picture.

Click.

2. On the Picture Format tab, in the Adjust group, click the Reset Picture button.

3. Choose the Reset Picture item.

If the image was also resized or cropped, choose instead the Reset Picture & Size item.

The picture is restored.

Picture Framing

Pictures are naked without a frame. Word understands this modesty, so it comes with a virtual clothing store which you can use to frame a picture in your document. These picture style effects apply to the picture and the space around it, setting it apart from the document's text and making the picture feel less vulnerable.

Selecting a frame style

The quickest way to frame a picture is to choose a preset style from the Picture Styles gallery. Heed these steps:

1. Click to select a picture.

2. On the Picture Format tab, in the Picture Styles group, choose a preset picture style from the gallery.

Or you can click the More button, illustrated in Figure 7-4, to display a whole rack of styles.

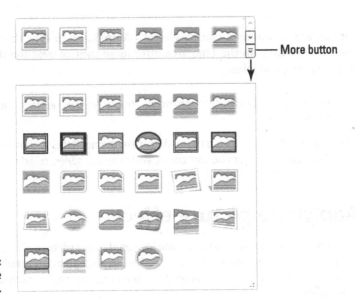

More button

FIGURE 7-4:
Various picture
frame styles.

3. **Choose a frame style from the gallery.**

If you point the mouse at the style, you see a preview of how it affects the
image inside the document. Click the style to apply it to the picture.

Though this method is quick, it's also what most other people use when they
desire to frame or modify a picture. To be unique, you can mix up the effects as
described in the next two sections.

Adding a border

The simplest form of picture frame is a border or line applied around the picture.
You can apply a specific color, weight (thickness), and style to the line in whatever
manner complements the image. Follow these steps:

1. **Select the image.**

2. **On the Picture Format tab, in the Picture Styles group, click the Picture
Border button.**

The Picture Border menu lists various colors, plus submenus to adjust the
border thickness and line style.

3. **Choose items from the menu to customize the picture border.**

You may need to choose from the menu several times to create the
border desired.

** For border superpowers, choose Weight ⇨ More Lines to view the Format Picture pane. The settings in the Line area offer more control over the line color, type, style, corners, and joins.

>> To remove the border from an image, choose No Outline from the Picture Border menu.

>> Border colors are related to the document theme. If the document theme is changed, the image's border colors, and even line styles, could change as well.

Applying a picture effect

To complement a picture border, consider applying a picture effect. These include fun items such as a drop shadow, reflection, bevel, and other attributes applied to a picture's border (see the preceding section). To add a picture effect, heed these steps:

1. **Click to select the image.**

2. **On the Picture Format tab, in the Picture Styles group, click the Picture Effects button.**

3. **Choose a category, and then choose an effect.**

   The effect is applied to the picture.

As with other picture manipulation tools, you can point the mouse at an effect to preview what it does to the image in your document. You can also double up on effects — add perhaps soft edges as well as a reflection.

To remove all effects, use the Picture Reset button, as described in the earlier section "Restoring an image (removing effects)."

Caption That Picture

Not all pictures in a document need captions. An initial image of a map of Africa may help introduce the reader to your subject (assuming that the subject is Africa). If you need to reference the picture, however, it helps to have a caption. By doing so, you can write *See Figure 1* and the reader knows where to look.

Although Word has a Captions command (see Chapter 18), it's rather inflexible. As an alternative, I suggest creating a text box and grouping it with an image, which serves as a caption. Such a concoction is shown in Figure 7-5.

Picture

Objects grouped

Jonah at the Independence Day Parade, 2013

FIGURE 7-5:
A caption below
a picture.

Text box

Follow these steps to group a text box with a picture to act as a caption:

1. **Set a picture in your document and select it.**

After it's selected, the picture's bounding box appears, which helps with drawing the text box (Step 3).

2. **On the Insert tab, in the Text group, click the Text Box button and choose the Draw Text Box command.**

3. **Drag the mouse below the selected picture to set the location and size of the text box.**

Use the picture's bounding box (the frame around the picture) to help set the text box's width.

4. **Type and format the caption inside the text box.**

All text and formatting commands apply in a text box. In Figure 7-5, I pressed Ctrl+E to apply center paragraph alignment and Ctrl+B to create boldface text.

5. **On the Shape Format tab, in the Shape Styles area, click the Shape Outline button and choose No Outline from the menu.**

This step removes the line around the text box. If you want to keep the line, skip this step. Likewise, if you want to shade the text box or apply other effects (which I don't recommend), use the tools in the Shape Styles group. Refer to Chapter 6 for specifics.

6. **Set the text box's layout to match the picture's layout.**

Choose something other than In Line with Text. For example, Square or Tight. See Chapter 5 for more details on selecting a layout.

7. **Select both the text box and the picture.**

Click the first item, and then Ctrl+click the second. Both items are now a unit.

If you're unable to select both items, they probably feature incompatible layout options. Choose Tight or Square for the best results.

TIP

8. **Click the Shape Format tab.**

Or you can click the Picture Format tab, as both tabs feature the same commands.

9. **In the Arrange group, click the Align button and choose Align Center.**

10. **In the Arrange group, click the Group button and choose the Group command.**

The picture and its caption (text box) are now aligned and grouped into a single unit.

Now that both the picture and caption are lined up and grouped and the proper layout applied, you can move them around together. Thanks to their common layout option, text flows around both items.

» Captions also explain what's going on in the image, name people who are pictured, and describe other details that are helpful to the reader.

» Beyond pictures, you can use the techniques in this section to add a caption to a table or any number of objects you can stick into a document.

IN THIS CHAPTER

» Saving time with SmartArt

» Inserting a whole Word document

» Adding an equation

» Pasting from Excel

» Creating a worksheet link

» Sticking Excel into Word

» Adding a chart

Chapter **8**

Insert Objects Weird and Amazing

What are the limits of the things that Word can stick into a document? Text is understandable. Pictures are fun and interesting. Anything else?

Of course! Word is a virtual department store of non-text objects, surprising and delightful. These include specific items like charts and equations, but also unexpected weird stuff, like the entire Excel program. If that doesn't show the Excel snobs who's in charge, I don't know what else will.

More Than Plain Text

At the Word salad bar, text is only the lettuce. Piled atop of this low-cal base is a rich assortment of other goodies — more than anyone would expect from a mere word processor. This variety doesn't mean that you must load up your plate with everything available, not like that way-too-slow little old lady in front of you who can't figure out how to use tongs. No, the variety is there for your choosing.

The goal is to make your document look its best, especially when you need something more than plain text.

Adding SmartArt

Before using multiple shapes to cobble together artwork, consider using the SmartArt feature instead. This tool contains a collection of multiple shapes, arranged in common and useful ways. Adorning some of the shapes are text boxes, which further helps save time over creating all that nonsense yourself.

To slap SmartArt into a document, follow these slappy steps:

1. **On the Insert tab, in the Illustrations group, click the Smart Art button.**

The Choose a SmartArt Graphic dialog box appears, illustrated in Figure 8-1. It lists categories on the left, examples in the middle, and descriptions on the right.

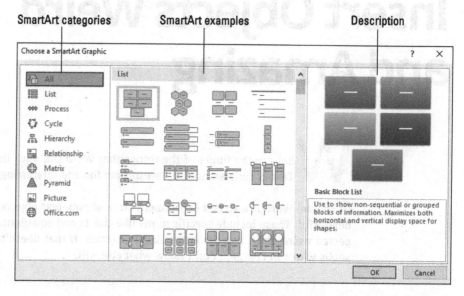

2. **Choose a category.**

For example, choose Process to create a type of flowchart.

3. **Select a SmartArt design from the center portion of the dialog box.**

4. **Click OK.**

The selected SmartArt is placed into your document.

Your next task is to add text to the SmartArt. Available text boxes already contain sample text, which you can replace with your own scrivening, including any formatting.

The SmartArt object itself is a drawing canvas, inside of which are placed shapes. You can move the shapes around within the canvas. You can even change the shapes' coloring and styles.

To complete the SmartArt operation, click on the drawing canvas border to select the entire object. At that point, you can apply layout settings to arrange the artwork in your text. Refer to Chapter 5 for layout options.

Also refer to Chapter 6 for information on shapes.

Inserting a whole 'nuther Word document

One of the less obvious things you can stick into a Word document is another Word document. Rather than open both documents and copy-and-paste, you can quickly shove text (and formatting and everything else) from one document into your current document. This may save you time, and it's one method of boiler-plating common text. Follow these steps:

1. **Set the insertion pointer at the location where you want the other document's text to appear.**

2. **On the Insert tab, in the Text group, click the Object button.**

3. **Choose Text From File.**

   The command says *text,* but the entire contents of another Word document are placed inside the current document.

4. **Use the Insert File dialog box to hunt down the Word document you want to insert.**

5. **Click to select the document icon, and then click the Insert button.**

The document appears at the insertion pointer's location (refer to Step 1), complete with formatting, styles, and any graphics or other objects.

The other document's text isn't updated when you change the other document. To do so, choose Object in Step 3. Then choose Microsoft Word Document in the Object dialog box. This procedure works like inserting a live Excel worksheet. See the section, "Copying and linking a worksheet."

Summing up equations

When it comes to math, Word is ever ready to present the formulas. It won't calculate anything or verify results, but it lets you present the mathematical hieroglyphics without much effort on your part.

On the Insert tab, in the Symbols group, you find the Symbol command (icon shown in the margin). Pluck from its menu a recently used symbol or choose the More Symbols command to bring forth the Symbol dialog box. From this dialog box you can insert into your document just about any character imaginable.

Yet the ultimate nerd-out tool is the Equation command, found on the Insert tab in the Symbols group. Choose this command (icon shown in the margin) and pluck out a ready-made high-IQ equation from the list. Or — if you're a Vulcan — you can choose the Insert New Equation command from the Equation button menu and craft your own equation, as I've done in Figure 8-2.

Content control handle   Content control menu

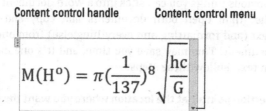

$$M(H^o) = \pi(\frac{1}{137})^8 \sqrt{\frac{hc}{G}}$$

FIGURE 8-2:
An equation
content control.

When you choose the Insert New Equation command, the Equation tab appears on the Ribbon. You probably need a PhD to fully understand all the items on this tab. They're available to help you build a complex equation, slapping it right into Word as shown in Figure 8-2.

>> Secretly, equations dwell inside a content control, which acts as a tiny container for special text in a document. See Chapter 21.

>> Whilst visiting the Symbol dialog box, click that Special Characters tab. Behold the variety of common symbols available, many of which have a (admittedly bizarre) associated keyboard shortcut.

>> The Equation keyboard shortcut is Alt+=. This command sticks an equation content control into your document, selects its text, and displays the Equation tab so that you can start solving problems — or writing equations that prove problematic.

>> To convert the content control to document text, click its menu button (refer to Figure 8-2) and choose the command Change to Inline.

TIP

TECHNICAL STUFF

» The equation shown in Figure 8-2 was written by Homer Simpson in *The Simpsons* episode "The Wizard of Evergreen Terrace." It predicts the mass of the Higgs boson, which was proven and verified 14 years later by real scientists working at CERN laboratories in Switzerland.

Where Word Meets Excel

Sometimes a table isn't good enough. Especially if you've already done the work in Excel, why bother re-creating your efforts in Word? Or perhaps you need Excel's power within a table inside Word. All these things are possible, providing you know the forbidden secrets of how Word and Excel can comingle.

Pasting part of an Excel worksheet into a document

The most obvious way to get data from Excel into your Word document is to copy-and-paste the table. This process involves some legerdemain with regard to positioning two program windows on the screen at once. Carefully heed these directions:

1. **Open both Excel and Word.**

2. **Create the document and work on the spreadsheet.**

   Perform whatever magic you need in both programs to get ready to copy from one to the other.

TIP

   Use the Alt+Tab key combination to switch between each app.

   If possible, keep both windows visible, as illustrated in Figure 8-3.

3. **Select the cells you want to copy in Excel.**

   Drag the mouse over the cells to select them.

4. **Press Ctrl+C to copy.**

5. **Switch to the Word window.**

6. **Position the insertion pointer where you want the Excel data to be pasted.**

7. **Press Ctrl+V to paste.**

   The Excel cells appear as a table inside your Word document.

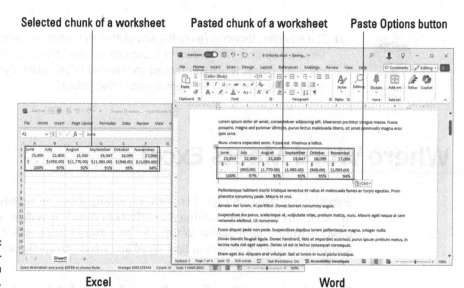

FIGURE 8-3:
A copy-and-
paste from
Excel to Word.

Excel   Word

As with any pasted item, a Paste Options button appears in Word, as shown in Figure 8-3. This button has a higher level of importance when pasting between Excel and Word than it does when pasting plain text. I recommend carefully considering the choice you make from this button. This decision determines how the Excel data works in your document.

To keep the Excel data as a Word table, click the Paste Options button and choose either the option Keep Source Formatting (K) or Use Destination Styles (S). The difference between the two is whether the table contains Excel's styles (K) or Word's styles (S).

Other choices available on the Paste Options menu are illustrated in Table 8-1.

If you just want the text from the worksheet, tap Ctrl and then the T key to choose the Keep Text Only option. The text is pasted in with each cell separated by tab characters.

The Picture option takes the worksheet chunk and pastes it in as a static image. As with any picture in a Word document, you can flow text around the object, resize it, and so on. The picture, however, doesn't update if you change the worksheet in Excel.

The Link options, which parallel the style/formatting paste options, are covered in the next section. These options update the table in Word as you change the data in Excel.

TABLE 8-1   **Excel Worksheet Pasting Options**

Icon	Shortcut	Command	Description
	K	Keep Source Formatting	A table is pasted using Excel's text format.
	S	Use Destination Styles	A table is pasted using Word's text format.
	F	Link & Keep Source Formatting	A linked table is inserted using Excel's text format.
	L	Link & Use Destination Styles	A linked table is inserted using Word's text format.
	U	Picture	A graphical image is created of the Excel data and is pasted into the document as a picture.
	T	Keep Text Only	The cell's data is pasted in as tab-separated text.

>> When you choose the paste options described in this section, the table in Word contains only plain text, not formulas. The formulas are retained in the Excel worksheet.

>> Refer to Chapter 3 for more information on tables in Word

Copying and linking a worksheet

The standard copy-and-paste operation is static. After you paste an Excel worksheet into Word, it becomes a table (plain text) or a graphic, depending on how it's pasted. The problem here is that when you update the worksheet in Excel, you must repeat the operation: copy and paste, as described in the preceding section. This step is unnecessary, however, when you choose to paste and link.

To paste and link, choose one of the two linking options presented in the Paste Options menu, shown in Figure 8-4: Link & Keep Source Formatting or Link & Use Destination Styles. Both options keep the data fresh. The difference lies in which styles are used — Excel's or Word's.

Paste and link commands

Paste Options:

Set Default Paste...

Link & Use Destination Styles (L)

Link & Keep Source Formatting (F)

To paste and link, follow these directions:

1. Create the spreadsheet in Excel and the document in Word.

WARNING

Save both documents before you proceed. If you don't save the worksheet, the linking operation might not be successful.

2. In Excel, select the cells that you want to copy and link.

3. Press Ctrl+C.

4. Switch to the Word window.

5. Click to position the insertion pointer at the location in the document's text where you want the Excel data to be pasted.

When you link the data from Excel, it appears in Word as a table. My advice is to place the table in a paragraph by itself, on a blank line.

6. Press Ctrl+V to paste.

7. Tap the Ctrl key and press the F or L key.

Or you can click the Ctrl button that appears to the lower right after you paste, as shown in Figure 8-4. The L key uses Word's styles for the pasted cells. If you press the F key, you retain Excel's formatting. Either key pastes the table as a link to the Excel worksheet.

The rows and columns of cells from the worksheet appear as a table in your document. The data, however, is linked to Excel. This link explains why the table's text looks more like a document field than plain text. For example, when you click in the table, the entire table becomes highlighted, just like a field.

Linking means that when you change the Excel worksheet, any updates are reflected in Word. To refresh the pasted table, right-click its text and choose the Update Link command. The table is refreshed to reflect the current data in Excel.

» When both Excel and Word are open at the same time, with the linked data appearing in both program windows, you don't need to click the Update Link button. As you work in Excel, any changes are instantly reflected in Word.

» If you need to edit the data, right-click in the table and choose the command Linked Worksheet Object ➪ Edit Link. Excel opens, displays the worksheet, and lets you modify the data.

» See Chapter 21 for information on fields.

Creating an Excel worksheet inside of Word

One of the quirkiest things you can do in Word is to create an Excel object inside of a document. The effect is that you transform Word into Excel without opening Excel directly. This operation has boggled the minds of Word users for centuries.

1. **Save your Word document.**

   Saving often is a proper thing to do, especially when you're superstitious.

2. **Place the insertion pointer on a blank line.**

   The embedded Excel object works like a table in Word. Tables are best set on a line by themselves.

3. **On the Insert tab, in the Text group, click the Object button and choose Object.**

   The Object dialog box appears. The items listed in the dialog box can be inserted "live" into your Word document.

4. **Select Microsoft Excel Worksheet and click OK.**

   A snippet of an Excel worksheet roosts in Word, as illustrated in Figure 8-5. The Excel Ribbon replaces Word's Ribbon. At this point, you're effectively using Excel within Word.

5. **Create the worksheet.**

   Use Excel to place fun and interesting items into the worksheet's cells, manipulating them in a manner that involves all the thrills and danger of whatever it is that spreadsheets do best. I wouldn't know; I'm a writer.

The embedded Excel worksheet is part of the Word document. When you're done using the worksheet, click the mouse outside of the worksheet's heavily armed border. At this point, Word recovers, and you can continue to work on your document.

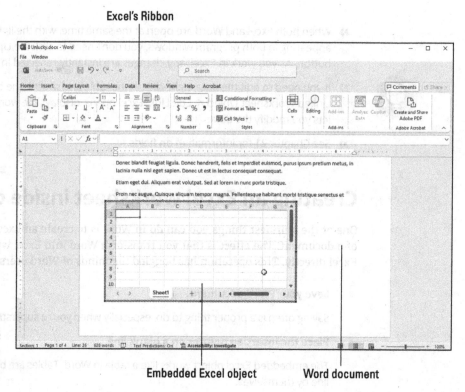

Excel's Ribbon

FIGURE 8-5:
An Excel object,
embedded in a
Word document.

Embedded Excel object   Word document

The Excel object resembles a table in Word. It's not a graphical object, so it remains in-line with the rest of the document's text. To edit the worksheet, double-click on its object. Excel takes over the Word window again, and you can modify the worksheet's data. Click in the document to exit Excel and return to Word.

TIP

If you find the experience of Excel-in-Word to be a threat to your understanding of reality, refer to the preceding section and use the paste-link option instead.

Whipping up a chart

Another way that Excel and Word mix it up is with the Chart command. This command allows you to build a pie chart, bar chart, or similar graphic inside a document. The process works the same in Word as it does in Excel because, once again, Excel is called upon from within Word to help you build the chart.

To add a chart graphic to your document, follow these richly illustrated steps:

1. On the Insert tab, in the Illustrations group, click the Chart button.

The Insert Chart dialog box appears. It lists a wide variety of chart types, and specific examples of each chart type.

2. Choose a chart category from the list on the left side of the dialog box.

3. Select a specific chart type shown the right side of the dialog box.

4. Click OK.

A chart sample is inserted into the document. You also see the Edit Data window, which looks like an Excel worksheet. (It is.) The worksheet is preset with labels and values, which are reflected in the sample chart, as illustrated in Figure 8-6.

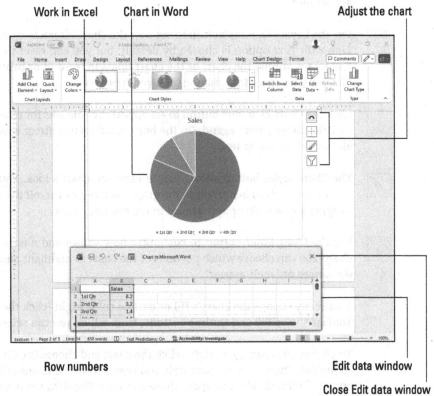

Work in Excel   Chart in Word   Adjust the chart

FIGURE 8-6:
Creating
the chart.
     Row numbers   Edit data window

Close Edit data window

5. Edit the chart data.

Click the mouse in the Edit Data window to modify the labels and corresponding data for your chart.

If you need to add a row, type it into the mini-worksheet. The row's data instantly appears in the chart.

If you need to remove a row, click the row number and press the Delete key. The row is removed and the chart is updated.

6. **Close the Edit Data window when you're done editing the data.**

The chart stays selected. You can continue to customize it, adjust its layout, and so on. Or click elsewhere in the document to continue editing.

If you need to update the chart or change the data, right-click in the Chart and choose the command Edit Data⇨ Edit Data. The Edit Data window appears again, and you can modify the values.

The buttons to the right of the chart object help you adjust the chart's layout and appearance.

Use the Layout Options button to set how the chart interacts with the text. The In Line with Text option is chosen by default, but you can reset this option so that text wraps around the chart or the chart floats in front of or behind text. Refer to Chapter 5 for more information on layout options.

Click the Chart Elements button to set appearance options for chart elements such as Title, Labels, and Legend. On the button, submenus direct which parts of each element show up, or not.

The Chart Styles button allows you to reset the chart's look. You can't reset the chart type, such as bar graph to pie graph, but you can scroll the menu presented to apply a new style or appearance to the existing chart.

Use the Chart Filter button to customize how values and names are used in the chart. You can choose which portions of the chart to highlight and where and how the names or labels appear.

To directly change the chart's fill or outline color, right-click the chart. The Mini Toolbar shows Fill and Outline buttons, from which you can select new colors.

To change the chart type, right-click the chart and choose the Change Chart Type command. Choose a new chart style and layout from the Change Chart Type dialog box, and then click OK to apply those changes. The data remains the same; only the chart's appearance changes.

To remove a chart, click to select it, and then press the Delete key.

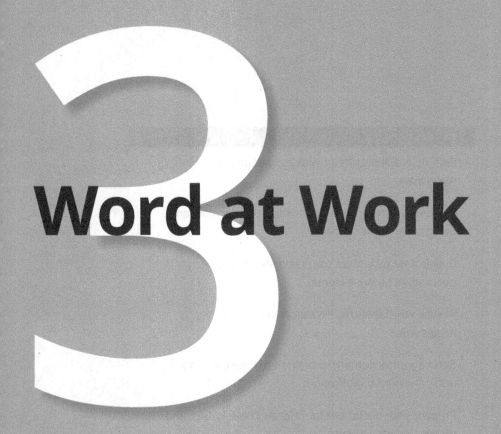

3
Word at Work

Spiff up a dull document with a cover page or watermark.

Explore exporting documents into other formats and using fancy printer tricks.

Collaborate with other users and share your documents on the Internet.

Review Word features necessary in the legal profession.

Secure your document to prevent malware attacks and unwanted modification.

Prepare your document for release, check issues, and recover lost documents.

IN THIS CHAPTER

» Creating a cover page

» Aligning cover page content

» Placing text boxes on the cover page

» Applying watermarks to a document

» Putting a border around the page

» Adjusting binding options

» Printing document properties

Chapter **9**

Beyond Routine Documents

Consider Edmond in Accounting. His documents are as dull as he is. They lack snap and pizzazz. That's probably why he's in Accounting. Oh, and he's good with numbers. Also knock-knock jokes.

My hope is that you're good with words. Unlike Edmond, when you're done writing, formatting, and sprucing up a document, you can add some final touches to truly make your efforts shine. These are items that go beyond the basics and the routine, and they're often required for professional documents in a business setting. These improvements are appreciated, especially when you're not in Accounting.

Cover Pages

The first page of an important document is called the *cover page* or *cover sheet*. It serves as an introduction, like a handshake or an awkward blind date. You can use Word's Cover Page command to quickly add a preset introduction to your document, or you can craft your own cover sheet that may better fit with your document's design.

> >> It doesn't matter whether you create the cover page first or add it later. It's easier to create it first.

> >> Word's preset cover pages are found on the Insert tab, in the Pages group. Choose one from the Cover Page button menu. Try not to yawn. Preset items contain placeholder text, which you can replace with your own brilliant musings.

> >> See the section "Setting a page border," later in this chapter, if you want to put a border around the cover page.

Designing a custom cover page

Word's preset cover pages are okay, but you probably don't want to use a prefab template that everyone else is using — especially if Edmond in Accounting figures out this trick. No, if you're going to make the effort, you might as well design your own cover page.

As the first page in your document, a cover page must be treated as a special element, separate from the document's text. I recommend that the cover page dwell in its own section, separate from the document's headers, footers, and page numbering. Here is how to create such a beast:

1. **Press Ctrl+Home to move the insertion pointer to the tippy-top of the document.**

2. **On the Layout tab, in the Page Setup group, click the Breaks button.**

3. **Choose Next Page from the Breaks menu.**

The Next Page break creates a new section in your document. This step isn't required; you could use a standard page break, but the section break makes it easier to control headers/footers and page numbers.

After creating the Next Page break, the insertion pointer is positioned on the second page of the document, in Section 2. The cover page is ready for festooning with whatever decorations you desire; the following two sections offer some suggestions. The immediate task, however, is to further separate the cover page from the rest of the document.

4. **On the Insert tab, in the Header & Footer group, click the Header button and choose Edit Header from the menu.**

The document window changes to reveal the Section 2 header, illustrated in Figure 9-1. The Header & Footer Design tab appears.

Unlink from cover page   Separate cover page

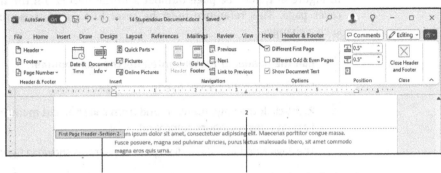

Second page is in the second section   Page number in the header

 5. **In the Navigation group, click Link to Previous to deselect that item.**

The Link to Previous setting copies the header/footer from the previous section to the current section. You don't want this setting active.

6. **You can edit the header now, adding whatever reference you need, such as a page number.**

The information in the header (First Page Header – Section 2 in Figure 9-1) is applied to all pages in the document after the cover page. You must repeat these steps for the document's footer.

 7. **Click the Go to Footer button.**

8. **Click the Link to Previous button.**

 9. **Click the Close Header and Footer button.**

You're done separating the document's header and footer from the cover page.

At this point, you can edit the cover page: add text, slap down some graphics, and create other fun design derring-do. The cover page is now separate from the rest of the document, so changes made elsewhere won't affect it.

Resetting page numbering

It's odd to number the cover page. In fact, the cover page isn't even counted in the document's page count. The second physical page in such a document is numbered starting with 1 and not 2. To effect that change, you must direct Word to renumber the document's pages.

In Figure 9-1, you see page number 2 in the header, on the first page after the cover page. This reference must be reset to 1. Heed these directions to make such a change:

1. **Edit the header or footer containing the page number.**

Double-click in the header to edit.

2. **Right-click the page number, and from the shortcut menu, choose the Format Page Numbers command.**

The Page Number Format dialog box appears, as shown in Figure 9-2.

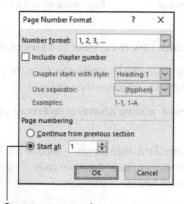

Set new page number

FIGURE 9-2:
The Page
Number Format
dialog box.

3. **At the bottom of the dialog box, choose Start At and set 1 as the value.**

4. **Click OK.**

The pages in the document are renumbered. The first page after the cover page is now numbered as page 1.

5. **Close the document header when you're done making changes.**

Click the Close button on the Header & Footer toolbar or double-click the mouse in the document's text.

Changing page numbers on the second page works when the header is held in its own section. The second page of the document starts in a new section. Effectively, you reset the page number values for the second section in the document; the first section (the cover page) lacks page number references.

Centering a page from top to bottom

Word features plenty of text and paragraph formatting tools to help you craft a marvelous document title for the cover page. The only tools that aren't readily available are those that let you position the title centered top-to-bottom on the page. To achieve this feat, you must set the page's vertical alignment.

In Figure 9-3, you see two versions of a title page. Both pages dwell in their own section at the start of a document. On the left, a title appears centered as a paragraph, aligned vertically at the top of the page. The same title appears on the right, but vertically aligned at the center of the page. Follow these steps to duplicate this effect:

1. **Write and format text on the title page.**

   The text is written in paragraphs, just like normal text. You can apply paragraph alignment, if you like, because it doesn't affect vertical alignment.

2. **On the Layout tab, in the Page Setup group, click the Launcher icon.**

   The Launcher icon appears in the lower right corner of the group, as illustrated in the margin.

3. **In the Page Setup dialog box, click the Layout tab.**

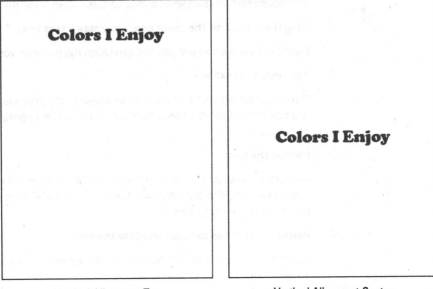

FIGURE 9-3:
Vertically
aligning a page.

Vertical Alignment Top   Vertical Alignment Center

4. **In the Page area, choose Center from the Vertical Alignment menu.**

   You're not done yet! You want this change to apply only to the cover page.

5. **From the Apply To menu, choose This Section.**

6. **Click OK.**

The page's contents are centered top to bottom, as illustrated on the right in Figure 9-3.

Using text boxes for titles

For cover pages with multiple text items, I recommend you use text boxes to hold the cover page text as opposed to messing with the page's vertical alignment. The text boxes can be positioned precisely. The resulting layout may be more to your liking.

The following steps apply a generic approach to using text boxes on a cover page. For more details on text box formatting and layout, refer to Chapter 6.

1. **On the Insert tab, in the Text area, click the Text box button.**

2. **Choose the Draw Text box command.**

   The mouse pointer changes to a plus sign, as shown in the margin.

3. **Drag the mouse on the cover page to create a text box.**

   Don't fret over the size just yet. You can resize the box after you add text.

4. **Type into the text box.**

   Type your title or subtitle. I type titles as shown in the preceding section. I use a text box for subtitles or other information as it's easier to position separately on the page.

5. **Format the text.**

   All character and paragraph formatting is available inside of the text box. Choose the font, size, and other attributes. You probably want to apply center alignment to the paragraph.

6. **Resize the text box to accommodate the text.**

   Drag one of the handles to stretch or shrink the box; the handles are illustrated in Figure 9-4.

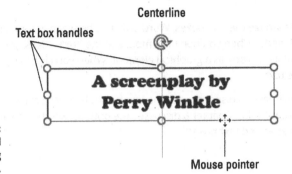

Centerline

Text box handles

A screenplay by Perry Winkle

Mouse pointer

FIGURE 9-4:
Resizing and positioning the text box.

7. **Point the mouse at the text box so that the mouse pointer changes to a four-way arrow.**

   The four-way arrow mouse pointer is shown in the margin. Use it to drag the text box to a specific location on the cover page. If you can't drag the text box, change its layout to In Front of Text.

TIP

   As you drag the box, you see green guidelines appear on the screen. These lines serve as your clue that the text box is properly aligned with the page. In Figure 9-4, the centerline appears, lining up with the center of the text box.

   If the green guidelines don't appear, on the Shape Format tab, in the Arrange group, click the Align Objects button. From the menu, choose the item Use Alignment Guides.

8. **Remove the text box's border.**

   I find the text box border to be jarring (refer to Figure 9-4). To remove it, right-click on the box's edge and from the pop-up click the Outline button and choose No Outline. The text box's outline vanishes, leaving only the text. (The outline shows up when the text box is selected; click elsewhere to preview the box.)

9. **Fix the text box's position on the page.**

   To keep the text box in the same location, select it and click the Layout Options button (icon shown in the margin). From the Layout Options palette, select the option Fix Position on Page. This option ensures that none of the text on the page affects where you've positioned the text box.

Repeat these steps to create additional text boxes, if necessary. For example: the title, your name, a headline, an address box, and so on. These items are appropriate on a cover page, but don't let it get too junky.

» As you manage the text boxes, Word switches between graphics mode and editing mode. When you point the mouse at the box's edges, you can manipulate the box as a graphical element. When you click in the text, you edit the text.

» You don't have to dispense with the text box outline. You can even add a background color. Chapter 6 discusses the options, which apply equally to both shapes and text boxes.

Word's Phony Watermarks

A *watermark* is a feature found on fancy paper. If you're unable to see it directly, hold up the paper to a bright light to view the watermark. Typically, the water-mark is an image, logo, or text embedded in the paper. Watermarks exist to impress.

Word has the capability to simulate a watermark — a phony watermark. Instead of being embedded in the paper, Word's watermark is really nothing more than a faint background image. It's not used to impress, but it's another way to identify a document as a draft or copy. This use of Word's watermark is common in office environments.

Adding a preset watermark

To stick a watermark on the background of all pages in your document, heed these directions:

1. **Press Ctrl+Home to position the insertion pointer at the start of a document.**

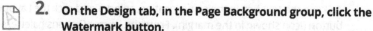 **2.** **On the Design tab, in the Page Background group, click the Watermark button.**

You see the Watermark gallery showing a scrolling list of preset, commonly used watermarks.

3. **Choose a watermark from the list.**

For example, DRAFT appears to be popular in windy offices.

The watermark is applied to all pages in the document.

To remove the watermark, follow Steps 1 and 2 in this section, but in Step 3, choose the command Remove Watermark.

>> Watermarks are seen in the document window when Print Layout view is chosen.

>> A document can have only one watermark. If you choose another watermark (for example, to set it on one page only), all the watermarks are changed in the document.

>> The watermark prints with the rest of the document. If not, see the later section "Printing background objects."

>> If you can't get the watermark to work properly, follow the steps in the next section, which might work better.

TECHNICAL STUFF

>> I've witnessed funky behavior after applying the watermark when the insertion pointer is not at the start of the document. I've seen the watermark apply to only one page or to a group of pages. To ensure that the watermark is applied to all pages in the document, follow the steps as outlined in this section.

Customizing the watermark

The most common watermark I see in Word is Draft. Other preset watermarks are useful, including Copy and Sample. Even TOP SECRET is available, but don't tell anyone.

Word lets you use an image as a watermark. The secret is to access the Printed Watermark dialog box, shown in Figure 9-5.

Remove watermark   Preset watermark text

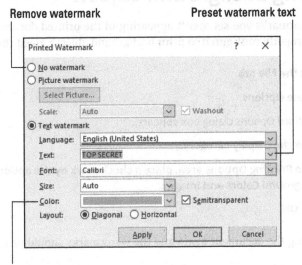

FIGURE 9-5: The Printed Watermark dialog box.

Watermark color

To customize the watermark, on the Design tab, in the Page Background group, click the Watermark button and from the menu choose the Custom Watermark command. The Printed Watermark dialog box shows up, illustrated in Figure 9-5.

To change the watermark's color, click the Color menu and choose a new color. If you keep the Semitransparent check box selected, the watermark fades into the background. When this option isn't selected, the watermark appears as a solid color.

Choose Picture Watermark to set an image as the watermark. Use the Select Picture button to find an image. This is the technique you use in Word to set a background image on a page. Keep the Washout item selected, lest the image overwhelm the document's text.

TIP

Before you finish making your settings, click the Apply button. The watermark effect is added to the document window, which you can preview behind the Printed Watermark dialog box. If you need to make further adjustments, do so. Click the OK button when you're pleased.

I'm not a graphic artist and I don't understand etiquette, but I believe that creating a company logo watermark in Word would be tacky. If you want to impress people, pay a stationer to craft your organization its own custom watermarked paper.

Printing background objects

If the watermarks you set aren't appearing in the printed document, ensure that Word is properly configured to print background objects. Heed these directions:

1. **Click the File tab.**

2. **Choose Options.**

   The Word Options dialog box appears.

3. **Select the Display category.**

4. **In the Printing Options area, place a check mark by the option Print Background Colors and Images.**

5. **Click OK.**

Try printing the document again and the watermarks should print.

Document Tricks

Word's selection of document tricks is as extensive as items you'll find up a magician's sleeve. Like several dozen handkerchiefs, some doves, and a few playing cards, not all tricks are particularly useful. Still, they may amaze you.

Setting a page border

Page borders are tricky because sometimes they show up and sometimes they don't. For example, your printer may not print where you set the board. Even so, I have a solution. Heed these steps:

1. **On the Design tab, in the Page Background group, click the Page Borders button.**

   The Borders and Shading dialog box appears with the Page Border tab forward. The page border application works exactly like a paragraph border, though the effects are added to the entire page.

2. **Choose a setting, such as Box.**

   The Box setting encloses the entire page.

3. **Choose a line style from the Style list.**

4. **Set a color.**

   The Automatic color is usually black, though it could be different, depending on the document theme.

5. **Set the line width.**

   Use the Preview window to see how the border is applied to the page.

6. **Use the Apply To menu to set whether the border is applied to every page in the document or only to the current section.**

   For example, if the cover page is its own section and that's the only part of the document to which you want to apply the page border, choose This Section from the menu.

7. **Click OK to apply the page border.**

   The border appears in Print Layout view. You can also see it on the Print Preview screen just before you print.

To remove the border, choose None in Step 2 and then click OK.

TIP

>> To apply the border only to the cover page, click the mouse on that page before completing the steps in this section. This trick works only when the cover page is set in its own section.

>> If the border doesn't print, bring up the Borders and Shading dialog box and click the Options button. In the Border and Shading Options dialog box, click the Measure From menu and choose Text. Click OK (twice) to close the dialog boxes. This change moves the page border inward a tad, which may help it to show up when printed.

Placing the document's filename in a header or footer

To help identify a printed document's location in the digital realm, many office workers put its filename in the header or footer. This trick is easy to accomplish, if you follow these steps:

1. **On the Insert tab, in the Header & Footer group, click the Header button.**

2. **Choose Edit Header from the menu.**

    The document's header is revealed.

    You could also choose Edit Footer if you prefer the filename located in the footer.

3. **Position the insertion pointer to the location where you want the filename to appear.**

    Preset tab stops exist center and right.

4. **On the Header & Footer tab, in the Insert group, choose Document Info ⇨ File Name.**

    The document's filename is inserted into the header.

TECHNICAL STUFF

    The File Name command inserts the FILENAME field into the document. If you instead choose the File Path command, the same field is inserted but adding the \p switch. This switch directs Word to display the full pathname. See Chapter 21 for details on fields.

5. **Continue editing the header, or click the Close Header and Footer button to return to the document.**

Filenames routinely appear on draft documents, but not on the final version. To remove the filename, follow Steps 1 and 2 in this section and delete the FILENAME field to remove the filename from the document's header.

The document header is affected by sections. If you want to ensure that the filename appears in all sections, you must link the sections. Refer to the section "Designing a custom cover page" earlier in this chapter for information on the Link to Previous command.

REMEMBER

Printing for three-ring binding

Whether you print on three-hole-punch paper or punch the holes yourself, you notice something: Your document's text could scoot over a notch to accommodate the holes. Rather than adjust the page margins or paragraph indents, you need to create a binding area in the page format. This area is known as the *gutter*. Follow these steps to add a gutter to your document:

1. **On the Layout tab, in the Page Setup group, click the Launcher icon.**

   The Page Setup dialog box appears.

2. **Click the Margins tab.**

   The Margins area is located at the top of the dialog box, shown in Figure 9-6. The *gutter* is an extra margin, as illustrated in the figure. Its position is set to the left or top of the page, depending on the binding.

3. **Set the Gutter Position box to Left or Top.**

   The Top option works when using the three-hole punch on the short end of the paper, for example with Landscape page orientation. (Refer to Figure 9-6.)

4. **Set the size in the Gutter box.**

   For three-ring binding, I set an extra half inch for the gutter.

   As you set the Gutter value, observe how the Preview part of the dialog box adjusts to accommodate the binding.

TIP

5. **Click OK.**

   When Word is in Print Layout view, you can see the wider space on the side of the page. This space is the combined page margin and gutter.

The gutter affects either the current section or all your document's pages. This setting is made at the bottom of the dialog box, in the Apply To menu.

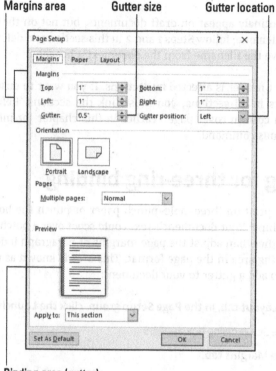

Margins area   Gutter size   Gutter location

Binding area (gutter)

FIGURE 9-6:
The Page Setup
dialog box.

If you print the document on both sides of the page, the gutter is applied left and right, depending on how the page lays out. This setting is made automatically when you print the document.

Accessing document properties

You can round up the information stored with a document in several ways. This data, collectively known as a document's *properties,* is accessed from the Info screen in Word: Click the File tab and choose the Info item from the categories listed on the left side of the window.

The document's properties list appears on the right side of the window, below the Properties heading. This list may seem trivial, but in a business environment it's an activity record.

You can set some of the properties by clicking on the Properties heading. Choose Advanced Properties and then fill in the various fields presented. Items include the document title and subject, comments, and so on. Click OK after setting the document's properties.

A document's properties are stored digitally with the document, though these details can be printed. Follow these steps:

1. **Press Ctrl+P.**

   The Print screen appears.

2. **Below the Settings heading, choose Document Info.**

   Click Print All Pages button to view the menu and locate the Document Info item. This button is known as the "Print What" button, though no label appears nearby.

3. **Click the Print button.**

   A single sheet prints, listing the document's properties.

Any items you add are printed as described in this section. They also stick to the document, even if you copy the document's file to another computer. In fact, some might consider the information to be a security risk. See Chapter 13 for information on document inspection.

IN THIS CHAPTER

» **Reviewing oddball document formats**

» **Saving documents in other formats**

» **Working with PDF files**

» **Opening non-Word documents**

» **Collating multiple documents**

» **Using duplex printing**

» **Printing multiple sheets on a page**

Chapter **10**

Document Formats and Printer Control

Knowing about files and their organization makes you a better computer user, like knowing about seasoning makes you a better cook. It's entirely possible to whip up a meal without flavor, just as it's possible to know how to use a computer without understanding files. For Word, the document is a file. It's stored on the computer for later retrieval. Specifically, it's stored in a format (call it a "flavor") that Word can easily digest.

Like a talented chef who's disciplined in multiple cuisines, Word can cook up documents in formats other than its own, as well as read from those alien formats. This flexibility allows you to edit documents created by other programs while enjoying the power and familiarity of Word. The details are covered in this chapter, along with some document printing tips.

» Documents you create in Word are saved as files on your PC's storage system or on the cloud. The files are not saved in Word; they are unique and separate items.

» Managing files falls under the reign of Windows, the PC's operating system. You use Windows to copy, move, delete, and organize document files.

Documents Formats Strange and Alien

Word's document file format is officially known as just that: the Word *document file format*. It's an organized set of data stored inside a computer that, when read properly, becomes a lovely document. Word isn't the only program that uses a specific format. And, just to be kind, Word has the capability to save documents in other formats.

Understanding document formats

Much to Microsoft's chagrin, Word isn't the only word processor available. Many competitors exist, each sporting its own document format. Add in to the mix various common file formats, such as the popular Adobe Acrobat or PDF format, the HTML or web page format, and you find the computer world bursting with different types of document files.

Table 10-1 lists common document file formats. These formats can be read by Word.

TABLE 10-1   **Common Document File Formats**

Format	Filename Extension	Description
Acrobat	pdf	The Adobe Acrobat file format, known as the Portable Document Format, or PDF.
OpenDocument	odt	A document created by the LibreOffice suite.
Plain text	txt	A text-only document without formatting or graphics.
Rich text format	rtf	A plain-text document, but with formatting information included.
Web page	htm, html	A plain text document using Hypertext Markup Language formatting.
Word document	doc	An older Word document file format.
Word document	docx	A Word document file format; Word versions 2007 to present.
WordPerfect	wpd, doc	A WordPerfect document.
XML	xml	A text document formatted with the eXtensible Markup Language, which is similar to HTML.

SHOWING THE FILENAME EXTENSIONS

TECHNICAL STUFF

A document's file format is related to a filename's extension. This extension describes the file type to Windows and determines which program opens the file and which icon represents the file. Because this association is critical to opening and identifying files, Windows hides the filename extension by default.

To show the filename extensions, start the File Explorer program: Press the Win+E keyboard shortcut.

In Windows 10, on the View tab, place a check mark by the item File Name Extensions.

In Windows 11, click the View menu and choose Show ⇨ File Name Extensions.

WARNING

Avoid the temptation to change a filename extension. Doing so doesn't change the file's format or alter its contents. Instead, use a program like Word to save or export the file to another format.

Word can also save documents in any of these formats, though I recommend that you first save the document normally just to keep a native copy. For example, you save your résumé in Word and then save it as a PDF document for uploading to a potential employer.

TIP

>> In many programs, the art of saving a document in another format is called *exporting*. In Word, you use the standard Save As or Save a Copy commands, though an Export command is also available just to keep you guessing.

>> Don't let the abundance of document saving formats boggle you. Online guides suggest specific document formats, such as PDF (Adobe Acrobat) or HTML. Even so, many sources accept Word documents as-is.

>> File formats for no longer supported programs are known as legacy formats. It's often possible to recover text from these files; see the section "Recovering text from any old file," later in this chapter.

Saving a Word document in another format

Word offers a few commands on the File tab to save your document in another format. Popular are the Save a Copy and Save As commands, as well as the Export command. I prefer to use the traditional Save As dialog box, which may not be as fancy as those other, newfangled commands, but it takes fewer steps to get the job done. Obey these directions:

1. **Save the document one more time.**

   It's best to keep a Word document file separate from its generated text file version.

2. **Press the F12 key.**

   The traditional Save As dialog box appears.

3. **From the Save As Type menu, choose the file type.**

   For example, choose Plain Text if you need only the text from your document. Choose OpenDocument Text if you need to save a copy of the document for editing in OpenOffice. To save the document in the older Word format, choose Word 97-2003 Document.

TECHNICAL STUFF

   Each file format description lists its associated filename extension, such as (*.doc) for the older Word document format. See the nearby sidebar "Showing the Filename Extensions" for more information.

4. **If necessary, choose a folder for the file.**

   I recommend keeping the file in the same folder as the Word document. You can copy it elsewhere later.

5. **If necessary, type a new name for the file.**

   Word assumes you want the same filename as the original document. This name is okay as Windows won't overwrite the Word document or confuse the two, thanks to their differing filename extensions.

6. **Click the Save button.**

For some file formats, you may see a File Conversion dialog box. For example, for a Plain Text file, the conversion dialog box is shown in Figure 10-1. The most important option is the End Lines With menu. Despite their ubiquity, text files can differ in how they represent the Enter key press. In Windows, it's CR/LF, which means carriage return and line feed characters — two characters. On Linux systems and for macOS, it's LF (line feed) only. Click OK to close the File Conversion dialog box and save the file.

When saving to an older Word document format, a compatibility checker dialog box appears. This dialog box flags items available in newer Word documents that are incompatible with the older file format.

Set the end-of-line character

File Conversion - pain in the plain text.txt

Warning: Saving as a text file will cause all formatting, pictures, and objects in your file to be lost.

Text encoding:
◉ Windows (Default)   ○ MS-DOS   ○ Other encoding:

Wang Taiwan
Western European (DOS)
Western European (IA5)
Western European (ISO)
Western European (Mac)

Options:
☐ Insert line breaks
End lines with: CR / LF ▾
☐ Allow character substitution

Preview:

Lorem ipsum dolor sit amet, consectetuer adipiscing elit. Maecenas porttitor congue massa.
Fusce posuere, magna sed pulvinar ultricies, purus lectus malesuada libero, sit amet commodo
magna eros quis urna.
☐Nunc viverra imperdiet enim. Fusce est. Vivamus a tellus.
☐Pellentesque habitant morbi tristique senectus et netus et malesuada fames ac turpis egestas.
Proin pharetra nonummy pede. Mauris et orci.
☐Aenean nec lorem. In porttitor. Donec laoreet nonummy augue.
☐Suspendisse dui purus, scelerisque at, vulputate vitae, pretium mattis, nunc. Mauris eget

OK   Cancel

FIGURE 10-1: Setting options for a text file.

>> A plain-text document isn't a Word document. In Windows, plain-text documents are associated with the Notepad program (unless another program is selected). If you double-click the text document's icon, it opens in Notepad, not Word. You can open text documents in Word: See the later section "Choosing a specific document format."

>> Plain text files lack formatting, graphics, and all the fun stuff you can do with a document in Word. Yet sometimes information is required in plain text format, probably for the same reason that many people seem to enjoy vanilla pudding.

>> The most common file format for exchanging documents between different word processing programs is probably Word's own document file format. Coming in second is the web page or HTML document.

>> The RTF, or Rich Text Format, document uses plain text but also describes formatting.

TECHNICAL STUFF

>> The plain text format is referred to as ASCII. This acronym stands for the American Standard Code for Information Interchange. This standard ensures that text files from one computer are readable by another. To avoid conflict, the text is limited to upper- and lowercase letters, numbers, and a few symbols.

Creating a PDF

Perhaps the most compatible form of document available today is the Adobe Acrobat Portable Document Format file, also known as a *PDF*. This format is the best way to electronically distribute your Word documents; just about every computer and mobile device hosts the Adobe Acrobat Reader program, which opens and displays PDF documents.

Word offers two ways to create a PDF: You can save a document in the PDF format, or you can print the document to a PDF "printer." The following steps use Word's Export command to create the PDF:

1. Save your document.

I recommend saving your work as a standard Word document before you export to the PDF format.

2. Click the File tab.

3. Choose Export.

4. With the Create PDF/XPS Document item chosen, click the button Create PDF/XPS.

The Publish As PDF or XPS dialog box appears. It's a modified version of the Save As dialog box, but in this instance the file type is chosen as PDF.

5. Optionally type a new name for the file.

It's not necessary to give the file a new name as both the Word document and PDF can dwell in the same folder with the same name. It's the filename extensions that make them different.

6. Remove the checkmark by the item Open File After Publishing.

If you forget this step, Word may open a web browser or prompt you to select a file to open the freshly created PDF.

7. Click the Publish button.

TIP

Windows features a "printer" called Microsoft Print to PDF. If your computer has the Adobe Acrobat program installed, an Adobe PDF "printer" is also available. These virtual printers can also be used to generate a PDF document: From the Print screen, choose Microsoft Print to PDF or Adobe PDF to digitally print your document. You're prompted for a name and a location where to save the PDF file. I find this approach easier than using the Export command as described in this section.

>> PDF documents render the content consistently on all computers and devices. This reason is why the PDF file format is so popular.

>> The XPS document format is specific to Microsoft Office. It was an attempt to create a rival universal document format. The attempt was less than successful.

>> You can obtain a free copy of the Acrobat Reader from get.adobe.com/reader.

>> I have more success using the Print to PDF "printer" than using the Adobe PDF "printer."

Open Strange Document Formats

Perhaps you're like me and you have file archives from generations back. These archives include documents created by word processing programs long since discarded in the digital dumpster of technology. It's a sad story, but with a happy ending: Word does its best to not only open documents saved in unusual formats but also to recover text from just about any file. It's an amazing trick.

Choosing a specific document format

The key to opening a document in a strange format from a strange program developed on a strange planet by strange alien nerds is to know its file format. Providing that you know the file format, you can follow these steps to open the document and view its contents in Word:

1. **Press the Ctrl+F12 keyboard shortcut.**

The traditional Open dialog box appears.

2. **Use the File Type menu to choose the document's type.**

For example, choose Text Files (*.txt) and the Open dialog box displays only text files.

TIP

If the file you want doesn't show in the Open dialog box, or its type isn't listed, choose All Files (*.*) as the file type.

3. **Navigate to the folder containing the text file you want to open.**

Only the document file types of the sort chosen in Step 2 appear in the folder.

4. **Click to select the file, and click the Open button.**

The alien file is opened and ready for action in Word.

If it's your desire to continue working with the imported document in Word, I recommend that you save it right away. Pressing the Ctrl+S keyboard shortcut may cause Word to want to save the document in its native format. Instead, choose to save the file as a Word document to avoid any compatibility issues later.

If necessary, press Ctrl+F12 to use the traditional Save As dialog box to save the document in the Word Document (*.docx) file format.

TIP

» PDF files open easily in Word, though the conversion may not be exact. An info dialog box appears as you open the PDF, reminding you that the translation may not be as pretty as the original.

» Older Word documents you open can be converted to the current Word document format. Your clue is that you see the text "Compatibility Mode" appear in the window's title bar. To update the document, click the File tab and choose the Info category. Click the Convert button to update the document.

» To save a document in another format, refer to the earlier section "Saving a Word document in another format."

» An advantage of opening a plain text document in Word is that you have the power of document proofing. Many text editors lack this feature.

Recovering text from any old file

It amazes me which antique word processing files Word recognizes. For example, I used WordPerfect 5.1 to write *DOS For Dummies* in 1991. I still have the document files, though their format is unknown to Word. If you have such older files still around, or whenever you encounter a document file format that Word stubbornly refuses to recognize, follow these steps to recover text from the file:

1. Press Ctrl+F12.

The traditional Open dialog box appears.

2. In the Open dialog box, from the File Type menu choose the option Recover Text From Any File.

All files in the current folder are displayed, including oddball graphics files and other files that don't contain any text whatsoever. Word is indifferent at this point.

3. Browse to the folder containing the file to open.

4. Select the file.

5. Click the Open button.

The file opens in Word, translated from whatever file format Word recognizes into a document.

When the file type isn't recognized, Word displays the File Conversion dialog box, as shown in Figure 10-2. Work the controls in that dialog box to see whether you can massage the text into a digestible format. If so, click the OK button. If not, click Cancel and accept that the file can't be opened.

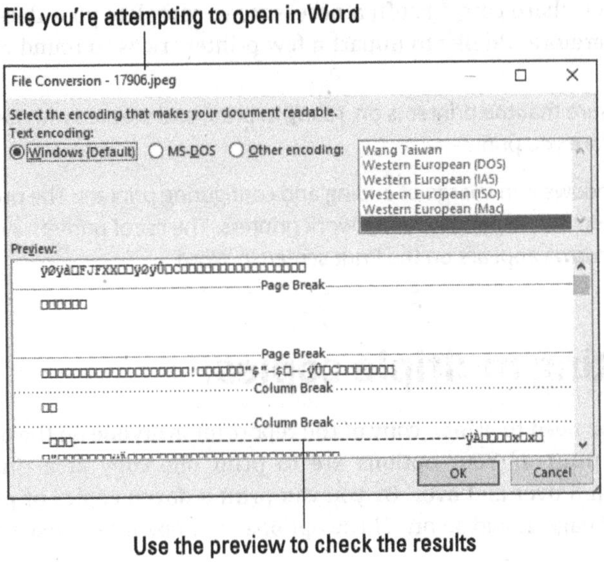

File you're attempting to open in Word

FIGURE 10-2:
Word attempts to read text from a graphics file.

Use the preview to check the results

>> Word may refuse to open some files for security reasons, specifically older Microsoft Word documents. See Chapter 13 for details on how to temporarily lower Word's security paranoia to access the files.

>> I'll be honest: The controls in the File Conversion dialog box are rather limited. If you don't see what you want immediately in the Preview window, click Cancel.

>> In Figure 10-2, I attempt to open a graphics file. The proper way to insert graphics into a document is to use the Insert Pictures command. Refer to Chapter 7. Even if the graphics file contains a text image, Word cannot read it as described in this section.

>> Word's capability to recover text from older files is one reason I retain my old word processing files.

TECHNICAL STUFF

>> If you don't see the Recover Text from Any File option (Step 2), try using All Files instead. A strange bug exists in Word where the Recover Text from Any File option may appear in a foreign language. For example, on my computer it shows up as *Récupérer du texte de n'importe quel fichier*. This command probably appears because I have the French language proofing tools installed in my personal copy of Word. It's a bug.

Printer Tricks

Once upon a time, printing was a necessary computer activity. These days, things aren't printed as much as they're digitally shared on the Internet. Still, word processing is one computer activity where printing is required at some point. That printed or "hard copy" is often necessary to complete your document's preparation. Therefore, I'd like to impart a few printer tricks to round out this chapter.

>> Ensure that the printer is on, ready to print, and stocked with paper and ink before you print.

>> Windows is in charge of adding and configuring printers. The process is automatic, especially for network printers. The list of printers available in Windows appears on the Print screen in Word.

Printing multiple copies

When you need to print a copy of the report for everyone on the board, how do you want it printed? Your options are to print one copy at a time — say, pages 1 through 8 over and over. Or you can print a dozen copies of page 1, and then a dozen of page 2, and so on. These options are known as *collated* and *uncollated*.

On the Print screen, illustrated in Figure 10-3, use the Copies gizmo to set the number of copies, such as 6 or however many people attend the meeting.

Ensure that the Collation button shows collated (refer to Figure 10-3). This option, chosen by default, ensures that you don't have to shuffle all the pages after you print.

Printing on both sides of a sheet of paper

Unlike the old hand-cranked computer printers of the 1990s, today's printers can easily print on both sides of a sheet of paper, what's known as *duplex* printing. Word is happy to accommodate this printer feature, but you, the human, must remember to activate it.

After pressing the Ctrl+P key, look for the Duplex Printing item on the Print screen (refer to Figure 10-3). Click this button to display a menu of options as illustrated in Figure 10-4. Available options depend on the printer.

The Print One Sided option is the standard, boring, 1990s version of printing.

Duplex Printing

Select Printer

Number of copies

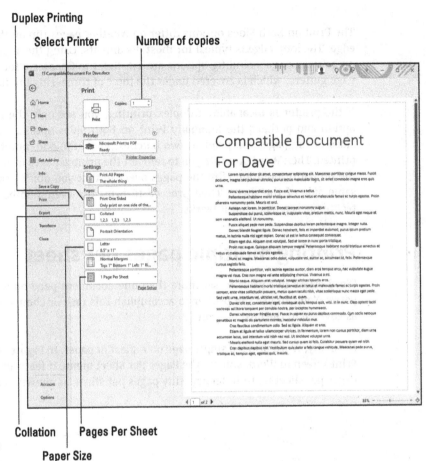

Collation

Pages Per Sheet

FIGURE 10-3:
The Print screen.

Paper Size

Binding on the sides

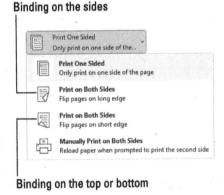

FIGURE 10-4:
Options for
printing on both
sides of a
sheet of paper.

Binding on the top or bottom

The Print on Both Sides options differ on whether pages flip on the long or short edge. The long edge is typical for most documents. Using the short edge depends on how the page's binding options are set. Refer to Chapter 9 for information on page gutters, which is covered under the topic of three-ring binding.

If the printer is incapable of duplex printing, you see only the Print One Sided option and perhaps the Manually Print on Both Sides option. To print on both sides of the page, you print in two batches: First, the odd-numbered pages are printed. Then Word prompts you to reinsert the printed pages into the printer. Use the proper orientation (flip the pages over) so that you don't print twice on the same side of the sheet. Then proceed to print the even-numbered pages. This technique is a pain, but it works.

Printing multiple pages per sheet

Word offers two ways to set more than one document page on a single sheet of paper. You can use the printer to accomplish this task or change the page layout as covered in the next section.

Normally, Word prints a single page on a sheet of paper. In Figure 10-3, and on the Print screen in Word, you see the Pages Per Sheet menu. It features options from 2 pages per sheet up to 16 teensy-tiny pages per sheet, as shown in Figure 10-5.

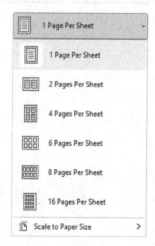

FIGURE 10-5: Setting pages per sheet.

Choosing a different number of pages per sheet doesn't alter what you see in the Print screen's preview window. It does, however, affect what's printed. Word reduces a page to fit on a sheet of paper in the quantity you select. The printing can get very tiny, which is why I don't see this option as very useful.

Formatting multiple pages per sheet

If it's your desire to print multiple pages per sheet and have it look good, my advice is not to use Word's printing command to set multiple pages per sheet (refer to the preceding section). Instead, change the page layout to accommodate multiple pages per sheet.

For example, to print two document pages per sheet, obey these instructions:

1. **On the Layout tab, in the Page Setup group, click the Launcher icon.**

   The Page Setup dialog box appears.

2. **Ensure that the Margins tab is forward.**

3. **In the Orientation area, choose Landscape.**

   Two-pages-per-sheet looks better in landscape orientation.

4. **From the Multiple Pages menu, choose 2 Pages Per Sheet.**

   The Preview window shows the pages side-by-side on a sheet of paper.

5. **From the Apply To menu, choose Whole Document.**

6. **Click OK.**

The document presents itself in Print Layout view, but at half-width. This effect is how Word visually displays printing one page on half a sheet of paper, which is really two pages per sheet of paper. The document prints these pages side by side on a single sheet of paper.

> » The other options on the Multiple Pages menu may not affect your document. Especially if you use Portrait orientation, you may see no printed effect at all.
>
> » To reset Word to print a single page on a sheet of paper, choose Normal from the Multiple Pages menu.
>
> » This feature makes sense when you think of a page in Word and a sheet of paper as different things.

TIP

IN THIS CHAPTER

» Adding comments to a document

» Reviewing comments

» Using the Track Changes feature

» Perusing changes to a document

» Approving document changes

» Comparing document versions

» Collaborating online

Chapter **11**

Collaboration and Sharing

Many consider writing to be a solitary art. Even so, the publishing process involves more than a single person. Plus, good writers desire feedback. This process involves more than one set of eyes — hopefully, a competent editor and copy editor. For a project in a business or office setting, several people might contribute to the final document — even Randy in shipping, who is probably high on something all the time.

Word's collaboration tools help you interact with others during the document production process. You can provide feedback and comments, track who-changed-what, and even collaborate in real time on the Internet while Randy is home playing *Call of Duty* completely sober.

Here Are My Thoughts

Teachers and editors have historically demanded that primitive, typewritten documents feature ample margins and double, or even triple, line spacing. The reason is simple: Room is required in order to write comments and make corrections. In the digital realm, however, tools are available for providing feedback inside the document, saving the document's margins and spacing from the lusty desires of overzealous contributors.

Highlighting text

The basic feedback tool is the Text Highlight Color command, commonly known as the highlighter tool. Like its real-world counterpart, the Text Highlight Color command applies a background shade to text.

 To use the Text Highlight Color tool, on the Home tab, in the Font group, click the Text Highlight Color tool.

 While the tool is active, the mouse pointer changes, as shown in the margin. You can drag over any swath of text to apply the highlight.

The tool deactivates after you've selected text. To go into hyperactive scribble mode, double-click the Text Highlight Color tool. The mouse pointer remains in highlighting mode until you press the Esc key or choose the tool again to disable it.

To remove the highlight, use the same color to highlight the text again. You can also choose No Color from the Text Highlight Color menu and then drag over the highlighted text to erase.

TIP

>> Highlighting is good to reference material in addition to adding comments to the text. The comment can refer to the highlighted text, for example, to draw attention to repeated words or phrases. See the next section for details on inserting comments.

>> To change the highlight color, click the menu button next to the Text Highlight Color button. Choose a color from the list. I often use different colors to highlight different issues with the text.

TECHNICAL STUFF

>> Highlighted text isn't a text formatting attribute. It's neither a foreground nor background color, you cannot search for highlighted text, and you cannot use the Clear All Formatting command (Ctrl+spacebar) to remove it.

Inserting a comment

The traditional way to comment on someone else's document was to scribble text in the margin. When word processing, doing so damages the computer screen. Rather than do so, Word offers a comment feature. Put away that red pen, and follow these steps:

1. **Select a chunk of text.**

   The text is the subject of your comment, such as that horrible run-on sentence that doesn't seem to stop and just goes on without ever seeming to reach what would otherwise be considered a positive and satisfying conclusion.

2. **On the Review tab, in the Comments area, click the New Comment button.**

   A comment area appears on the right side of the document window. Your name appears in a comment bubble, as illustrated in Figure 11-1.

Relevant text   Comment   Your name

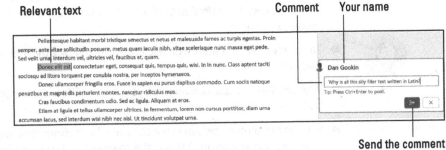

Send the comment

FIGURE 11-1:
A comment is pending resolution.

3. **Type the comment text.**

   Be brief. Be descriptive. Be supportive.

4. **Click the Send icon or press Ctrl+Enter to post the comment.**

   The Send icon is illustrated in Figure 11-1.

After sending, or posting, the comment box changes as shown in Figure 11-2. Its new appearance allows others to reply to the comment, mark it as resolved, or delete it, as illustrated in the figure.

The comment/reply box can become quite busy, though its purpose is to resolve the issue. Once resolved, click the overflow button and choose Resolve Thread. You can also choose to delete the comment (also found on the overflow button menu).

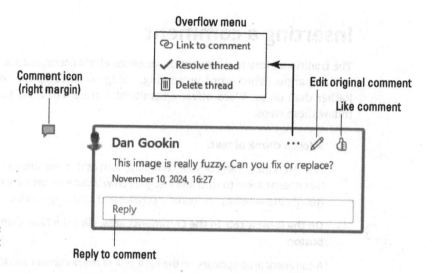

Overflow menu

🔗 Link to comment
✓ Resolve thread
🗑 Delete thread

Comment icon
(right margin)

Edit original comment

Like comment

Dan Gookin   ••• ✏ 👍

This image is really fuzzy. Can you fix or replace?
November 10, 2024, 16:27

Reply

FIGURE 11-2:
A comment
awaits resolution.

Reply to comment

TIP

» Although it may be tempting to select large chunks of text to reference in a comment, keep the selection brief. I would never select more than one sentence at a time.

» To quickly select a sentence of text, press Ctrl and click the mouse in the sentence.

» When multiple people comment on your text, a different color presents each person's comments.

» You can tag another person in the comment by prefixing their username or email address with an @ sign in the comment. This trick works only when the document is shared online or locally on the organization's network. An email alert is sent to the recipient, informing them that a comment requires attention.

Reviewing comments

With the comment area visible, it's easy to peruse what others have written about your text. An easier way is to page through the comments one a time, which is a good choice for a particularly long document.

The comment review buttons are found on the Review tab in the Comments group. The two you want to mess with are Previous Comment and Next Comment, but probably not in that order.

Click the Next Comment button to hop to the next chunk of commented text in your document. If the comment area is hidden, a card appears with the comment, including any replies.

Click the Previous Comment button to review comments between the insertion pointer and the start of the document — to "go back" if you're paging forward through the comments.

When you arrive at a comment, you can add text, resolve the thread, or delete the comment. Refer to Figure 11-2 for where to find these commands in the comment box.

Showing and hiding comments

Perhaps all those meddling editors vex you. Their comments are a distraction. If so, hide them!

On the Review tab, in the Comments group, click the Show Comments button to hide the comments.

Be aware that even when hidden, a comment icon appears in the document's right margin, as illustrated in Figure 11-2. You can't blot out this blemish until the comment is deleted. (If the comment is marked as "resolved" the same icon appears, but with a teensy green checkmark added.)

When comments are hidden, you can view them by clicking the Show Comments button again. This button features a menu with two items, Contextual and List. The Contextual choice shows comments as they appear, positioned on the same page with the comment. The List shows all the comments piled atop each other. Try not to let them overwhelm you.

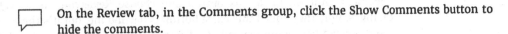

Look What They Did!

Some editors harbor a malevolence to do more than just comment on your text. No, they see fit to edit your efforts with reckless abandon. Imagine the nerve! Then again, they could either tell you what's wrong or fix it. The issue is knowing what has changed. To best determine where and how text was modified, Word offers the Track Changes feature.

Activating the Track Changes feature

Before some weirdo or editor (is that redundant?) begins hacking away at your text, implore this person to activate Word's Track Changes feature. It's simple, and regardless of what you think about the other person, you will thank them for employing this useful feature.

To activate the Track Changes feature, follow these steps:

1. **On the Review tab, in the Tracking group, click the Track Changes button.**

   The Track Changes button becomes highlighted.

2. **Begin editing the document.**

   As you edit, type, delete, or reformat the text, the changes appear highlighted on the screen.

If you're in a hurry, look for the Editing button in the upper right corner of the document window. Click this button and choose Reviewing to activate Track Changes. Why they added this extra button is beyond me, but it's there. And seeing it labeled Reviewing instead of Editing is a good clue that the Track Changes feature is active.

When editing a document with the Track Changes feature active, any new text you add appears <u>colored and underlined</u>.

Any text you remove appears colored and ~~strikethrough~~.

The text color is related to the person who edited the text. When multiple people are mangling your document, each of their additions or removals appears in a unique color. The Reviewing pane is used to determine who added or removed what. See the later section, "Showing or hiding the revision marks." In fact, the revisions may not appear if you've selected the option to hide the revisions.

>> The Reviewing pane is also useful to see when others have changed formatting or styles, as these modifications don't appear directly in the text.

>> When text has been modified, the Track Changes feature sets a vertical bar in the left margin next to the line of text that's been changed. You cannot delete this bar, though after the changes are accepted or rejected, it vanishes. See the later section, "Accepting or rejecting changes."

>> To temporarily disable Track Changes, click the Track Changes button a second time. The Track Changes button returns to normal (its highlight disappears), and the middle button in the upper-right corner of the window changes back to read "Editing." Feel free to edit your text without evidence.

Locking the changes

If you dislike seeing those red underlines and strikethroughs in your text, you can always hide the revisions. See the next section. But you can also lock your document to prevent the Track Changes feature from being used. Or, conversely, you can lock your document to prevent someone from disabling Track Changes when you want to keep this feature active. Obey these directions:

1. **On the Review tab, in the Tracking group, click the Track Changes button and choose Lock Tracking from the menu.**

The Lock Tracking dialog box appears.

2. **Type a password twice.**

The same password is typed twice to ensure that you know the password.

3. **Click OK.**

The Track Changes button is dimmed; the feature can no longer be deactivated.

To remove the lock, repeat the steps in this section, but in Step 2 type the password. Click OK to unlock the Track Changes feature.

WARNING

The Lock Tracking feature is not a document security tool. The only thing it prevents is anyone from disabling the Track Changes feature. See Chapter 13 for information on document security.

Showing or hiding the revision marks

How revision marks appear in your document depends on your preferences. You can choose to see every dang detail, just hints, or no revisions at all — despite them being recorded anyway. The secret is to access the Display for Review menu.

On the Review tab, in the Tracking group, click the Display for Review button (icon shown in the margin). The Display for Review button shows the current option for revision marks. Four choices are available:

Simple Markup: A vertical line appears in the left margin next to altered paragraphs.

All Markup: In addition to the vertical line, revision marks appear in the text as colored underline and strikethrough, with each editor/mangler assigned a color.

No Markup: All revisions are hidden in the text. They still exist, but you don't see them. I find this option best for editing the text because the revision marks don't get in my way.

Original: All changes (additions and removals) are all hidden, and the document is presented as it was before the Track Changes feature was activated.

To see who did a revision, point the mouse at the revision. A pop-up bubble appears with the editor's name, the time of the edit, and a description of what was changed.

 If you want to see a summary — which can get quite lengthy — activate the Reviewing pane: On the Review tab, in the Tracking group, click the Reviewing Pane button. The Revisions pane appears, showing a summary of all the document's changes since the Track Changes feature was activated.

Click on an item in the Revisions pane to instantly hop to that location in your document.

REMEMBER

» The underline and strikethrough text, as well as the text color, indicate revision marks. These are not text attributes or formatting.

» Two options from the Display for Review menu make the Revisions pane appear horizontally or vertically in the document window.

» Yeah: Don't ask me why the command is called Reviewing Pane when the actual gizmo is called the Revisions pane.

Accepting or rejecting changes

Those revision marks need not linger in your document, the brutal marks from a whip-wielding, overzealous editor. Seriously, the Track Changes feature is designed to show suggestions, not mortal changes. As the document's author, it's your choice whether to accept or reject the changes.

Obey these steps to approve or disapprove revisions:

1. Press Ctrl+Home to visit the tippy-top of your document.

 2. On the Review tab, in the Change group, click the Next button.

Word moves the insertion pointer to the location in your document where the next change occurred.

3. **Click the Accept button to agree with the change; click the Reject button to dismiss the change.**

These buttons are found on the Review tab, in the Changes group.

No matter which button you choose, the revision mark is removed. If you choose Accept, the change becomes part of the text. If you choose Reject, the change is removed.

4. **Continue to click the Accept or Reject buttons to move through the document.**

You no longer need to click the Next button as you accept and reject revisions.

If you're impatient, or just angry, you can employ two shortcuts to expedite the process: From the Accept button's menu, choose Accept All Changes. Or, from the Reject button's menu, choose Reject All Changes. Poof! The document review is complete.

You can also choose the variation on those commands: Accept All Changes and Stop Tracking, or Reject All Changes and Stop Tracking. In both cases, the document is scoured, and the Track Changes feature is mercifully deactivated.

WARNING

» It's easy to get confused! When you click the Accept button for a deletion, you are deleting the text. When you click the Reject button for an insertion, you are removing the inserted text. Sometimes, you might find yourself clicking Reject when you meant to accept a deletion.

» The revision marks stay with your document until you accept or reject them.

Comparing two versions of a document

Your document has made the rounds, and even Vicky in Accounting got her hands on it. She's never liked you, probably because she has no sense of humor, and you enjoy the occasional bon mot. Regardless, Vicky didn't bother to activate the Track Changes feature to record her edits. Whether her decision was negligent or vindictive is for HR to decide. Your job is to discover what she has changed.

To the rescue comes Word's Document Compare tool. It automatically applies revision marks to show you the exact differences between two documents. To use the tool, you must have two copies of the document available: the original and the copy. You must know both filenames. When you're set, follow these steps to compare the documents:

1. **On the Review tab, in the Compare group, click the Compare button.**

2. **From the menu, choose Compare.**

   It doesn't matter which document is currently open. You could be working with a blank document; Word doesn't care.

   The Compare Documents dialog box appears, as shown in Figure 11-3. Your goal is to specify the original document and the copy or revised document as illustrated in the figure.

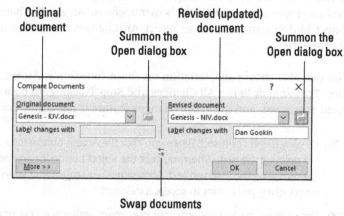

Original document

Revised (updated) document

Summon the Open dialog box

Summon the Open dialog box

Swap documents

FIGURE 11-3: The Compare Documents dialog box.

3. **Click the Original Document menu and choose the original document.**

   You must choose the name even if the original document is currently shown in the Word document window. Click the folder icon if you need to access files in a specific folder.

4. **Click the Revised Document menu and choose the updated document.**

   This document is the one that has the changes. The revision marks shown in the final document display what the revised document has added or removed.

   If you get the original and revised documents reversed, click the Swap icon in the Compare Documents dialog box. (Refer to Figure 11-3.)

TIP

5. **Click OK.**

   Word opens both documents, compares the original with the revised version, and displays a new document with the changes shown in revision marks.

Figure 11-4 shows the results, with both documents appearing on the right side of the window (original top, revised bottom) and the merged document in the center part of the window with the changes marked.

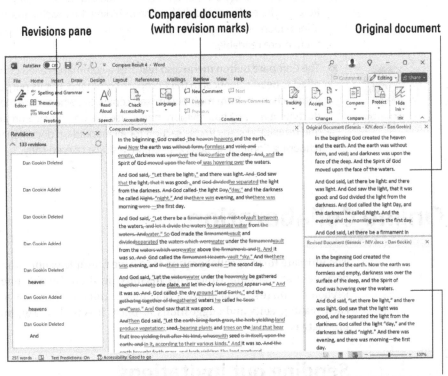

Revisions pane

Compared documents (with revision marks)

Original document

Revised document

FIGURE 11-4:
The compared documents.

All documents shown in the window are synchronized, so that they scroll together. This feature allows you to peruse all three to see what is changed.

At this point, you can proceed as described in the preceding section "Accepting or rejecting changes." Peruse the revision marks to see which to keep or which to toss out.

When you're done, save the compared result document as you would any other document.

>> The Compare command is unavailable if the document has been protected. See Chapter 13 for information on text editing restrictions.

>> If you accidentally close one of the document panes (shown in Figure 11-4), use the Compare button menu on the Review tab to restore it: Choose Compare ⇨ Show Source Documents ⇨ Show Both.

>> The Display for Review menu is set to All Markup for the compared document. Refer to the earlier section "Showing or hiding the revision marks" for information on changing the view, which might make the compared document more readable.

TECHNICAL STUFF

>> The Compare button menu also features a command called Combine. Its effect is nearly identical to the Compare command, but its purpose is to gather changes from multiple revised copies. So, when more than one document already has revision marks, use the Combine command in Step 2 and repeat the steps in this section for all marked-up document copies (choosing Combine in Step 2) to create a single revised copy.

Online Collaboration

The ultimate form of collaboration is to have multiple people working on the same document at the same time. This insanity need not involve one PC with several keyboards. Instead, you share a document online and host several contributors, each making edits and suggestions at once. It sounds crazy, but it can be quite productive.

Sending out invitations

The part of online collaboration involves gathering a virtual group of people to edit or view the same document. Just as you might send out invitations to a party, you send out invitations to work on the document. Cake, balloons, and silly hats are optional.

To invite online humans to participate in your document's creation and editing, heed these steps:

1. **Open the document you plan on sharing.**

   The document must be saved to your OneDrive account. If it hasn't been, you'll be prompted to save a copy there before you can proceed.

2. **Click the File tab and choose Share.**

If you haven't yet saved the document on your OneDrive storage, you'll be prompted to do so now. And, if you're not logged into your Microsoft account, you'll be prompted to do so.

TIP

The shortcut to share is to click the Share button in the upper-right corner of the document window. Choose Share ⇨ Share.

3. **Fill in the Send Link or Share dialog box.**

Your job is to supply names, provide a message, and set the access level, as shown in Figure 11-5. Or you can choose to share the link, in which case anyone with the link can access the document, as illustrated in the figure.

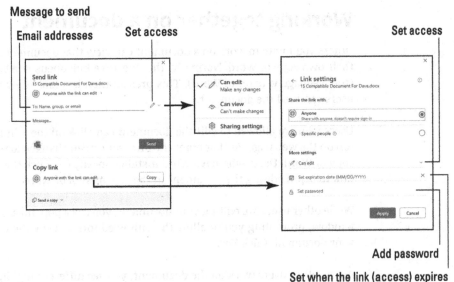

FIGURE 11-5:
Sharing a
document.

4. **Choose whether to share the file directly or share a link.**

- *Share the file directly.* If you choose to share the file directly, type your collaborator(s) email into the To field, as illustrated in Figure 11-5. Set their access level to Can Edit or Can View. (A viewer cannot edit, but can make comments.) Add a message. Click the Send button to send.

- *Share a link to the file.* Click the item Anyone With The Link Can Edit (refer to Figure 11-5). Fill in the Link Settings dialog box: Choose Anyone, set the access level, and optionally set a link expiration date and password. Click the Apply button, then click the Copy button to access and copy the link to the file.

If you choose to share the file directly, an email message is sent to the recipient(s) provided. This message shows a Word file icon, the filename, and a View In One-Drive button. The recipient clicks the button to edit the document, either on the web or in a local (not online) copy of Word. See the next section.

TIP

>> Don't be concerned about keeping the original document. OneDrive has a history feature that retains all copies of a document. Click the document's filename in the window's title bar and choose the Version History command to review previous editions of the document.

>> Email invites are sent from your Microsoft account, which is why you must be logged in to this account to use the Share feature.

Working together on a document

Others you invite to work on a document can view that document on the web or in their own copy of Word. Normally, the OneDrive link opens in a Word on the Web (the webpage version of Word). This presentation is a look-only thing; the other users can read the document.

Users who are allowed to edit the document can click on the Edit in Browser button on the web page. At that point the browser screen changes to reflect the online copy of Word. Users who have Word installed locally can click the OPEN IN WORD link to begin editing the document in the full version of Word.

While other users are editing your document, you see a pop-up appear in the Word window, prompting you to allow the online editors to view the changes made to your document. Click Yes.

As the other users work on the document, you see different highlights representing text selected or perhaps the other user's cursor location. Any changes are made are reflected by an Update icon appearing in the document's margin. Save the document to update the text and highlight what was changed.

>> Sharing works better while you're communicating. Word presently lacks any real-time chat mode for editing, so I assume you'll be on the phone or chatting with some app while you collaborate on the document.

>> Don't bother activating the Track Changes feature while a document is shared; it won't work. Instead, you can compare the document after it's shared with an original copy. Refer to the earlier section "Comparing two versions of a document."

Ending collaboration

Collaboration continues until you direct the document to stop being shared: Click the Share button in the upper right corner of the document window and choose the Manage Access command. Use the Manage Access dialog box to control sharing, determine who has access and what type of access (view or edit).

If you choose to stop sharing a document, your collaborators receive a notice saying that the document is no longer shared. Any further edits a collaborator makes can be saved to a new document on their own computer, but not to your copy.

IN THIS CHAPTER

» **Putting line numbers on a page**

» **Changing the line number format**

» **Creating citations**

» **Building a table of authorities**

» **Setting aside a paragraph of text**

» **Creating a redaction style**

» **Updating WordPerfect documents**

» **Dealing with the WordPerfect transition**

Chapter **12**

Word for Lawyers

'm prepared to pack this chapter with as many lawyer jokes as the pages will allow. Alas, the real reason for including a For Lawyers chapter in a *For Dummies* book (har!) is that the legal profession requires special word processing tools. These tools were once found — and showcased — in the popular WordPerfect word processor. Sadly, in the Word Processor Wars, WordPerfect came in second, which for computer software is like not coming in at all.

All that aside, lawyers need special word processing tools that were once found readily in WordPerfect program. These tools exist in Word, too. So before you jump out of your chair with the eagerness to shout "I object!," consider plunging into Word's more obscure tools designed specifically for those in the legal profession.

Line Numbers on the Page

I'm not an attorney, which has made both my parents proud. As a writer, however, I know that one thing required in the legal profession is a document with line numbers marching down the page. This feature is also used in radio scripts, just in case you're a lawyer who moonlights writing midnight radio drama.

Adding line numbers

Line numbering can restart at the top of each page or be continuous for the entire document. To add line numbers, follow these steps:

1. **On the Layout tab, in the Page Setup group, click the Line Numbers button.**

   A menu appears, from which you can choose line numbering options. All Word documents are preset with the None option chosen, for no line numbers.

2. **Choose Continuous to number all lines in the document consecutively, or choose Restart Each Page to start the first line of the page at number 1.**

   The lines in the document are numbered sequentially, top-down, in the left margin of the page, as shown in Figure 12-1.

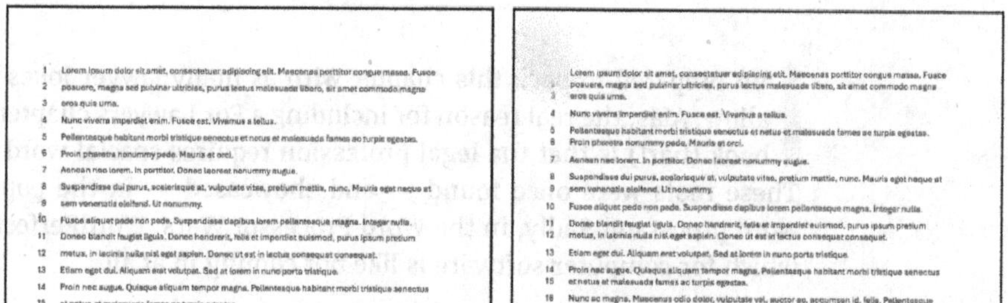

FIGURE 12-1: Line numbers on a page.

Line numbers without paragraph spacing   Line numbers with paragraph spacing

TIP

The same line numbering is applied in both page examples shown in Figure 12-1. The difference between them is that the page on the left is formatted with *no* paragraph spacing and 1.5 line spacing. The page on the right uses 8-point spacing after each paragraph, which is single spaced. The before and faster spacing is what makes the line numbering appear uneven.

Line numbering is affected by document sections. If you need only a portion of the document numbered, set those pages into their own section and apply the line numbering to that section only. In Step 2, choose Restart Each Section.

Formatting line numbers

If you desire to format the line numbers, you can bring up the Line Numbers dialog box to set some options, such as how far away from the text the numbers appear. Obey these directions:

1. **On the Layout tab, in the Page Setup group, click the Line Numbers button and choose Line Numbering Options.**

The Page Setup dialog box appears with the Layout tab forward.

2. **Click the Line Numbers button.**

The Line Numbers dialog box appears, as shown in Figure 12-2.

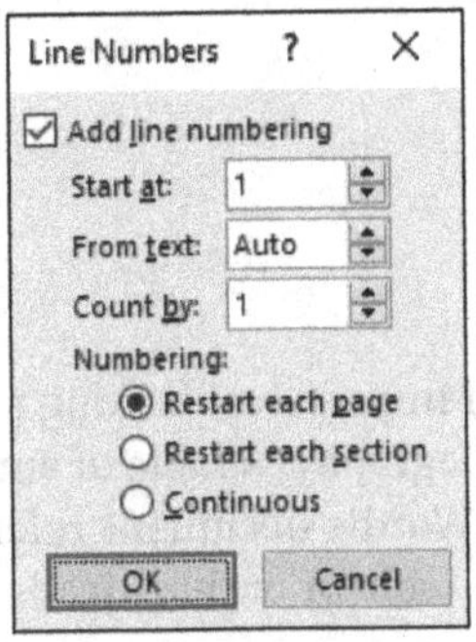

FIGURE 12-2: The Line Numbers dialog box.

Most of the options you can set in the Line Numbers dialog box are already represented by choices available on the Line Numbers menu, described in the preceding section. One item you won't find, however, is the From Text distance.

To set how far to the left of the page margin the numbers appear, enter a value in the box. For example, the value 0.5" sets the numbers half an inch from the left page margin. The Auto value sets the numbers about ¼-inch from the page margin.

Avoid setting line numbers closer than ½-inch to the page edge. That's because not every printer is capable of printing information toward the edge of the paper.

Removing line numbers

To zap all line numbers from a document, on the Layout tab, in the Page Setup group, click the Line Numbers button and choose None. The line numbers are gone — though only from the current section if the document is split into multiple sections.

To remove line numbering from a single paragraph, follow these steps:

1. Click to place the insertion pointer in the given paragraph.

You can also select a group of paragraphs.

2. On the Layout tab, in the Page Setup group, click the Line Numbers button and choose the command Suppress for Current Paragraph.

The line numbering is skipped for the given paragraph(s).

Numbering resumes at the following paragraph.

The line numbering is suppressed for an entire paragraph. Even when each line of the paragraph is numbered, the command removes all numbered lines in the paragraph.

The Table of Authorities

No, a table of authorities is not a group of impressive-looking people surrounding the defendant in a courtroom. Like a bibliography, a table of authorities is a list of legal references and sources. It's one of Word's document reference tools, which are covered in Chapter 18. But because a table of authorities is typically found in legal documents, it's mentioned here.

Marking citations

Word doesn't write the citations in a table of authorities for you; that's your job. It can help you organize and list them. To make that happen, you must first mark the citations in your document. Obey these steps:

1. **Finish your document.**

   To best mark citations, it helps to have the document completed with all the citations written. Though you can mark citations as you go, it's more effective to finish the document first. Oh, and:

2. **Save your document.**

   Always save.

3. **Select a citation.**

   Select the first instance of a citation in the document. If the citation is inside parentheses, don't select the parentheses (though you can edit them out later).

4. **On the References tab, in the Table of Authorities group, click the Mark Citation button.**

   The Mark Citation dialog box appears, with the text you selected from Step 3 shown inside, as depicted in Figure 12-3.

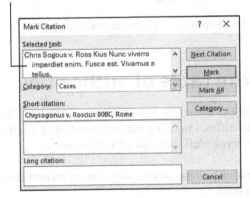

Text selected in the document

5. **Choose a category, such as Cases or Statutes.**

6. **If a longer citation is required, type it in the Long Citation text box.**

7. **Click the Mark button to mark the citation.**

   If you want to mark all instances of the citation in the document, click the Mark All button instead. This button directs Word to track the pages on which the same citation appears. These pages are referenced in the table of authorities.

8. **Keep the Mark Citation dialog box open, and repeat Steps 3 through 7.**

   When you click the Next Citation button, Word hops forward in the document to the next bit of text it believes to be a citation.

TIP

9. **When you're done marking citations, click the Cancel button.**

The dialog box goes away.

 A side effect of using the Mark Citation tool is that Word activates the Show/Hide feature, revealing the document's codes. Specific to the citations, you see a field displayed "in the raw" next to the citation text. That's okay! Don't delete the field, though you can turn off the Show/Hide feature: On the Home tab, in the Paragraph group, click the paragraph button, icon shown in the margin.

>> To remove a citation, erase its text.

>> Editing a citation is tricky. You can't just re-mark it — you just activate the Show/Hide command to reveal the citation's secret text. Delete that secret text, contained between the curly brackets. Then mark the citation again as described in this section.

>> Marking citations is similar to marking items for inclusion in an index. In fact, creating an index is similar to creating a table of authorities: You mark text for inclusion in a list, and then Word creates the list for you. See Chapter 18 for information on creating an index.

TIP

>> See Chapter 21 for information on document fields.

Inserting the table of authorities

The goal of marking citations in your document is to have Word automatically build a table of authorities. Providing that you've marked all citations and done all that other attorney-type stuff, proceed with these steps:

1. **Place the insertion pointer on the page where you want the table of authorities to start.**

I would recommend starting the page with a hard page break or even a section break.

You might also consider adding a title to this page — something clever, like *Table of Authorities.* If you want that text included in a table of contents, ensure that you use the Heading 1 or similar style for the title.

 2. **On the References tab, in the Table of Authorities group, click the Insert Table of Authorities button.**

The Table of Authorities dialog box appears. It shows a preview of what the table looks like, as shown in Figure 12-4.

Preview

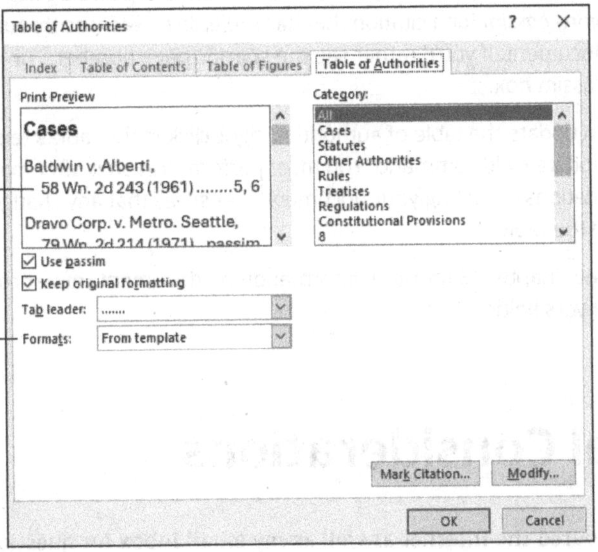

FIGURE 12-4:
The Table of
Authorities
dialog box.

Select format

3. **Choose a table format from the Formats menu.**

As you select formats, the Print Preview window updates to reflect how the table of authorities appears.

You can also choose an underline style from the Tab Leader menu. Again, the Print Preview window updates to show you the Table of Authorities style and presentation.

4. **Click OK to insert the table of authorities into your document.**

Take a moment to look at it. If it's not correct, press Ctrl+Z to undo and start over at Step 2.

Sidebar! The table of authorities is secretly a document field. You don't edit it; Word creates it for you, based on the text you've marked as citations. (Refer to the preceding section.)

» To edit the table of authorities, right-click in the table's text and choose the Edit Field command. In the Field dialog box, click the Table of Authorities button. You see the Table of Authorities dialog box (refer to Figure 12-4), where you can make changes to the format or layout.

» Yes, you can add more citations to the table at any time: Refer to the preceding section for details on marking citations. You need to update the table of authorities after you add or change citations.

TIP

» The Use Passim setting in the Table of Authorities dialog box substitutes the word *passim* for a citation that has multiple references throughout the document. If you'd rather see the specific page numbers, un-check the Use Passim box.

» To update the table of authorities, right-click in the table's text and choose the Update Field command. You must perform this step after marking new citations or editing your document. It ensures that any changes are included in the table.

» See Chapter 18 for more information on document references. Chapter 21 covers fields.

Other Legal Considerations

I've scoured the Internet as well as my email inbox for questions from law offices regarding specific issues with Microsoft Word. I have a bunch of them, and many of the answers are addressed in this book — specifically, in this chapter. Two additional topics are left-right block indent and text redaction.

» Also see Chapter 10 for information on saving Word documents in other file formats. These formats might be required for electronic submission of documents.

» Information on footnotes and endnotes is found in Chapter 18.

Setting a left-right block indent

The *left-right block indent* is a paragraph format, frequently found in legal documents. Also known as a *block quote*, this style involves increasing a paragraph's left and right indentations by equal values. Figure 12-5 illustrates how such a format might look.

To scrunch in a paragraph's left and right indentation, follow these steps:

1. **Place the insertion pointer in the given paragraph or select a group of paragraphs.**

2. **On the Layout tab, in the Paragraph group, type 0.5 in the Left Indentation box.**

Paragraph's left indentation   Paragraph's right indentation

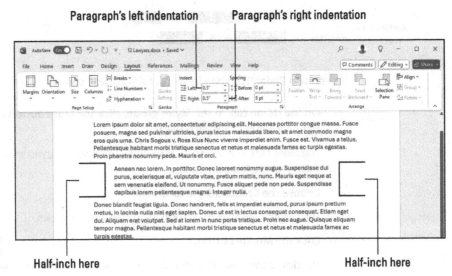

FIGURE 12-5:
Indenting a
paragraph.

Half-inch here   Half-inch here

3. **Type** 0.5 **in the Right Indentation box.**

The paragraph's left and right indentations move toward the center of the document, setting that text aside from the text above and below it.

You can set a value other than half-an-inch in Steps 2 and 3. Set whatever looks good.

TIP

>> Word features a "half-inch indent" command: Press Ctrl+M. This keyboard shortcut affects only the paragraph's left indentation.

>> If you plan on using the left-right block indent frequently, I recommend that you create a block indent style and include that style with your document templates.

>> Paragraph indentation is not the same thing as adjusting a page's margins. In Word, page margins are measured from the edge of the page. A paragraph's indent starts where the page margin ends.

Redacting text

When you need to remove information from a document, I recommend that you create and apply a Redaction style. This style doesn't remove text, and it doesn't blank it out. Instead, it sets the text's foreground and background colors to black. The result is that the text doesn't show up in the document, similar to what's shown in Figure 12-6.

FIGURE 12-6:
Redaction
in action.

But, Mr. Spock! You can't ████████████to the ███████!
We need your ███████████ on the ███████████!

To create a Redaction style in Word, follow these steps:

1. **On the Home tab, in the Styles group, click the More button in the lower right corner of the Style Gallery.**

   The More button is shown in the margin. Upon success, you see the full Style Gallery, plus a few commands.

2. **Choose the Create a Style command.**

   The Create New Style from Formatting dialog box appears.

3. **Click the Modify button.**

   The dialog box expands to show more options, as illustrated in Figure 12-7.

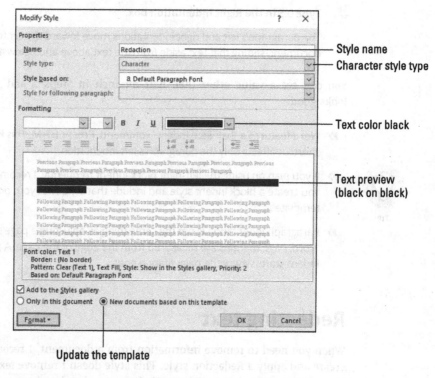

FIGURE 12-7:
Building the
Redaction style.

4. **Type** Redaction **in the Name box.**

5. **From the Style Type menu, choose Character.**

6. **In the Formatting area, click the Font Color button and choose black.**

    On the Font Color menu, the blackest black color is located below the first *e* in the word *Theme.*

7. **Click the Format button and choose Border.**

8. **Click the Shading tab in the Borders and Shading dialog box.**

9. **Click the Fill button.**

    You see a color menu like the one shown in Step 6.

10. **Choose black as the fill color.**

    Choose the same black, the one located below the first *e* in the word *Theme.*

11. **Click OK.**

12. **If you want to add the Redaction style to the template, place a check mark by the item New Documents Based On This Template.**

    This style is probably something you'll use again and again, so it makes sense to add it to the template.

13. **Click OK to create the Redaction style.**

To apply the style, select text in your document and then choose the Redaction style from the Home tab's Style gallery or from the Styles pane.

>> Your inclination might be to simply set the text's foreground and background colors to black, which can be done in Word: The text color is set in the Font dialog box, and the background color is part of the Borders and Shading command. Instead, I urge you to build a Redaction style, as recommended in this section.

>> The automatic font color is usually black, but when you create the Redaction style, you want to assert a true black color. That's because if you later edit the default text color or style, the Automatic option may change to a color other than black. That change would render text visible in the Redaction style.

>> By setting both the text color and background shading to black, you not only redact the text but also prevent someone from selecting that chunk of text and viewing its contents "inversed" in the selected block.

WARNING

>> Creating a Redaction style is useful only when printing. The information isn't truly redacted because anyone can reset the style to see what the text originally stated.

TIP

>> When you truly need to redact text, I recommend that you consider exporting the document (non-redacted) as a PDF. Refer to Chapter 10. The Adobe Acrobat program has a feature that redacts text to professional standards.

IN THIS CHAPTER

» **Reviewing document warnings**

» **Visiting the Trust Center**

» **Adding a trusted location**

» **Allowing Word to open older documents**

» **Restricting editing in a document**

» **Setting a document as final**

» **Applying password protection to a document**

Chapter **13**

Document Security

One of the most famous computer viruses was called Melissa. It sent out emails to your contact list, each with a copy of the virus attached. The virus's genius is that the message appeared to be sent from your account, which increased trust. This alarming event is mentioned in this book because the Melissa virus was spread via a Microsoft Word document.

Don't worry! Your documents are safe. Though the evil that created the Melissa virus is still out there, Microsoft has added higher levels of security to Word. Plus, various ways are available to further protect your document, restrict editing, and even add encryption and password protection.

Warnings Galore!

The most obvious effect that the Melissa virus had on Word is a warning you may see when you open a document. This warning appears just below the Ribbon. Several examples are shown in Figure 13-1, though each represents a different type of warning.

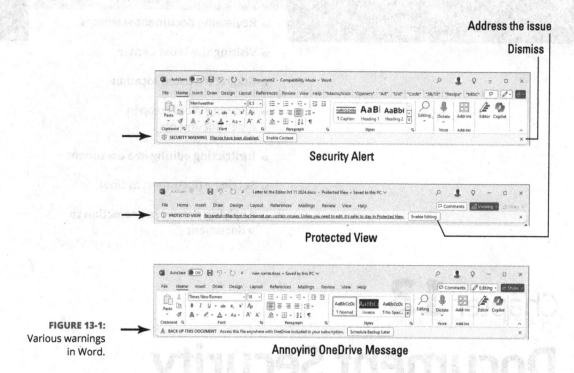

FIGURE 13-1:
Various warnings
in Word.

Here are some common warnings that may appear below the Ribbon when you open a document:

Hyperlink Warnings. The document contains links to suspicious websites.

Policy Tips. These warnings are based on your organization's policy settings. If the document violates a policy setting, for example when a document may contain a full social security number, an alert appears.

Privacy Options. The document may contain links to external files or websites that could compromise your privacy. For example, a field may share information with an external source, which could compromise your privacy.

Protected View. This warning appears most often if you've downloaded the document from the Internet — or even if it's shared over the local network.

Security Alerts. The document contains macros or other controls that are deemed suspicious. These warnings can be yellow or red, depending on the severity of the concern.

Information appears for each of these alerts, informing you of your options. For example, in Figure 13-1, the Security Alert identifies that macros have been disabled. You can dismiss the warning; in which case the macros stay disabled. Or you can click the Enable Content button to activate the macros.

For a Protected View warning, click the Enable Editing button if you're assured that the document was downloaded from a reliable source.

TIP

The Back Up This Document warning appears when the document you opened isn't saved to OneDrive cloud storage. The prompt is urging you to use OneDrive, which is up to you. (A similar prompt appears in the Windows Settings app.) If you click the button, the document is moved to OneDrive, though it could also activate OneDrive backup which moves all documents and files on your PC to OneDrive. I just dismiss this warning.

>> These settings are controlled in the Trust Center. See the next section.

>> Policy Tip warnings are based upon settings made by your organization's IT department. These can cover document content as well as other items.

>> I use OneDrive, but I also prefer to keep files stored locally on my computer. I just put up with the OneDrive warnings, though I do believe them to be misleading. I have several backup programs running on my computer. Just because the warning implies that your document isn't being backed up doesn't necessarily mean it's not backed up in other ways.

The Trust Center

To keep your documents safe, Microsoft Word features a Trust Center. It's a centralized location for reviewing and settings and options related to document security. You can ratchet up security if doing so makes you comfortable. Or you can remove some restrictions if you find them unduly burdensome.

Visiting the Trust Center

Microsoft didn't put the Trust Center somewhere obvious, probably because they don't trust you. To summon it, heed these directions:

1. **Click the File tab.**

2. **Choose Options.**

   The Word Options dialog box appears.

3. **From the categories on the left side of the Word Options dialog box, choose Trust Center.**

No, you're not there yet.

4. **Click the Trust Center Settings button.**

Now you're there.

The Trust Center window is illustrated in Figure 13-2. Categories appear on the left side of the window, with settings on the right.

Categories   Content

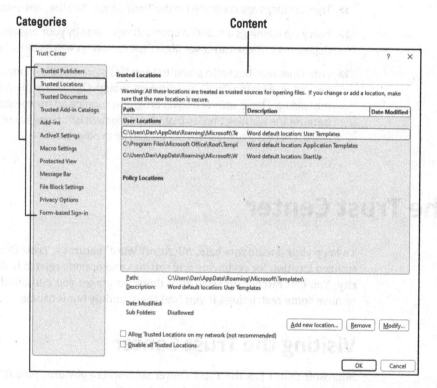

FIGURE 13-2:
The Trust
Center window.

Close the Trust Center window when you're done, then close the Windows Options dialog box to return to your document.

The following sections cover some options presented in the Trust Center window.

Setting trusted locations

By default, Word doesn't want you to lurk in strange folder neighborhoods to open documents. When you attempt to do so, you may see a warning or Word just may flat-out refuse. To add known — and safe — locations where Word can trust your documents, follow these steps:

1. **Open the Trust Center window.**

   Refer to the preceding section.

2. **Choose the category Trusted Locations.**

   You see details as shown in Figure 13-2. A list of User Locations appears, folders local to your account that contain items safe for Word to open.

If you find yourself accessing documents from a specific folder on your computer, but you get an error message or cannot open the document, add its location: Click the Add New Location button. Use the Browse button in the Microsoft Office Trusted Location dialog box to locate the folder you frequent and let Word know that this location is safe. You might also consider checking the item to allow sub-folders for the location as well.

TIP

Consider adding local network storage to Word's safe list. But rather than add each individual network folder, click the Trusted Documents category. On the Trusted Documents page, put a check mark by the item Allow Documents on a Network To Be Trusted.

Removing the downloaded documents restriction

When you download a document from the Internet or save it from an email attachment, a warning appears as shown earlier in this chapter. This warning is set in the Protected View category in the Trust Center window. Refer to the section "Visiting the Trust Center" for steps on accessing this window.

Three items are available for Protected View settings, as shown in Figure 13-3.

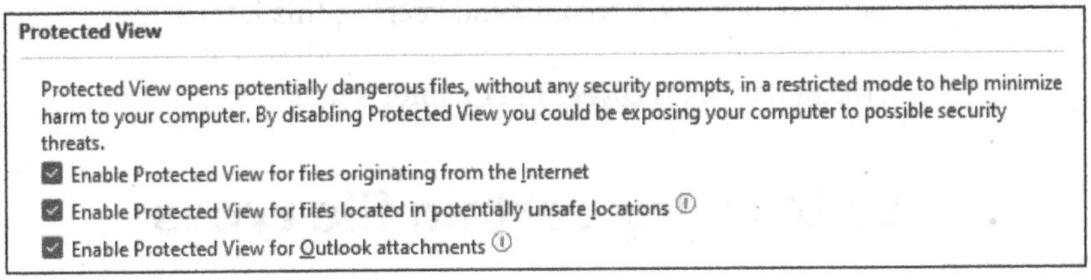

Protected View

Protected View opens potentially dangerous files, without any security prompts, in a restricted mode to help minimize harm to your computer. By disabling Protected View you could be exposing your computer to possible security threats.

☑ Enable Protected View for files originating from the Internet

☑ Enable Protected View for files located in potentially unsafe locations ⓘ

☑ Enable Protected View for Outlook attachments ⓘ

FIGURE 13-3: Protected View warnings.

I recommend keeping all three options active (checked). Even so, Word lets you remove protected view, which allows any document downloaded from the Internet to be viewed with no warning. Macro warnings, however, still appear. See the next section.

WARNING

If you disable the protected view item, ensure that you have an anti-virus program installed on the computer. Follow safe computing practice, such as not downloading a document from a shady website or opening an unexpected document file attachment.

Controlling macro security

The Melissa virus was launched from a macro, back in the days before Word came with a Trust Center. To deal with this type of threat, the Trust Center disables all macros with a notification, as shown in Figure 13-1. Yes, even good macros are disabled in this manner, so don't let the warning freak you out.

You can use the Trust Center window to allow all macros (not recommended), allow only those that are digitally signed, and control whether Word displays notifications when all macros are disabled. These options are available in the Trust Center window, in the Macro Settings category shown in Figure 13-4.

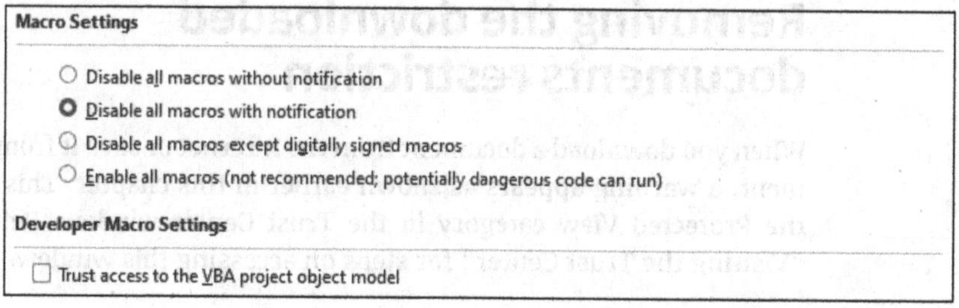

Macro Settings

○ Disable all macros without notification

◉ Disable all macros with notification

○ Disable all macros except digitally signed macros

○ Enable all macros (not recommended; potentially dangerous code can run)

Developer Macro Settings

☐ Trust access to the VBA project object model

FIGURE 13-4:
Macro settings.

The default option is to Disable All Macros With Notification. Even when you write your own macros, I recommend keeping this item set.

Writing macros is covered in Chapter 22.

Unblocking certain file types

I never paid heed to the Trust Center until I tried to open an ancient Word document. Though I created the document, and I knew it was safe, Word flat-out refused to open it. I could extract text from the document (foretold in Chapter 10), but I wanted to see the document as I wrote it in Word long ago.

The reason older Word documents, as well as other file types, are restricted is due to security. Due to the old file format, no guarantee can be made the opening the document won't lead to mischief. Therefore, you must specifically instruct Word that older documents are safe for you to open. Follow these steps:

1. Open the Trust Center.

Refer to the steps presented earlier, in the section "Visiting the Trust Center."

2. Choose the category File Block Settings.

The Trust Center shows a list of file types with check boxes for Open and Save permissions, as illustrated in Figure 13-5.

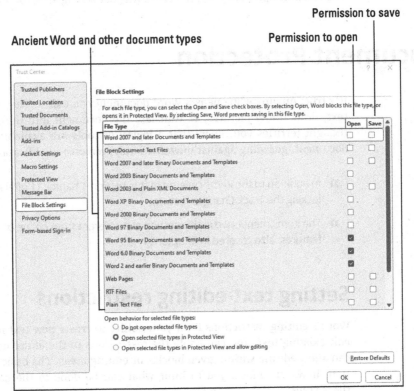

FIGURE 13-5: File Block Settings.

3. Select a file type from the list.

For example, my old Word documents use the Word 6.0 Binary Document file format.

4. Set a check mark to open or save the document type.

I wanted to open my old Word documents, so I clicked on Open. (Refer to Figure 13-5.)

5. Ensure that the option Open Selected File Types In Protected View is chosen.

With this item on, you see a warning displayed as you open the document. I recommend this setting just to ensure that you're aware it's an older document or could potentially compromise your security.

6. Click OK.

You can now open the given file types without seeing an error message displayed.

Document Protection

It's true: Anyone who opens a Word document can edit it. They can mangle your text, draw funny pictures, or translate the document into German. If the mere thought terrifies you, know that a legion of tools are available to protect your document, guarding against unwanted, nay, *verboten* modification by others.

>> In addition to the items covered in this section, Chapter 11 offers tips on locking the Track Changes feature.

>> The items mentioned in this section are different from online collaboration features, also covered in Chapter 11.

Setting text-editing restrictions

Word's editing restrictions limit your ability to create new text in a document or edit existing text. You can apply the restrictions to the entire document, or you can allow editing within given blocks, or editing areas. The basic form of restriction, however, allows you to limit what can be done to the document. Follow these steps:

1. Save your document.

2. Click the File tab.

3. On the Info screen, click the Protect Document button.

A menu of document protection features appears.

4. **Choose Restrict Editing.**

The Restrict Editing pane appears.

5. **Place a check mark in the box below Editing Restrictions.**

The Editing Restrictions area expands, as shown in Figure 13-6. Specifically, the list of exceptions appears, but your focus for now is on the menu, as illustrated in the figure.

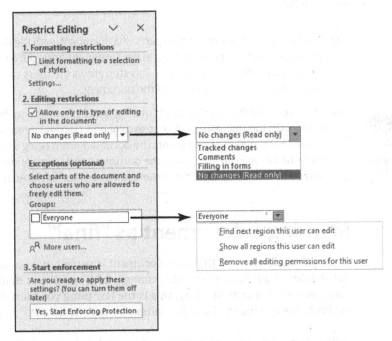

FIGURE 13-6: Applying editing restrictions.

6. **Choose a restriction level from the menu.**

The options are

No Changes (Read Only): The document cannot be edited or changed.

Tracked Changes: Modifications can be made, but only with the Track Changes feature active.

Comments: Other authors can insert only comments.

Filling in Forms: Only content controls are available for typing text or adding information to the document.

If you're collaborating and you want to ensure that your text is unmolested, choose Tracked Changes or Comments.

7. **Click the button Yes, Start Enforcing Protection.**

8. **Type a password into the dialog box: once to set the password and again to confirm.**

9. **Click OK to begin enforcing the editing restrictions.**

The document is now protected against making any changes.

To stop this restriction, open the Restrict Editing pane again: Follow Steps 1 through 4. Click the Stop Protection button, type the password (from Step 8) and click OK.

>> To restrict editing to just certain parts of a document, with the Restrict Editing pane open, select a chunk of text. In the Exceptions area, put a check mark by Everyone (refer to Figure 13-6). This step allows the users to modify the selected block, but not the rest of the document.

>> The traditional Open dialog box (Ctrl+F12) features a menu on the Open button. On this menu you can choose to open a document read-only, however this option only prevents the document from being saved under the same name; you can still modify the document and save it under a new name. The protection covered in this section, however, restricts all editing.

Marking a document as "final"

When you're determined that your document is perfect, or you just desire to limit the abilities of others to write, edit, change, fold, spindle, or mutilate your document, you mark it as *final*. Truly, this is the last thing you must do to a document in Word, like locking the back door after you put out the cat.

Follow these steps to mark a document as final and apply read-only protection:

1. **Click the File tab.**

2. **On the Info screen, click the Protect Document button and choose the command Mark As Final.**

   A warning dialog box appears.

3. **Click OK to confirm.**

   If you haven't yet saved the document, you'll be prompted to do so now. And shame on you for not saving!

   Another dialog box appears with some complicated explanations about marking a document as final.

4. **Don't read the information in the dialog box and just click OK.**

What the dialog box says in Step 4 is that the document's status property is set to Final and that all editing and proofing and such is deactivated. The document's title (at the top of the window) is suffixed with the text Read Only, which is a visual clue that no further changes can be made. Also, the Ribbon is hidden, and you might see a banner displayed, as shown in Figure 13-7.

FIGURE 13-7: Perhaps "final" needs a new definition?

That's correct: To remove a document's "Final" status, you just click the Edit Anyway button. But at least the steps outlined in this section might make you feel better about finally finishing something.

You can also remove final protection by repeating Steps 1 and 2 in this section.

Adding a password to your document

To lock up your document with a password, which also encrypts the document, follow these steps:

1. **Save your document.**

2. **Click the File tab.**

   Ensure that Info is chosen from the list of items on the left side of the window.

3. **Click the Protect Document button and choose Encrypt with Password.**

   The Encrypt Document dialog box appears.

4. **Write down the password you plan to use.**

   I'm serious: Before you type the password, write it down somewhere obvious to you but not apparent to someone out to snoop for passwords. You need this backup password because if you forget it the document remains forever locked.

5. **Type the password into the Encrypt Document dialog box.**

   The password is case-sensitive.

6. **Click OK.**

7. **Retype the password to ensure that you know it.**

8. **Click OK.**

   The document is encrypted when it's saved.

You can use an encrypted document just as you would any document in Word. Unless you've further applied editing restrictions (covered in Chapter 13), you'll notice little difference between working on an encrypted document and working on a regular Word document.

When you open an encrypted document, a password prompt appears on the screen. Type the document's password and click the OK button. The document opens and you can do whatever with it.

>> As a file, a password-protected document can be copied, renamed, moved, or deleted. You cannot, however, use the Preview pane in a File Explorer window to peek at an encrypted document's contents.

WARNING

>> There is no ability to recover a lost password. I can't do it. Microsoft can't do it. Apparently, even the FBI can't do it. Do not forget the password!

Removing the password

To free your document from an encrypted and password-protected state, obey these steps:

1. **Open the password-protected, encrypted document.**

2. **Type the password when prompted; click OK.**

The document is open. The key is to save it in a nonprotected state.

3. **Press the F12 key.**

The traditional Save As dialog box appears.

4. **Near the bottom right part of the dialog box, click the Tools menu and choose General Options.**

The General Options dialog box appears, shown in Figure 13-8. It contains locations to set an encryption password and a modification password.

5. **Delete the password from the Password to Open text field.**

You don't need to know the password because Word assumes you knew it when you opened the document. Still, I consider the lack of double verification to be a security risk.

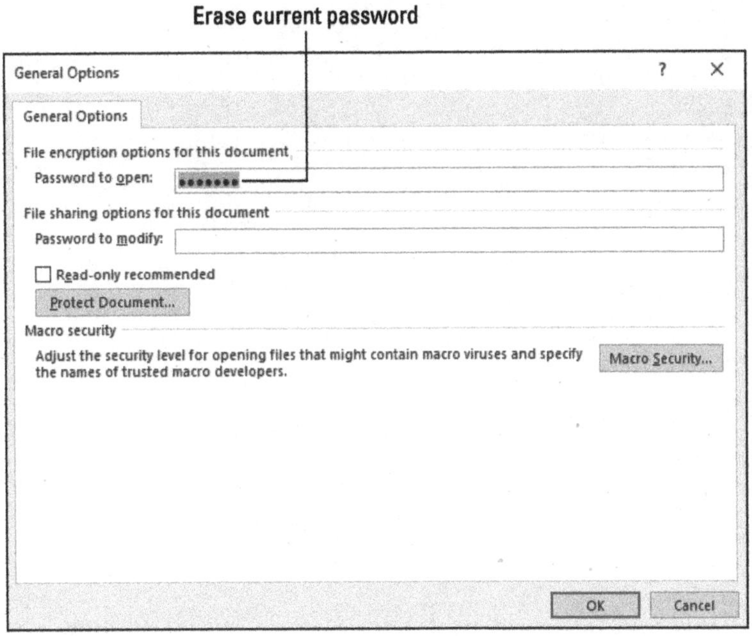

Erase current password

FIGURE 13-8:
The General
Options
dialog box.

6. **Click OK.**

Document encryption is removed, as is the document's password.

7. **In the Save As dialog box, click the Save button to resave the document.**

8. **Click the Yes button.**

The document is saved in a nonencrypted, non-password protected state.

Chapter **14**

Final Document Preparation and Review

You may think that the final task for writing a document is to print. Or, better, to *save* and then print. That's fine, but it's not the bottom line when it comes to features Word offers for final document preparation. If you have the Copilot tool installed, you can obtain document summaries and other evaluations. Word can assist you in locating missing items. You can even hunt down lost documents and recover older versions. Word is more than happy to assist you as you cross the document finish line.

Some AI Assistance

Microsoft's artificial intelligence companion is named Copilot. At the time this book goes to press, Copilot is not included with either Windows or Microsoft Office. It's a subscription service you pay for, which then becomes available as a tool in Windows as well as a writing assistant in Microsoft Word.

If you don't have Copilot installed, you may merrily skip this section. Otherwise, pay heed to those marvelous AI tools that will help you craft a better document, at least until AI takes over the world and decides that humans are a bothersome nuisance.

Finding Copilot in Word

 After installing Copilot, you must restart Word. When you do, you find the Copilot icon on the Ribbon's Home tab, far right end. The icon is shown in the margin.

 Copilot also lurks in the document's left margin, as shown in this book in the left margin. This icon appears when you start a new paragraph or whenever text is selected. It's called the Draft with Copilot icon.

At the top of each document, you see the Copilot Summary box. Click this box to see a description of the document's text, highlighting its contents.

Finally, when you first start a document, you see the Draft with Copilot icon in the left margin, but also the faint text, "Select the icon or press Alt+I to draft with Copilot" appearing on the page. This text disappears as you start to type, though the Alt+I keyboard shortcut remains to instantly summon Copilot as described elsewhere in this section.

Working the Copilot pane

Choosing the Copilot button on the Ribbon displays the Copilot pane, illustrated in Figure 14-1.

Use the Copilot pane to ask a question or gain insight into your document. Sample questions and examples are provided, as shown in the figure. For example, you can type, "Who is this document written for" to see a summary. You can also ask general questions, such as, "Why is the dessert Napoleon named after Napoleon?"

 » When a response is generated in the Copilot pane, you may see tiny numbers appear in the text — like footnotes, as shown in the margin. Click one of these numbers to see a relevant reference in the document or web page link.

» Although you can ask Copilot to generate an image for you, you cannot copy or drag the image into your document. (If you drag in the image, you instead drag in a webpage link that doesn't help your document much.) Further, Copilot can be busy elsewhere on the Internet and may be unable to generate an image.

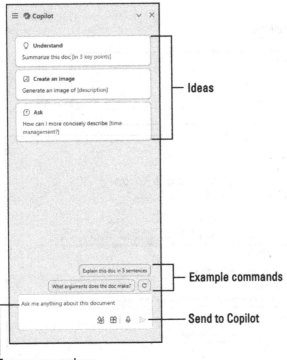

Ideas

Example commands

Send to Copilot

FIGURE 14-1:
The Copilot pane. Type your query here

>> The Copilot pane is more of a research and reference tool. For interaction directly with text in your document, use the Draft With Copilot icon that appears to the left of a paragraph.

Writing that first draft

When words fail you, and that demon writer's block is begging you to go outside and wander aimlessly, beckon Copilot to provide you with a spark of inspiration: Press the Alt+I keyboard shortcut. Type a request for the draft, such as the example shown in Figure 14-2. In a few moments, you see the results written in the document.

The document generated is selected and awaiting your approval. Click the Keep It button (refer to Figure 14-2) to accept the proposed text, or type a further refinement into the box provided.

Results

Type directions

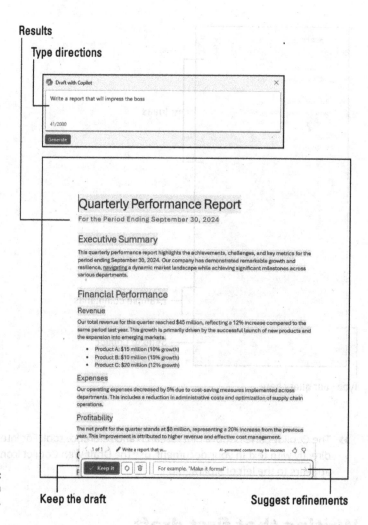

Quarterly Performance Report

For the Period Ending September 30, 2024

Executive Summary

This quarterly performance report highlights the achievements, challenges, and key metrics for the period ending September 30, 2024. Our company has demonstrated remarkable growth and resilience, navigating a dynamic market landscape while achieving significant milestones across various departments.

Financial Performance

Revenue

Our total revenue for this quarter reached $45 million, reflecting a 12% increase compared to the same period last year. This growth is primarily driven by the successful launch of new products and the expansion into emerging markets.

- Product A: $15 million (10% growth)
- Product B: $10 million (15% growth)
- Product C: $20 million (12% growth)

Expenses

Our operating expenses decreased by 5% due to cost-saving measures implemented across departments. This includes a reduction in administrative costs and optimization of supply chain operations.

Profitability

The net profit for the quarter stands at $8 million, representing a 20% increase from the previous year. This improvement is attributed to higher revenue and effective cost management.

Keep the draft

Suggest refinements

FIGURE 14-2:
Copilot creates a
draft for you.

WARNING

TIP

» All the information shown in Figure 14-2 is fabricated. Like all AI-generated information, it's designed to inspire you and help you get started.

» Generating any type of report with AI is prone to errors. Always check the data to confirm that what the AI has produced is valid.

» AI is very good at writing stories. For example, you can ask Copilot to write a story about kids at summer camp and it does a fair job. It can also do your homework for you, though relying on AI to do your job isn't recommended. People are becoming keenly aware and suspicious of AI-generated content.

» Always flag AI-generated content as such in your text. In the future, it may be a legal requirement to do so.

Rewriting some text

When you struggle to find the right words, consider getting some help from Copilot. Follow these steps:

1. Select the text you want Copilot to examine.

For example, select a paragraph you're working on and need suggestions, as shown in Figure 14-3.

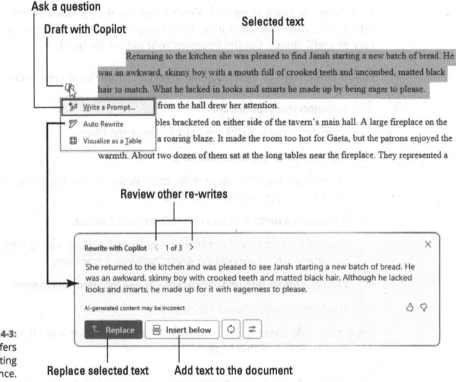

FIGURE 14-3: Copilot offers some rewriting assistance.

2. Click the Draft With Copilot icon.

The icon appears to the left of the selected text, as shown in the margin.

3. From the pop-up menu, choose Auto Rewrite.

A dialog box appears with replacement suggestions, as illustrated in Figure 14-3. Use the left and right chevrons to page through various examples.

4. **Click the Replace button to replace the selected paragraph with Copilot's rewrite.**

   Or you can instead click the Insert Below button to have Copilot's suggestion added to your document for further editing.

Hopefully, one of Copilot's suggestions can inspire you to improve your draft.

Adding an AI image

In addition to fabricating text, Copilot can dream up fancy images and let you insert them into your document. For example, when you desperately need a picture of a jelly donut, Copilot becomes your digital pastry chef.

Follow these steps to direct Copilot to add an AI image to your document:

1. **Summon the Copilot pane.**

   From the Home tab, click the Copilot icon on the Ribbon.

2. **Type in a description of the image.**

   For example, type "Create an image of a jelly donut." The Copilot Designer generates images, as illustrated in Figure 14-4.

3. **If the image isn't what you want, describe it further.**

   You need not start over, just continue your Copilot conversation. Type something like, "Show only the donut" or "Make it grape jelly."

4. **Click the Insert button to thrust the image into your document.**

   This button is illustrated in Figure 14-4.

Once in the document, you can adjust or otherwise manipulate the image as described in Part 2 of this book.

REMEMBER

>> Copilot's Designer is frequently busy or unavailable. If so, try again later.

>> The public, as well as various legal experts, are sensitive to AI content. Ensure that you properly label any image in your document as being created by AI, as was done in Figure 14-4. The sample text was also generated by using Copilot.

Image description

AI-generated image in the document

Copilot command

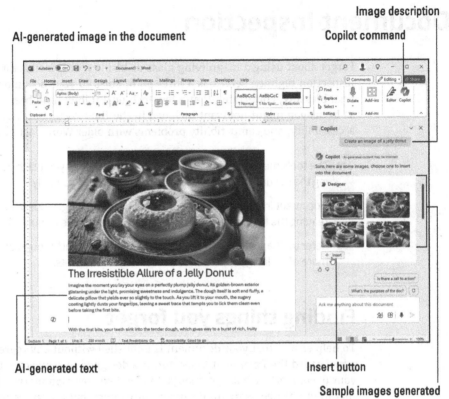

The Irresistible Allure of a Jelly Donut

Imagine the moment you lay your eyes on a perfectly plump jelly donut, its golden-brown exterior glistening under the light, promising sweetness and indulgence. The dough itself is soft and fluffy, a delicate pillow that yields ever so slightly to the touch. As you lift it to your mouth, the sugary coating lightly dusts your fingertips, leaving a sweet trace that tempts you to lick them clean even before taking the first bite.

With the first bite, your teeth sink into the tender dough, which gives way to a burst of rich, fruity

AI-generated text

Insert button

Sample images generated

FIGURE 14-4:
An AI-generated
image.

Summarizing your document

One thing that Copilot aways seems eager to do is to create a document summary for you. The summary box appears atop the first page in every Word document when Copilot is installed. Click in this box to view a summary.

References at the end of each summary sentence provide links to the relevant parts of the document. For example, click on the [4] reference to visit the fourth item summarized.

You can also obtain a summary from the Copilot pane. One of the suggestions listed above the input box is to "Summarize this document." When this suggestion doesn't appear, just type **Summarize this document** and Copilot does so in an eager manner.

Regrettably, Copilot will never tell you that your document lacks pizazz or that your ideas are stupid. It may be artificial intelligence, but it's not cruel. Not yet, at least.

Document Inspection

Forget about using a magnifying glass or hiring a drill instructor. The document inspection regimen serves as a farewell of sorts to your document. Consider it a final blessing, confirming that a few technical tidbits have been addressed, such as items you might not want included in the final document, issues surrounding accessibility, and compatibility problems with older Word documents.

>> The tools mentioned in this section are the last ones you use before publishing the document, especially when publishing electronically.

>> Document inspecting isn't the same thing as proofing. It doesn't involve reading the text, looking for mistakes, or checking the layout.

>> Refer to Chapter 13 for marking a document as "Final," though this step is more of a (flimsy) approach to preventing further edits.

Finding things you forget

To help ensure that your document is published without any regrets, Word offers a tool called the Document Inspector. It's designed to remove certain items from your document, such as comments, hidden text, revision marks, and other items that might be necessary for document production but unwanted for publication.

Follow these steps to give your document one last sweep before you commit it to paper or silicon:

1. **Save your document.**

Always save before performing a document inspection. Some of the changed items cannot be reversed, in which case the saved copy serves as a backup.

2. **Click the File tab.**

3. **Choose Info.**

The Info screen appears.

4. **Click the Check for Issues button and choose Inspect Document.**

5. **If you haven't recently saved your document, you're prompted to do so; click Yes.**

The Document Inspector dialog box appears, shown on the left in Figure 14-5. It lists items you might have overlooked or forgotten about. You can add or remove check marks to direct the inspector to find or ignore specific items.

6. **Click the Inspect button.**

Word scours the document, checking for those items you selected in the Document Inspector dialog box. A summary appears, listing items of concern, as shown at the right in Figure 14-5.

Choose items to inspect   Results   Remove issues

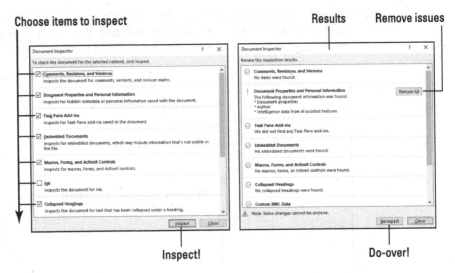

FIGURE 14-5:
The Document Inspector dialog box.

Inspect!   Do-over!

7. **Click the Remove All button to purge your document of the unwanted items.**

Repeat this step as necessary for each flagged category (refer to Figure 14-5).

8. **Click the Reinspect button to scour the document again.**

9. **When you're satisfied, click the Close button.**

At this point, you can further examine the document to ensure that none of the changes did something unintended.

In case something untoward happens, and you can't undo the action, do not save the document! Close it, and then open the copy you saved in Step 1. That's your best avenue for recovery. Otherwise, refer to the section "Viewing an older version of your document," later in this chapter.

REMEMBER

The purpose of the Document Inspector is to ensure that unwanted items don't remain in your document before you release it into the wild. This admonition holds true especially for electronic documents.

Sizing up your writing

When you truly practice writing as a solitary art, consider summoning Word's electronic editor to review your document before you release it on a judgmental public.

 To see how judgmental Word can be, on the Home tab, in the far-right group, click the Editor button (icon shown in the margin). Word evaluates your document's contents, with the results appearing in the Editor pane as illustrated in Figure 14-6.

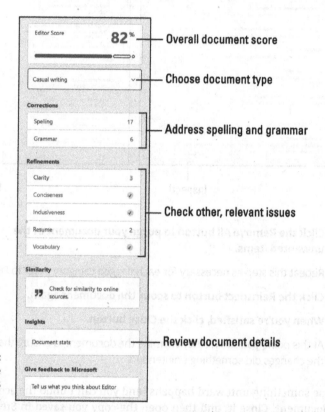

Editor Score 82%	── Overall document score
Casual writing ⌄	── Choose document type
Corrections	
Spelling 17	
Grammar 6	── Address spelling and grammar
Refinements	
Clarity 3	
Conciseness ✓	
Inclusiveness ✓	── Check other, relevant issues
Resume 2	
Vocabulary ✓	
Similarity	
99 Check for similarity to online sources.	
Insights	
Document stats	── Review document details
Give feedback to Microsoft	
Tell us what you think about Editor	

FIGURE 14-6: The Editor pane cruelly judges your work.

The Editor Score (shown as 82 percent in Figure 14-6) is a summary of all the items that the Editor evaluates. Ensure that you choose the proper document type from the menu just below the score. Writing categories are Formal, Professional, and Casual.

To address an issue that the Editor found, click on an item. For example, in Figure 14-6, click on the Spelling item to examine the 17 spelling errors found in the document. Under Refinements, click on the Clarity item to examine those issues. Word displays the relevant part of the document, along with a comment in the Editor pane that offers suggestions and a change to ignore further checking.

TIP

Below the Insights heading, click the Document Stats button to review further details about your document, as shown in Figure 14-7.

Readability Statistics	?	X
Counts		
Words		26
Characters		129
Paragraphs		1
Sentences		1
Averages		
Sentences per Paragraph		1.0
Words per Sentence		26.0
Characters per Word		4.8
Readability		
Flesch Reading Ease		56.7
Flesch-Kincaid Grade Level		11.7
Passive Sentences		0.0%
Readability statistics are based on your text selection.		
	OK	

FIGURE 14-7: The Readability Statistics dialog box.

The Reliability Statistics dialog box summarizes a word, character, paragraph, and sentence count in your document, as well as averages. It's been said that shorter sentences are more readable, which may help your overall score.

The final, Readability section in the Readability Statistics dialog box is most important. Newspapers are written to the sixth grade level with a high percentage on the Flesch Reading Ease scale. Also be mindful of passive sentences. These are the bane of most English language writers — something dreaded by editors.

Checking accessibility

Computers are more than eager to assist people with disabilities. The goal is to ensure that everyone's experience is equitable. For example, someone at a library may have a computer read your book — and even explain the illustrations, if you're thoughtful enough to provide this information in Word. The secret is to use Word's Accessibility Checker.

To check your document for accessibility issues, obey these directions:

1. **Save your document.**

2. **Click the File tab.**

3. **Choose the Info category.**

4. **Click the Check for Issues button, and choose Check Accessibility from the menu.**

The Accessibility Assistant pane appears on the right side of the document window, as shown in Figure 14-8. It lists any parts of the document that need addressing with regard to accessibility.

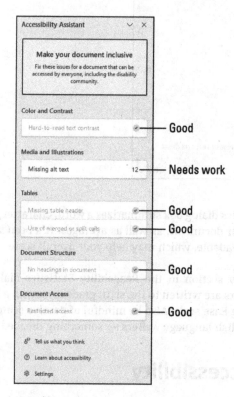

— Good (Color and Contrast / Hard-to-read text contrast)

— Needs work (Media and Illustrations / Missing alt text, 12)

— Good (Tables / Missing table header)

— Good (Use of merged or split cells)

— Good (Document Structure / No headings in document)

— Good (Document Access / Restricted access)

FIGURE 14-8:
The Accessibility
Assistant pane.

When an issue needs addressing, such as the Missing Alt Text shown in Figure 14-8, click the button. You're taken to the specific part of your document with the issue presented. For example, an image where you can type *alt text*, or text describing the image's contents. Or, if the image is for decoration, you can mark it as such.

The goal is to make your document accessible to as wide an audience as possible. Yes, even when you plan on printing a document and the alt text will never be read by a computer, I recommend that you consider adding this information.

Reviewing document compatibility

Not everyone is as up-to-speed with Word as you are. Some folks still use Word 2007. Scary as it seems, folks may be using Word 97! My point isn't to change anyone's mind about software upgrade choices, but rather to help you maintain compatibility with individuals or organizations that cling to those antique versions of Word.

To check your document's compatibility, you can run the compatibility checker. Heed these directions:

1. **Save your document.**

2. **Click the File tab.**

3. **Choose the Info category.**

4. **Click the Check for Issues button and choose Check Compatibility from the menu.**

   The Microsoft Word Compatibility Checker dialog box appears, as shown in Figure 14-9. It lists any issues your document may have for users of an older version of Word. For example, features such as special text attributes, content controls, or document add-ins would be incompatible with those users' software.

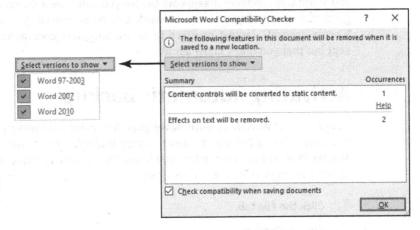

FIGURE 14-9:
The Compatibility Checker dialog box.

5. **Choose which versions of Word to check.**

Use the Select Versions to Show down menu to select specific Word versions. For example, the content controls (refer to Figure 14-9) are unavailable to Word versions 97 through 2003. The text effects attribute is available in Word 2010 but not in Word 2007.

6. **Click the OK button when you're done checking the document.**

The compatibility checker doesn't show you specifically where the items are located in the document, which isn't the issue. The point of checking for compatibility is whether you save the document in an older file format. When you do, the items listed in the dialog box are lost to that version, typically converted to plain text.

If you place a check mark by the item at the bottom of the dialog box, Word displays the Microsoft Word Compatibility Checker dialog box when you attempt to use an older Word file format to save the document. At that point, you can click the Cancel button to stop the save or click Continue to save the document with translated features.

Refer to Chapter 10 for details on using other file formats when saving documents.

Document Recovery

When disaster strikes, Word does its best to help you recover a lost document. Copies of your document are saved automatically. If anything suddenly happens, and Word unexpectedly disappears before you can save a document, chances are good that some of your unsaved work can be recovered. You can even peruse Word's deepest, darkest recesses to locate long-lost documents that Word has kept but that you don't know about.

Activating automatic backup

To ensure that Word frequently saves your document even when you forget — and you should be saving the document every few minutes — you can activate the AutoRecover feature. Even when you know that feature is active, it's good to confirm its settings. Heed these directions:

1. **Click the File tab.**

2. **Choose Options.**

The Word Options dialog box appears.

3. **On the left side of the dialog box, choose Save.**

4. **Ensure that a check mark appears by the option Save AutoRecover Information Every.**

5. **Ensure that the time setting shows 10 Minutes.**

   Or, if you find this duration too great, set it to 5 Minutes.

6. **Click OK to close the Word Options dialog box.**

The AutoRecover feature is appreciated when your computer decides to crash, or perhaps when Word decides to have an out-of-body experience and suddenly freezes. After these occurrences, you see a document recovery panel appear when you re-open Word. You're given the chance to restore an older version of a file or continue to work with the document as it was last saved by document recovery. If you choose to recover a document, save it specifically so that Word knows which version you're using.

>> When AutoRecover is set to a 10-minute interval, the largest chunk of information you can lose is whatever you typed during the last 9 minutes and 59 seconds of editing. For me, this interval is quick enough that the original material I typed is still in my brain. I'm not happy about the situation, but at least I don't have to redo the entire document.

>> See Chapter 25 for solutions to common Word problems.

Viewing an older version of your document

Once upon a time, Word diligently kept copies of your saved documents. You save again, Word creates a new copy. These copies were available for perusal, but when Microsoft started pushing its OneDrive cloud storage, this feature was removed from Word. Set aside some time to be angry.

If you use OneDrive cloud storage, however, your files are backed up and a version history is maintained. This feature works only when you store files on OneDrive.

To review previous versions of a document (saved to OneDrive), follow these steps:

1. **Click the file's name on the document window's title bar.**

   You see a drop-down menu, as shown in Figure 14-10. If the menu instead prompts you to get or save to OneDrive, version history isn't available.

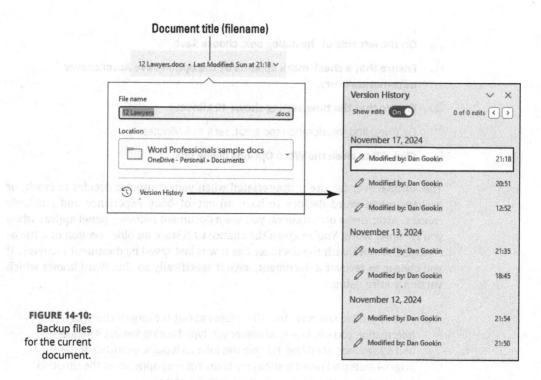

Document title (filename)

12 Lawyers.docx · Last Modified: Sun at 21:18 ⌄

File name

12 Lawyers   .docx

Location

Word Professionals sample docs
OneDrive - Personal » Documents

🕑 Version History

Version History   ⌄   ✕

Show edits On ●   0 of 0 edits ⟨ ⟩

November 17, 2024

✎ Modified by: Dan Gookin   21:18

✎ Modified by: Dan Gookin   20:51

✎ Modified by: Dan Gookin   12:52

November 13, 2024

✎ Modified by: Dan Gookin   21:35

✎ Modified by: Dan Gookin   18:45

November 12, 2024

✎ Modified by: Dan Gookin   21:54

✎ Modified by: Dan Gookin   21:50

FIGURE 14-10:
Backup files
for the current
document.

2. **Choose Version History.**

   A new, read-only version of the document opens with the Version History pane
   visible, as shown in Figure 14-10. It lists recent copies of the document by date
   and time last saved.

The read-only version of the document opened is the most recent version shown
in the Version History panel. Choose another item in the list to view that version
of the document.

No simple way exists to compare both versions of the document. You can copy
from the older version and paste to the newer version. You can also use the Save
As command (F12) to save the older version, in which case you can perform a
document compare as covered in Chapter 11. Otherwise, close the read-only his-
torical document when you're done with it.

Searching for lost documents

Word keeps a crypt of sorts, populating it with lost, dead, or not-recovered documents. It's not a feature you'll use often, but if you're hunting for a document
you've lost or misplaced, it's a place where you can look.

To peruse the purgatory of lost documents, obey these directions:

1. **Click the File tab.**

2. **Choose the Info item.**

3. **Click the Manage Document button and choose the Recover Unsaved Documents item from the menu.**

   A traditional Open dialog box appears. It reveals the location where Word places its unsaved files — the Word crypt.

4. **Click to select a file to open.**

   The filenames listed in the Open dialog box are similar to the original Word document names. They contain a special suffix, which Word uses to track the document's origins. Some, however, may simply say "AutoRecovery save of Document . . ." for those documents you never bothered to save in the first place. For shame.

5. **Click the Open button.**

   The file appears in a Word document window, but it's tagged as [Read Only]. A banner appears in the window. The banner features the Save As button.

6. **Peruse the document to determine whether it's worthy of recovery.**

   If you choose to recover the document, proceed with Step 7. If not, close the document and click the Don't Save button when prompted.

7. **Press the F12 keyboard shortcut to use the Save As dialog box to find a location for the document and to give it a proper filename.**

   You can continue working with the recovered document.

If the Recover Unsaved Documents feature doesn't help you locate the document you're looking for, use other, traditional Word tools. For example, check the list of recently opened documents in Word, use the Search command in Windows, or look in the Recycle Bin for the file.

4

Word for Writers

IN THIS CHAPTER

» Setting up the document window

» Grabbing a word count

» Reviewing spelling and grammar

» Working with your personal dictionary

» Fine-tuning the grammar checker

» Using the Thesaurus

» Working with foreign text

Chapter 15

Tools for Every Author

Word hosts an abundance of features to succor the budding scribe. It won't encourage you to write every day, help meet your quota, or reward you when your text is brilliant. Word will, however, help you locate spelling errors and fix common grammatical blunders, and it offers tools to assist any wordsmith with their writing duties.

TIP

Word's digital tools are no replacement for a second set of eyes on your text. Nothing helps a writer like a good editor, even an amateur editor. If you truly want to become a professional writer, you will welcome the opportunity for others to read and judge your prose.

Behold! The Document Window

Word's document window is a flexible thing. You can direct Word to show you lots of controls and options, or you can configure the window to be as reserved as a haiku. Your document can appear as it will print, or you can enjoy text-only Draft view. Optional panes appear to the left or right of the document. And the useful status bar is customizable to reflect your workflow. It's time to mess with the document window.

Showing or hiding the Ribbon

For pure writing tasks, you don't really need to see the Ribbon hanging at the top of the document window. To hide it, press the Ctrl+F1 keyboard shortcut. Press Ctrl+F1 again to bring it back.

When the Ribbon is hidden, only the tab headings appear atop the document window: File, Home, Insert, and so on. Click a tab to view its contents and access commands. The Ribbon disappears after you've chosen a command, or you can press the Esc key to hide the Ribbon again.

>> Some versions of Word feature a down-pointing chevron on the far-right end of the Ribbon. Click this chevron to view a menu that controls the Ribbon.

>> Some versions of Word feature an up-pointing chevron on the far-right end of the Ribbon. Click this chevron to hide the Ribbon. When the Ribbon is visible again, click the pushpin icon (shown in the margin) to keep the Ribbon visible.

TIP

>> If you desire lots of typing room, you can direct Word to fill the screen with your document and hide the Ribbon. The command, Full-Screen Mode, is available when the Ribbon's chevron points down. Otherwise, you can add this comment to the Quick Access toolbar. See Chapter 24 for details.

Setting the document view

Word offers five ways to view a document in its window. Three of the ways are popular enough to find a spot on the status bar; the rest are accessed from the View menu, found in the Views group. Here are all five views:

Read Mode: Best for reading text, but not editing. This icon, shown in the margin, is found on the status bar.

Print Layout: Good for editing text, especially when you need to view document formatting, graphics, tables, and other items. This icon is also found on the status bar.

Web Layout: Shows how the document would look if presented on a web page instead of on a sheet of paper. This icon is the third view icon found on the status bar.

Outline: Used for organizing topics, as covered in Chapter 16.

Draft: Great for writing, but not for final document preview or layout.

Of the five modes, the two used most frequently by writers are Print Layout and Draft, with Print Layout being the default. Draft mode is good when you desire fewer distractions while you write, but many Word features automatically switch the view to Print Layout.

Adding useful panes

Some Word features present themselves as floating windows or panes. These panes come and go, depending on what you're doing in Word. If not, you can dismiss them by clicking the X (Close) button in the pane's upper right corner.

Two panes I find handy for writing are the Navigation pane and Styles pane, shown in Figure 15-1, which is how I prefer to work.

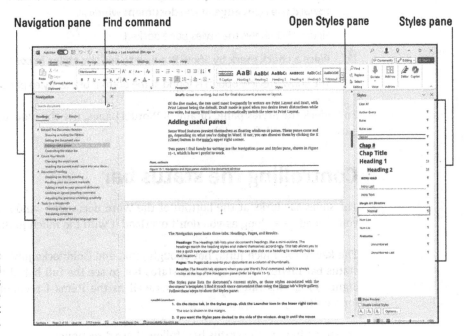

Navigation pane   Find command   Open Styles pane   Styles pane

FIGURE 15-1:
Navigation and
Styles panes
visible in the
document
window.

The Navigation pane hosts three tabs: Headings, Pages, and Results.

Headings: The Headings tab lists your document's headings, like a mini-outline. The headings match the heading styles and indent themselves accordingly. This tab allows you to see a quick overview of your document. You can also click on a heading to instantly hop to that location.

Pages: The Pages tab presents your document as one or more columns of thumbnails.

Results: The Results tab appears when you use Word's Find command, which is always visible at the top of the Navigation pane (refer to Figure 15-1).

The Styles pane lists the document's current styles, or those styles associated with the document's template. I find it much more convenient than using the Home tab's Styles gallery. Follow these steps to show the Styles pane:

1. **On the Home tab, in the Styles group, click the Launcher icon in the lower right corner.**

   The icon is shown in the margin.

2. **If you want the Styles pane docked to the side of the window, drag it toward the right edge of the document window.**

   Figure 15-1 shows the Styles pane docked.

3. **Place a check mark by Show Preview to see the styles in context.**

   The Show Preview option is found at the bottom of the Styles pane.

To undock the Styles pane, or any of Word's panes, use the mouse to drag the top part of the pane left or right.

Controlling the status bar

The *status bar* lurks at the bottom of the Word document window, and it can be your friend — as long as you don't overload it with too much junk.

The key to too much junk, not enough junk, and Goldilocks junk is found on the status bar menu: Right-click the status bar to see the full list of items available. Figure 15-2 illustrates the menu, as well as the items I recommend as useful for a writer.

To add an item to the status bar, follow these directions:

1. **Right-click the status bar to display its menu.**

2. **Click to choose an item to add.**

   Added items appear with a check mark to their left, as illustrated in Figure 15-2.

3. **Click elsewhere in the document window or press the Esc key when you're done adding items.**

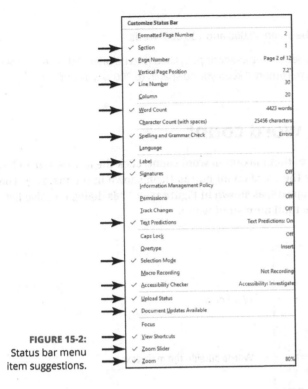

FIGURE 15-2:
Status bar menu item suggestions.

To remove an item, choose it from the status bar menu to remove its check mark. (Refer to Step 2.)

A lot of check marks are present in Figure 15-2, though not all these items appear on the taskbar. Some, such as Label and Selection Mode, show up only when their associated features are active in the document.

Count Your Words

Anyone who's written articles for a magazine or a letter to the editor knows about *word count*. It's a limit you don't want to surpass. For professional writers, word count is the way you get paid; the first article I sold paid me a nickel a word. Pulling a word count is a common activity for writers, and Word does the job for you automatically.

>> Publishers deal in word counts, not page counts. Page count varies depending on layout and design choices.

>> Word count is set as a maximum value, such as 1,000 words or 2,500 words.

>> Novels typically run between 40,000 and 100,000 words.

>> The best way to get a letter-to-the-editor published is to be brief. If the newspaper suggests "200 words maximum," keep your dispatch to 200 words or fewer.

Checking the word count

To see how near you are to that maximum word count, click the Review tab and in the Proofing group, click the Word Count button (icon shown in the margin). The Word Count dialog box appears, as shown in Figure 15-3. This dialog box also lists text statistics beyond the total number of words.

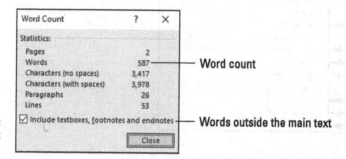

FIGURE 15-3:
The Word Count
dialog box.

— Word count

— Words outside the main text

The total number of words, such as 587 in Figure 15-3, includes any individual text tidbit, such as the title at the top of the document, and even footnotes and endnotes if you select the check box. (Refer to the figure.)

>> Rather than summon the Word Count dialog box, you can view an active, running word count total on the document window's Status Bar. Refer to the preceding section and choose the Word Count item from the Status Bar's pop-up menu. The word count appears on the status bar, updated as you type.

>> Click the word count on the Status bar to instantly view the Word Count dialog box.

>> If you select text, the word count on the status bar shows values for the selected text as well as the document's total word count.

Inserting the current word count into your document

The most accurate way to insert a document's word count into the document itself is to use the word count field. Follow these steps:

1. **Click to position the insertion pointer where you want the value to appear.**

   For example, after the text *word count =*.

2. **On the Insert tab, in the Text group, click the Quick Parts button and choose Field.**

   The Quick Parts button is illustrated in the margin.

3. **In the Field dialog box, from the Categories menu, choose Document information.**

4. **From the Field Names list, choose NumWords.**

5. **Click the OK button.**

The field shows the document's current word count, not including the field's text (which adds one to the count).

REMEMBER

>> If you edit the document, you must update the field: Right-click the word count and choose the Update Field command.

>> See Chapter 21 for further details on document fields.

Document Proofing

Fortunately for me, one of the qualifications for being a good writer is not the ability to win a spelling bee. I'm a horrid speller; most writers are. In the old days, editors corrected spelling errors. Since 1995, Word does the spell-checking job automatically as you type. In 1997, automatic grammar checking was added, though I'm not an enthusiastic fan of this feature.

>> Improperly spelled words appear with a red zigzag underline.

>> Improper grammar or word usage appears with a blue zigzag underline.

>> To correct a spelling error, right-click the word and choose the proper spelling from the shortcut menu. If the correct word isn't found, take another stab at spelling and try again. If all else fails, grab a dictionary.

>> To fix a grammar error, right-click the blue-underlined word and choose a replacement. If the grammar is fine, which happens often, choose the Ignore Once command.

>> When you're really stuck on spelling, open a web browser and type the word into Google's Search text box. Google might suggest the proper spelling or suggest a better word.

>> You must know the old adage by now: A spell check isn't the same as proof-reading. Words can be spelled properly but used inappropriately. Nothing beats having that second set of eyes look at your text.

TIP

>> To increase your English grammar kung fu, I strongly recommend that you read a copy of Strunk & White's *The Elements of Style*. It's an excellent book, short and pithy. It will help you understand and use English grammar far more than anything you've forgotten since high school.

Disabling on-the-fly proofing

Maybe you don't like to see either the red zigzag underline of spelling shame or the blue zigzag underline of garbled grammar. Maybe you intention is to be deliberate in your misuse of what's commonly considered proper English. Good. If you prefer, you can forbid Word from performing on-the-fly proofing, which may help you concentrate more on writing and less on correcting your text.

To disable automatic spell checking, grammar checking, or both, follow these steps:

1. **Click the File tab and choose Options.**

   The Word Options dialog box appears.

2. **On the left side of the dialog box, choose Proofing.**

3. **Remove the check mark by the item Check Spelling As You Type.**

4. **Remove the check mark by the item Mark Grammar Errors As You Type.**

5. **Click OK.**

Once disabled, Word refuses to show a proofing command's red or blue zigzag underlines. You can still proof your document, but it's a process you must do manually. See the next section.

Proofing your document manually

When on-the-fly proofing is disabled, the task falls upon your shoulders: You must run manual document proofing just like in the olden days. Perform these steps:

1. **On the Review tab, in the Proofing group, click the Spelling & Grammar button.**

The Spelling pane appears, as shown on the left in Figure 15-4. Each misspelled word is displayed one at a time. A tally of all spelling offenses appears near the top of the pane.

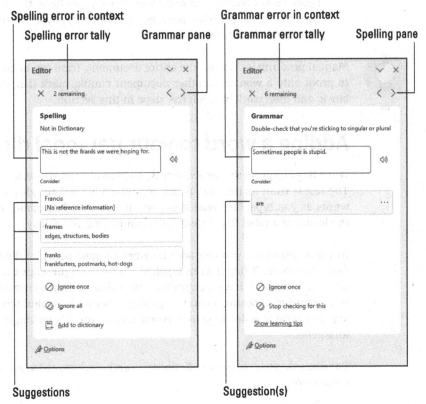

Spelling error in context

Spelling error tally   Grammar pane   Grammar error in context

Grammar error tally   Spelling pane

Suggestions   Suggestion(s)

FIGURE 15-4: The Spelling and Grammar panes.

2. **Deal with the issue.**

The options presented on the Spelling and Grammar panes differ, depending on the issue at hand. You can choose a suggested replacement as presented (refer to Figure 15-4).

You can also choose Ignore Once for a specific instance.

For spelling, choose Ignore All to ignore all instances, such as when you're writing science fiction and all the bad guys' names aren't in the dictionary — yet. Or, if you want their names to be in the dictionary, click the Add to Dictionary button.

For grammar, choose Stop Checking For This so that Word doesn't bug you with issues that seem trivial to you, which for grammar checking is most of them.

3. **Keep proofing.**

   After spell checking, you see the Grammar pane (shown in the right in Figure 15-4). Continue checking issues. When you're done, the Grammar pane changes to the Editor pane, listing a summary of your document's offenses — should any remain.

Manual proofing is done on the entire document, from top to bottom. If you need to proof only a word or another document chunk, mark that chunk of text as a block, and then work through the steps in this section.

Adding a word to your personal dictionary

Word flags improperly spelled words, but specifically words it doesn't recognize. The test is from its internal dictionary, which is used at lightning speed to check words as you type. But what about words like your last name, street address, or the leader of a rebel fleet intent upon conquering the galaxy?

In these instances, you can add the word to your personal dictionary, ensuring that Word doesn't flag it as misspelled. To do so, right-click the word flagged as misspelled just as if it were any other misspelled word, as illustrated in Figure 15-5. But instead of choosing a correct spelling, choose the menu item Add to Dictionary. The word is added to your personal dictionary. It's no longer flagged as being misspelled.

To witness your personal dictionary, and perhaps edit its contents, follow these steps:

1. **Click the File tab and choose Options.**

2. **In the Word Options dialog box, choose Proofing from the list of categories on the left.**

3. **Click the Custom Dictionaries button.**

   The Custom Dictionaries dialog box appears.

4. **Ensure that the personal dictionary is chosen.**

It's given the ridiculous name RoamingCustom.dic (Default).

5. **Click the Edit Word List button.**

The dictionary's word list appears.

Word that's not misspelled   Word's foolish suggestions

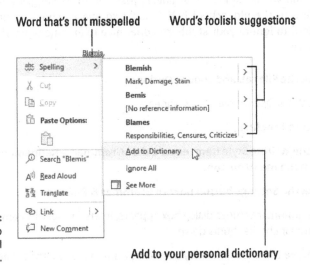

FIGURE 15-5:
Adding a word to
your personal
dictionary.

Add to your personal dictionary

The words you see were added to the dictionary. Some may have been added from other Office programs, including Excel and Outlook.

You can manually add a word to the dictionary by typing it into the Word(s) text box and then clicking the Add button. Likewise, if you've mistakenly added a word to the dictionary, click to select the word and then click the Delete button.

Undoing an ignore proofing command

Proofing a document is not for the impatient. When you're careless, you may choose to ignore a word that you didn't mean to ignore. When this goof happens, you must undo the operation and direct Word to start over with document proofing. Follow these steps:

1. **Click the File tab and choose Options.**

2. **Choose Proofing from the left side of the Word Options dialog box.**

3. **Click the Recheck Document button.**

4. **Click the Yes button to confirm.**

Any misspelled words you've chosen to ignore, or grammatical blunders you've forgiven, are once again flagged as incorrect.

Adjusting grammar checking sensitivity

Say that you value the grammar check, just not all its suggestions. For example, you adhere to the old-school belief that two spaces should follow a period. To direct Word to ignore your stubborn adherence to archaic typewriter rules, follow these steps:

1. **Click the File tab and choose Options.**

   The Word Options dialog box appears.

2. **Choose Proofing.**

3. **By the Writing Style item, ensure that Grammar & Refinements is chosen from the menu button.**

4. **Click the Settings button next to Grammar & Refinements.**

   The Grammar Settings dialog box appears. It lists the specific items the grammar checker hunts down.

5. **Remove the check mark by a specific item to disable that proofing feature.**

   For example, the Spacing item.

6. **Click OK to dismiss the Grammar Settings dialog box, and then click OK again to banish the Word Options dialog box.**

You can also disable on-the-fly grammar checking, as described earlier in this chapter.

REMEMBER

Tools for a Wordsmith

During typewriter times, and even in the early computer era, writers kept handy various references to help them craft the best text. Chief among the references were a dictionary and thesaurus. Also recommended were a book of quotations, foreign phrases, a rhyming dictionary — even the full-on encyclopedia. The modern computer provides digital alternatives to those references, but I must confess that reference books still look handsome on a shelf.

Choosing a better word

Every writer tends to use the same words over and over. To spice up your text, consider using Word's Thesaurus to pluck out a better term. Heed these directions:

1. **Right-click a word you want to improve.**

The best word choices are adjectives.

2. **Choose Synonyms from the pop-up menu.**

3. **Select a better word from the list.**

To explore additional synonyms in detail, choose Thesaurus in Step 3. You see the Thesaurus pane appear, shown in Figure 15-6. It shows far more word choices than the shortcut menu, including antonyms or words that describe the opposite of the selected term.

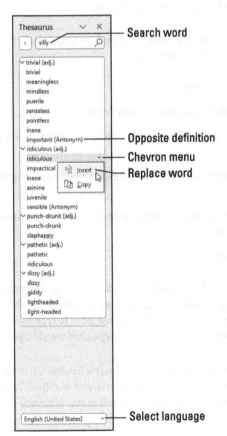

FIGURE 15-6:
The The-
saurus pane.

To replace the word you right-clicked (Step 1), click its chevron menu (refer to Figure 15-6) and choose the Insert command. Otherwise, if you click a term, you see additional synonyms.

>> Another way to view the Thesaurus pane is to click the Review tab and then click the Thesaurus button, icon shown in the margin.

>> Not every word features a synonym.

Translating some text

It sounds as though Word's Translate commands might help you spice up some text by adding foreign words. That's how it sounds, but how it works is clunky: If you want to use foreign words in your text, learn another language or buy a book full of foreign phrases. Otherwise, Word's language tool works best when translating text from another language into your own.

For example, you might use the term *bon mot* in your text. To confirm that it means what you intend, follow these steps:

1. **Select the foreign language text.**

2. **Right-click the selected text and choose Translate.**

3. **Click the Yes button to confirm that it's okay to send a chunk of text out to the Internet.**

   Word uses tools on the Internet to translate your text, displaying the results in the Translator pane.

4. **In the Translator pane, ensure that the proper languages are chosen in the From and To fields.**

   Behold the translation.

This tool is designed more to confirm that you're using the proper foreign language phrase than it is to translate text for you. In fact, with the Translator pane open, you can try typing text into the box to see how it translates. These types of translations may not always be what a native speaker would use.

>> To manually summon the Translate pane, on the Review tab in the Language group, choose Translate (icon shown in the margin) and then Translate Document from the menu. Click the Select tab in the Translate pane to play around with various translations.

>> Just in case you're curious, Klingon is listed as one of the language from and to which you can translate text.

Ignoring a span of foreign language text

If you're clever enough to add foreign text to your document, you'll note that Word flags the text (some or all) as obnoxiously misspelled. *Quel ridicule!* That red zigzag stain remains below the phrase, despite it being accurate in another language. Rather than ignore the words, you can direct Word to not proof that text. Here's how:

1. **Select the foreign-language text, or any text you want the proofer to ignore.**

2. **On the Review tab, in the Language group, click the Language button and choose the Set Proofing Language command.**

   The Language dialog box appears.

3. **Ensure that the Selected Text option is chosen.**

4. **Place a check mark by the option Do Not Check Spelling or Grammar.**

   The setting applies only to selected text, not to the entire document.

5. **Click OK.**

   The selected text, which may have been flagged as misspelled, is cleared of any proofing marks.

You can also direct Word to use a foreign-language proofer on the selected text: In Step 4, choose the language from the scrolling list, such as French (France). If the foreign-language dictionary is installed in Word, the text is proofed in that language. For short quips and quotes, however, I recommend that you direct Word to not proof the text, as described in this section.

REMEMBER

>> If the word is spelled correctly, add it to the dictionary. If the word is okay for the document, choose Ignore. Use the steps in this section only for text you don't want proofed, such as foreign-language text or quotes.

>> Refer elsewhere in this chapter for information on ignoring proofing or adding words to the dictionary.

IN THIS CHAPTER

» **Understanding Word's outline view**

» **Jotting down your thoughts**

» **Putting topics in order**

» **Adding subtopics**

» **Rearranging the outline**

» **Creating narrative text in an outline**

» **Changing the outline view**

» **Printing outline topic levels**

Chapter **16**

From Brainstorm to Outline

'm certain that some guy once sat down and instantly wrote, from front to back, a wonderful story. It was all in his head, and then he wrote it down. Such a writer is amazingly rare. For most of us, organization is required before anything is written. From a complex novel about aliens, zombies, and the Russian Revolution to a technical book on the intrigues of the Document Object Module, outlining is the vital first step taken by any serious writer.

The Outline Thing

If you've never used an outline program or even a stack of 3-by-5 index cards to create an outline, you're really missing out. Outlining tools aren't just for writers. They help you organize anything, from a simple shopping list to the complex-but-legal process whereby major political parties ignore election results.

The outlining process works like this:

1. **Jot down your ideas.**

   Start by writing a quick list, in any order. This is the brainstorming step.

2. **Continue to add ideas and organize them.**

   Organization is when you determine which ideas come first. Once you decide which ideas are related, group them into topics and subtopics. As you go, you rearrange things, move topics, combine and eliminate things as the outline develops.

3. **Finish the outline.**

   When you start writing content instead of organizing ideas, consider that the outline is complete.

Outlining can continue after you start writing. The changes may not be major, but they come as your thoughts solidify. When I write, I keep the outline document window open all the time. This approach allows me to reference other parts of the book or to jot down new information, relevant elsewhere, that may pop into my head. My outlines aren't complete until the project is done.

>> Items in an outline are called topics.

>> Topics are set at various levels. Related topics become subtopics of a general topic. These topics can be arranged several levels deep, depending on how organized you are.

>> It's possible for an outline to contain notes, though when you reach this level of organization, it's time to stop outlining and to start writing. See the later section, "Adding narrative."

REMEMBER

>> The outline is for you, the writer. It doesn't need to follow any rules or guidelines. Consider the outline as a tool to help you organize your thoughts.

Word's Outline View

A long time ago, an outliner was a program separate from your word processor. For my early books, I used an outliner called Acta on the Macintosh. On the PC, I used GrandView. Word incorporated outlining as a feature back in the early 1990s, so you no longer need to obtain special software. You do, however, need to know how to work with Outline view in Word.

Activating Outline view

 To switch to Outline view, click the View tab. In the Views group, click the Outline button, icon shown in the margin. You can also use the Ctrl+Alt+O keyboard shortcut, which seems obtuse but it's not that difficult to remember.

Word's document window changes. Handles appear to the left of each paragraph in the document. Dragging these handles with the mouse is how you organize the paragraphs, determine whether a topic has subtopics, and expand or collapse topics. The variety of handles is shown in Figure 16-1.

 Topic with subtopics

 Topic without subtopics

 Narrative (text) topic

Also visible in the window in Outline view is the Outlining tab. See the next section.

>> Outline view is yet another document presentation, one that works best for arranging and organizing paragraphs of text. You can switch to Print Layout view from Outline view and vice-versa.

>> In the big picture, an outline is just another Word document: Save it as you would any Word document. When you open an outline, it opens in either Print Layout or Web Layout view, depending on which of these views you used last. You must then switch to Outline view, as described in this section.

Exploring the Outlining tab

When Outline view is active, the Outlining tab appears on the Ribbon. This tab features controls to help you manipulate the outline, as illustrated in Figure 16-2. Though these controls are handy, it's often faster to use keyboard shortcuts to manipulate your outline, as discussed throughout this chapter.

One item on the Outlining tab that comes in handy is the Show Level menu. It allows you to quickly view the outline from any level, from major topics down to detailed topics. See the later section "Collapsing and expanding outline topics."

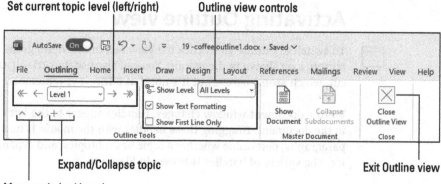

Set current topic level (left/right)   Outline view controls

Expand/Collapse topic

FIGURE 16-2:
The Outlining tab.   Move topic (up/down)   Exit Outline view

 The Close Outline View button exits Outline view and restores Print Layout view.

Using heading styles

To make Outline mode work, Word uses its built-in heading styles: Heading 1, Heading 2, and so on. Each heading style represents a topic level in the outline. Heading 1 is the top level; Heading 2, the next level; and so on.

The built-in heading styles present themselves visually in Outline view. The top-level Heading 1 style is larger and heavier than Heading 2. Each style gets smaller and has other unique attributes, which helps as a visual reference in your outline.

TIP

If you prefer to see the outline without text formatting, on the Outlining tab remove the check mark by the Show Text Formatting item. (Refer to Figure 16-2.)

Outline Construction

Building an outline is the part of the brainstorming process where you write down information. It begins haphazardly, as described earlier in this chapter. Keep in mind that an initially disorganized outline is part of the process. As brainstorming progresses, the outline takes shape, and your ideas acquire an order. Commands in this section help you to organize.

Creating top-level topics

In Outline view, the lines you initially type in a document are given the Heading 1 style. Each line, or topic, features a handle on the left. Your job is at this point is to type topics, to brainstorm. Don't worry about organization — just type some items related to the overall topic, as shown in Figure 16-3.

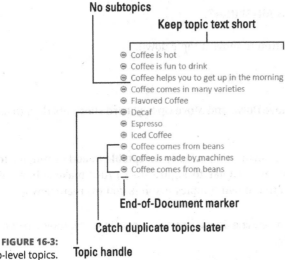

No subtopics

Keep topic text short

- Coffee is hot
- Coffee is fun to drink
- Coffee helps you to get up in the morning
- Coffee comes in many varieties
- Flavored Coffee
- Decaf
- Espresso
- Iced Coffee
- Coffee comes from beans
- Coffee is made by machines
- Coffee comes from beans

End-of-Document marker

Catch duplicate topics later

FIGURE 16-3:
Top-level topics.   Topic handle

>> Don't worry about the topic order just yet.

>> Don't worry whether a topic should become a subtopic.

>> Don't make the main topics too wordy. Subtopics can be more wordy.

>> If you need to add notes to a topic, see the later section "Adding narrative," though this step should come later.

>> That squat horizontal bar at the end of the outline marks the end of the document; it's not something you can edit or remove. The same bar appears when you edit a document in Draft view.

Moving topics

After brainstorming, you organize topics. The order depends on the subject, though you can choose whether it's chronological, from best to worst, from important to least important, or whatever the subject demands.

The easiest way to move a topic is to use the mouse: Drag the topic's handle up or down. This handle appears to the left of the topic, as illustrated in Figure 16-3.

On the Outlining toolbar, two command buttons move the current topic:

 Click the Move Up button to move a topic up.

The keyboard shortcut is Alt+Shift++↑.

 Click the Move Down button to move a topic down.

The keyboard shortcut is Alt+Shift++↓.

It's quicker to use the Move Down and Move Up keyboard shortcuts than to use the toolbar buttons.

As you move topics up or down, it's perfectly acceptable to add or remove topics. You can also catch duplicates. (Refer to Figure 16-3.) Also make subtle edits, if necessary. You may find that moving topics inspires you to create new topics.

>> To add a topic, type a new line as you normally would in Word. Topics exist as their own paragraphs.

>> To remove a topic, select the line and delete it, as you would any paragraph in Word.

>> To split a topic, place the insertion pointer into the topic's text at the point where you want to split the topic. Press the Enter key.

>> When you're outlining a novel, the top-level topics eventually become chapters.

>> Moving a topic up or down doesn't change its level. To change a topic's level, see the next section.

>> The topic-moving keyboard commands can be used to move any paragraph of text in Word, whether Outline view is active or not: Press Alt+Shift++@UA to move the current paragraph up; press Alt+Shift++@DA to move the current paragraph down.

REMEMBER

TIP

Demoting or promoting a topic

During your brainstorm, you may notice how some topics are related. If so, consider demoting these topics into subtopics. In Figure 16-4, the types-of-coffee topics are demoted and placed under a new topic, "Coffee comes in many varieties."

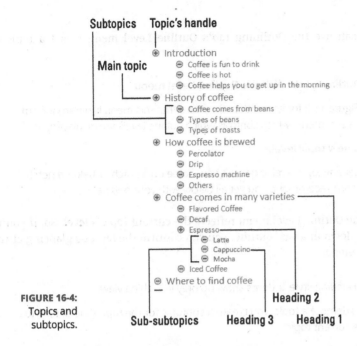

FIGURE 16-4:
Topics and
subtopics.

In Figure 16-4, see how topics and subtopics are set at a certain indent in Outline view. The text style is based on the heading style. You can see in the figure how each indent sports its own style, which makes viewing the outline easier. Also see the later section "Collapsing and expanding outline topics."

Promoting and demoting a topic are the official terms for moving a topic left or right in an outline.

To demote a topic (move it right one notch), click the Demote button on the Outlining toolbar.

The keyboard shortcut to demote a topic is Alt+Shift+→.

To promote a topic (move it left one notch), click the Promote button on the Outlining toolbar.

The keyboard shortcut is Alt+Shift+←.

One other button on the Outlining toolbar lets you move a topic: The Promote to Heading 1 button shifts a topic all the way up to a top level. This button has no keyboard shortcut.

Finally, you can use the Outlining tab's Outline Level menu to set a topic to any level:

1. On the Outlining tab, click the Outline Level menu.

Refer to Figure 16-2 for its location. Be aware that this menu is different from the Show Level menu, which controls which outline levels are displayed.

2. Choose a new topic level.

You can set any topic level; it doesn't have to be up a notch or below a notch, though I don't recommend you get all wacky with your outline.

As a bonus, the Outline Level menu reflects the current topic's level. So, if you're working deep down in a vast outline, you can confirm the level by glancing at the Outline Level menu.

>> Topic, or Heading style, indents show up only in Outline view.

>> When you demote a topic, you create a subtopic for the topic (line of text) just above the current topic.

>> You need a subtopic when two or more same-level topics are similar. When this similarity occurs, demote these topics into subtopics below a new, higher-level more general topic.

>> People who know more than I do claim that you can't have a topic with only one subtopic. If so, eliminate the subtopic, add a second subtopic, or promote the subtopic.

>> For a novel, you want to organize chapters as main topics. Subtopics within a chapter could cover what happens in that chapter, a list of characters involved, and so on.

>> The keyboard shortcuts to promote and demote topics are available at any time. Use them to convert text to the heading style or to change from one heading style to another.

TIP

Moving topics and subtopics in groups

Whether you're moving a topic up or down or promoting or demoting that topic, only the topic itself — a single line of text — moves. Any subtopics remain in their same positions. To move a topic and all its subtopics, you have two options.

First, you can collapse the topic. See the later section "Collapsing and expanding outline topics." When the topic is collapsed, all subtopics move with the topic.

Second, you can select the topic and its subtopics as a block. This type of selection works differently in Outline view than in Word's text-editing views. To move the topics, follow these steps:

1. **Click the topic's handle.**

   The topic and all its subtopics are selected as a block.

2. **Move, promote, or demote the topic and subtopics as a group.**

   You can use any of the commands mentioned in the preceding two sections to move the group. You can also use the mouse to drag the group in any direction, though that technique is a bit tricky to master.

You can also select multiple topics to promote or demote or move them as a group. Drag the mouse over the topics to select them.

WARNING

Text selection in Outline view works differently than in other Word document views. It's possible to select part of a topic's text, but you cannot select parts of text from two topics. When you select two or more topics, the full lines for both topics are selected. If you need to do fancy text selection, switch to Print Layout view or Draft view, manipulate the text, and then switch back to Outline view.

Adding narrative

When the urge to write something hits you in Outline view, do so: Write narratives when you feel compelled. The key is to set the paragraph's format to Normal, where it's treated differently in Outline view than the heading-formatted topics.

Word refers to narrative text as *body text*. I prefer the term *narrative* because the keyboard shortcut to convert a topic to body text is Ctrl+Shift+N.

In Figure 16-5, you see narrative text added to the coffee outline. A narrative paragraph sits below any topic level. You can even add a narrative paragraph as the first part of the outline.

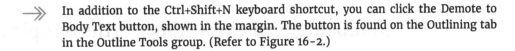

In addition to the Ctrl+Shift+N keyboard shortcut, you can click the Demote to Body Text button, shown in the margin. The button is found on the Outlining tab in the Outline Tools group. (Refer to Figure 16-2.)

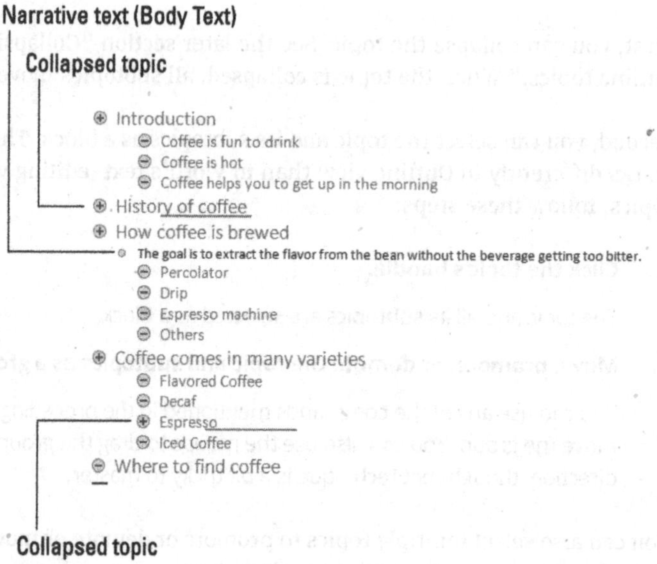

Narrative text (Body Text)

Collapsed topic

⊕ Introduction
   ⊖ Coffee is fun to drink
   ⊖ Coffee is hot
   ⊖ Coffee helps you to get up in the morning
⊕ History of coffee
⊕ How coffee is brewed
   ○ The goal is to extract the flavor from the bean without the beverage getting too bitter.
   ⊖ Percolator
   ⊖ Drip
   ⊖ Espresso machine
   ⊖ Others
⊕ Coffee comes in many varieties
   ⊖ Flavored Coffee
   ⊖ Decaf
   ⊕ Espresso
   ⊖ Iced Coffee
⊖ Where to find coffee

FIGURE 16-5:
Narrative text in
an outline.

Collapsed topic

>> A narrative is any text in an outline that adds more information or lets you jot down non-topic thoughts.

>> Narratives can be moved up or down or anywhere in the outline. See the earlier section "Moving topics."

>> To convert a narrative to a topic, promote or demote the paragraph. See the earlier section "Demoting or promoting a topic."

>> Ctrl+Shift+N is also the keyboard shortcut to apply the Normal text style.

**TECHNICAL
STUFF**

Outline Presentation

The goal of an outline is to eventually organize your thoughts and then do something with the results. To help you meet this goal, Word offers various ways to present the outline on the screen, on the page, or even in mini-outline view in any document.

Collapsing and expanding outline topics

Complex outlines, brimming with detail and information, are wonderful things. I finished writing the book *WordPerfect For Dummies* in only three weeks because I had spent months building a marvelously detailed outline. In fact, much of the final book's contents appeared in the outline as narrative text. Make your outlines just as detailed and you too will be equally blessed.

The problem with a detailed outline is that it consumes a lot of screen space. Scrolling a long outline becomes tedious and distracting. The job is made easier when you collapse portions of the outline.

— To collapse a topic and all its subtopics, double-click the mouse on the topic's handle. The keyboard shortcut is the minus key on the numeric keypad. You can also use the Collapse button found on the Ribbon's Outlining tab.

Collapsed topics appear with a fuzzy underline to the right of the topic's text. Refer to Figure 16-5 for examples of collapsed topics.

+ To expand a collapsed topic, double-click the mouse on the collapsed topic's handle. You can also press the plus key on the numeric keypad. On the Outlining tab, click the Expand button to expand the topic.

As an example, the outline to your book might show *Parts* as the top (Heading 1) level and *Chapters* as the next (Heading 2) level. To quickly see an overview of your book's table of contents, choose Level 2 from the Show Level menu. The outline is collapsed, hiding any Level 3 (Heading 3) topics and below.

>> To quickly expand all topics throughout the outline, choose All Levels from the Show Level menu on the Outlining toolbar.

>> The keyboard shortcut for showing a specific level in an outline is Alt+Shift+*n*, where *n* is a number 1 through 9. To show all topics, use the shortcut Alt+Shift+A (the letter A).

>> When you move a collapsed topic, you also move all the topic's subtopics.

>> Another way to shorten an outline is to place a check mark by the option Show First Line Only, found in the Outline Tools group on the Outlining toolbar. When active, this setting truncates long topics and narratives, showing only the first few words. It's not the same as collapsing topics, but it does tighten the outline's presentation.

Printing the outline

When you print an outline, Word automatically (and frustratingly) switches the document to Print Layout view and prints the entire thing. If you prefer to print only the visible portion of the outline, such as only the top-level headers, you must use the Quick Print command.

Don't bother looking for the Quick Print command. It's not on the Ribbon. You can, however, add it to the Quick Access toolbar, which is located above the Ribbon on the top left side of the window. Here's how:

1. Click the down-pointing arrow by the Quick Access toolbar.

Use Figure 16-6 as your guide.

2. Choose Quick Print.

The Quick Print icon is added to the Quick Access toolbar.

Quick Access toolbar   Quick Access toolbar menu

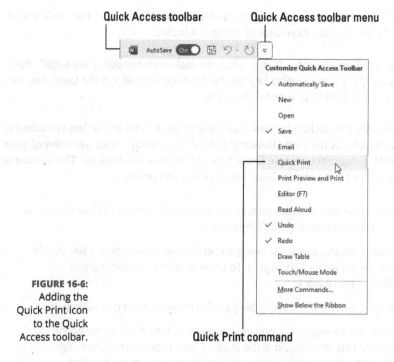

Quick Print command

FIGURE 16-6:
Adding the
Quick Print icon
to the Quick
Access toolbar.

To print the outline showing only visible topics, first arrange the outline so that it shows only what you want to print. Refer to the preceding section for information on expanding and collapsing topics. On the Quick Access toolbar, click the Quick Print button, shown in the margin, to print only the visible topics.

Using the navigation pane

TIP

I keep my manuscript's outline open in a separate window while I work. For the current document, however, you can summon a mini outline that's far easier to use. It's called the Navigation pane. To view it, On the View tab, in the Show group, place a check mark by the Navigation Pane item. The Navigation pane appears on the left side of the document window. (Refer to Figure 15-1 in Chapter 15.)

The Navigation pane, Headings tab, shows a list of headings in your document based on the Heading styles (or their equivalents). The pane isn't designed for organizing your thoughts; instead, it's best used as a way to jump around your document: Click a heading and Word instantly goes to that part of your document.

» The Navigation pane also contains the Find command's search box. In fact, pressing the Ctrl+F keyboard shortcut to summon the Find command instantly shows the Navigation pane.

» You can click the triangles in the Navigation pane to collapse or expand specific parts of the document's outline.

TIP

OUTLINE-MANIPULATION SHORTCUT KEYS

The best way to manipulate an outline is to use the keyboard. Of all Word's weirdo key combinations, it may behoove you to use and memorize the following:

Key Combo	What It Does
Alt+Shift++→	Demotes a topic
Alt+Shift++←	Promotes a topic
Alt+Shift++↑	Moves a topic up one line
Alt+Shift++↓	Moves a topic down one line
Ctrl+Shift+N	Adds a narrative (body text) to the outline
Alt+Shift+1	Displays only Heading 1 (top-level) topics
Alt+Shift+2	Displays only Heading 1 and Heading 2 topics
Alt+Shift+N	Displays Heading N topics
Alt+Shift+A	Displays all topics
Numeric keypad +	Expands the topic, showing all subtopics and narratives
Numeric keypad –	Collapses the topic
Numeric keypad *	Shows all topic levels

IN THIS CHAPTER

» **Creating a single, huge document**

» **Writing one chapter at a time**

» **Adding bookmarks**

» **Using a split window**

» **Juggling multiple document windows**

Chapter **17**

Humongous Documents

N o upper limit exists for a Word document's size, not a maximum page count or word count or any other text measurement. I don't know whether anyone is crazy enough to test this claim. The longest single document I ever created was over 240 pages long. Word seemed to deal with it well, but the document was just text — no graphics or fancy formatting. Though you may never write a document this long, you may someday desire to write a book or some other long manuscript. When you do, you'll find several ways to deal with all that text in Word, none of which are obvious.

Write That Novel!

Sit down, crack your knuckles, and be prepared to type the Great American Novel. Comfy? Good! Because you'll be sitting there for a while. The typical novel is between 40,000 and 100,000 words. Pages? Don't worry about pages. Instead, worry about how to best manage such a tremendous task on your word processor.

» The actual length of a novel depends on whom you ask; I've never seen any hard-and-fast rules.

» Refer to Chapter 15 for information on calculating a word count.

» Anything shorter than 40,000 words is considered a novella. Some novellas can be as short as 7,500 words.

>> Magazine articles run anywhere from 1,000 to 10,000 words, with 2,500 the average, depending on the publication.

>> Some publishers are reluctant to accept, let alone read, a first novel of greater than 100,000 words. The topic must be truly compelling for the word count to go higher.

>> *The Great Gatsby*, written by F. Scott Fitzgerald, considered the epitome of the Great American Novel, weighs in at about 50,000 words.

Building one long manuscript

Your first instinct when writing a long document might be to put all the manuscript into one file. This approach makes sense because Word trains you to see a written document as a single document file. For some manuscripts, this approach works best and might even be required. For others, the long-document method adds unforeseen complications.

Pros

>> With a single document, you can set formatting for the entire manuscript: headers, footers, page numbers, chapter titles, and other page-level formatting.

>> A long document gives you a complete word count.

>> Many publishers request that the manuscript be submitted as a single document.

>> An eBook must be formatted and submitted as one file.

>> It's easier to create hyperlinks in an eBook when you're working with a single document.

>> Creating a table of contents or an index is easy for a single document.

>> Managing one document file is less tedious than managing multiple documents (one per chapter). For example, reorganizing your book is a matter of copy-and-paste as opposed to renaming a slew of files.

Cons

>> The longer the document, the more difficult it is to move around within the document. See the later section "Splitting the window."

>> It's easier for a single file to become damaged, corrupted, overwritten, or lost. Efforts can be made to mitigate that problem; always back up your computer files.

>> Though it's easier to copy-and-paste to reorganize chapters, if you screw up, it's more difficult to undo the mistake.

>> If you decide to cut something, such as a chapter, it's gone unless you save that chunk in another document. When you cut a chapter as a document, you can use Windows to recover the deleted file.

>> At some point, Word slows down as the document grows. Especially if you add graphics, tables, and other objects, a long manuscript may tax the computer's capabilities to run Word.

Writing one chapter per document

The first book I wrote (unpublished) was a single document. It was murder working with such a long document. Since that time, I've split my books into separate documents, one for each chapter. Most professional writers work this way.

Pros

>> Shorter, chapter-size documents are easy to work on, quicker to search, and take less time to finish.

>> It's simple to track your progress, because the manuscript's folder shows more files (documents) as your writing progresses.

>> Working on multiple chapters at the same time is easy because each chapter naturally exists in its own document window.

>> You can add lots of graphics, tables, and other items to the document and not worry about their addition affecting Word's performance.

>> If you cut a chapter, you can save it in a backup folder. Doing so makes it easy to recover some or all of the chapter's text should you decide to do so in the future.

>> You can still generate a single document as the result of your efforts. See the later section "Collecting chapters into a final document."

Cons

>> If you reorganize your book, you need to rename the document files as well as edit individual files to reflect the new names, which requires a lot of overhead. (And it's why I recommend creating a good outline to start; refer to Chapter 16.)

>> Publishers may require you to consolidate the chapters for submission. eBook publishers require that you submit a single document.

>> Word's document-wide references, such as the table of contents, work only when you've combined the separate chapters into a master document.

>> To print the manuscript, you must open and print each individual chapter document. Ditto for converting the documents' file format.

>> Page numbering doesn't work across separate document files.

>> You can never obtain an overall word count or page count unless you examine each chapter document individually and tally the totals or you create a master document.

Collecting chapters into a final document

In practice, I write all my books with separate files for each chapter. When it comes time to publish the book, I combine the chapters into a single, master document. This step doesn't mean that you're done writing; the process continues until you think everything is perfect (which never happens) or someone tells you to stop, or you die.

To create a single, master document, follow these steps:

1. **Use your manuscript's template to start a new document.**

   Start the document just as you would another chapter-sized document, ensuring that you use the same template. This step guarantees that your formatting and layout remain consistent.

2. **On the Insert tab, in the Text group, choose Object ⇨ Text From File.**

   The Object button's icon is shown in the margin. This button features a menu chevron to the right. Click it to display the menu where the Text From File command is available. Upon success, you see the Insert File dialog box.

3. **Choose the next chapter to add to the master document file.**

   For example, if you're starting out, insert Chapter 1. Otherwise, insert the next chapter to build the manuscript.

4. **Repeat Step 3 for each chapter in the document.**

   Work consecutively, if you've followed my advice and named the chapters by number as opposed to naming them by title or something equally silly.

5. **Save the document!**

After combining the chapters, remember that any updates to the book must take place in the larger, master document. Work with this document until it's ready for whatever destination awaits it.

I recommend that you keep all the original, smaller chapter documents. What I do is create a subfolder for them and move them all there. Doing so keeps them handy (not deleted), but out of the way.

One Long Manuscript

Huge documents can just happen; they grow like bamboo. Or perhaps you have set out to write your manuscript as one long document on purpose. Either way, working on a humongous document presents some issues. Fret not! This section offers some helpful tricks, such as adding bookmarks and splitting or creating a new document window.

Bookmarking your text

Word's Bookmark command can help you locate a specific spot in a long document. For example, you can bookmark a chunk of text that needs more work so that you can return to it later. Or you can bookmark a passage of text that's quoted elsewhere in the book. Using a bookmark in this manner is more effective than writing yourself a note in the text, which you can forget about or not notice later.

To bookmark a chunk of text, follow these steps:

1. **Select the relevant chunk of text or just stab the insertion pointer into a specific location.**

2. **On the Insert tab, in the Links group, click the Bookmark button.**

   The Bookmark dialog box appears.

3. **Type a name for the bookmark.**

   Bookmark names cannot contain spaces, so use underlines instead. Be descriptive! For example, Fix_this_description or Belindas_confession.

4. **Click the Add button.**

   The bookmark is set in the document. It has no visual feedback — unless you've activated their visibility as described in the next section.

To use the bookmark, refer to the later section, "Visiting a bookmark."

>> Bookmarks are used to create hyperlinks in eBooks. See Chapter 19.

>> Bookmarks also come into play for certain document fields and cross-references. See Chapter 21 for information on fields; Chapter 18 covers cross-references.

>> You can also use Word's comment feature to write notes to yourself, though you may find that approach a bit distracting. See Chapter 11.

Showing the bookmarks

Bookmarks are normally hidden in a document. I prefer things this way, as I find them distracting otherwise. When you really want to know where a bookmark lurks in your text, but not the contents, heed these directions:

1. **Click the File tab.**

2. **Choose the Options command.**

   The Word Options dialog box appears.

3. **Choose the Advanced category.**

4. **Place a check mark by the item Show Bookmarks.**

   This item is located below the Show Document Content heading. (Scroll down.)

I   Bookmarks appear as a large I in your text, as shown in the margin. This is your only clue that a bookmark exists at a specific spot in the text; you cannot see the bookmark's name, nor can you delete the visible bookmark. For these reasons, I keep them hidden in my documents.

Visiting a bookmark

Even if you show bookmarks (see the preceding section), you can't tell what they represent by looking at them. Therefore, the best way to visit a bookmark in your document is to use the Go To command. Follow these steps:

1. **Press Ctrl+G.**

   Ctrl+G is the shortcut for the Go To tab in the Find and Replace dialog box, shown in Figure 17-1.

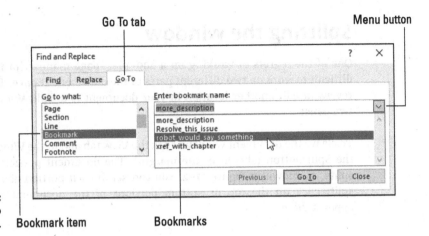

Go To tab

Menu button

Bookmark item

Bookmarks

FIGURE 17-1:
Jumping to
a bookmark.

2. Choose Bookmark from the Go to What list, as illustrated in Figure 17-1.

3. Click the menu button to choose a bookmark.

4. Click the Go To button to visit the bookmark's location in your document.

REMEMBER

Setting and visiting bookmarks doesn't guarantee that you'll remember them. Therefore, I suggest that you commit to memory the Ctrl+G keyboard shortcut and use it frequently to review any bookmarks you've set for editing purposes.

Removing a bookmark

Bookmarks aren't edited like regular text. Whether visible or invisible, to best remove a bookmark, return to the Bookmark dialog box by following these steps:

1. On the Insert tab, in the Links group, click the Bookmark button.

2. Select the bookmark you want to remove.

   All the document's bookmarks appear in the scrolling list portion of the Bookmark dialog box.

3. Click the Delete button.

4. Repeat Steps 2 and 3 to peel away additional bookmarks.

If you forget to remove bookmarks, it's no big deal. They don't show up in the text, unlike comments you may write to yourself in the body of the manuscript.

Splitting the window

One of the regrets of working on a 200-plus-page manuscript is that it's more difficult to work on two different parts of the document at once. The quick way to review or edit another location in your document is to split Word's window into two panes.

 To cleave the document window, click the View tab and in the Window group, click the Split button (shown in the margin). The document portion of the window splits, as shown in Figure 17-2. You can scroll each portion above or below the split; click on the top or bottom portions of the document to control what appears there.

One part of the document   Split bar

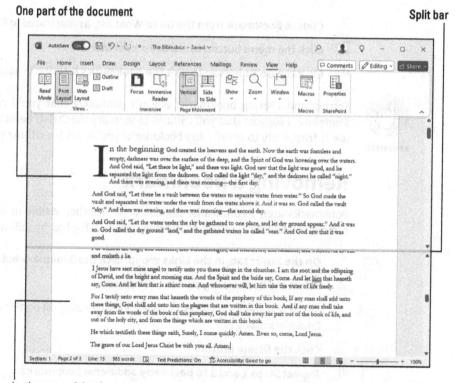

FIGURE 17-2:
A split window. 'nuther part of the document

 To adjust the size of the split, point the mouse at the split bar, as illustrated in Figure 17-2. When the mouse pointer changes as shown in the margin, drag the mouse up or down.

To remove the split, double-click the split bar. The top portion of the split remains.

Opening a second window

A split window is fine for a quick edit or fact-check. When you really need to hop between different parts of a long document, the best trick is to open a second document window. The result is that you have two Word document windows open, but each shows a different part of the same document.

 To open a second window and view a different part of a long document, on the View tab, in the Window group, click New Window (icon shown in the margin). A second Word document window appears, showing the same document as the first window, though each window works independently.

You can open as many windows for the current document as you need. Each window shows a specific portion of the document. It's the same document in every window, so edits in one window are updated in the others.

TIP

The window's title bar reflects which window you're viewing. The document's filename is suffixed with a colon and a number. The number references the window as opened in sequence.

Close the extra windows as you would any window. The main difference is that Word warns you to save an unsaved document only when you close the final window.

IN THIS CHAPTER

» **Creating a table of contents**

» **Working with footnotes and endnotes**

» **Adding bibliographical sources**

» **Inserting a bibliography**

» **Placing captions on figures**

» **Building cross-references**

» **Adding an index to your document**

Chapter **18**

Document References

Not every manuscript is a magazine article or novel. Many professional documents are created in the educational world or for industry professionals. These papers require reference features not normally found in your typical office memorandum, such as a bibliography, footnotes, a glossary, and other text tidbits. The good news is that Word provides tools that generate these references, automatically — providing you know where to find the tools and how to use them.

» Word keeps its automatic reference-creation tools on the References tab: Click the References tab to view the different groups.

» Most references work automatically. Numbered references are renumbered automatically as you change your text.

» Some references work as document fields. If you modify your document, you must update the reference field. Examples are provided throughout this chapter. Also see Chapter 21 for more information on fields.

» The References tab features the Table of Authorities group. The table of authorities is used primarily in legal documents. Refer to Chapter 12.

>> Those references Word doesn't create automatically must be built manually. Generally, these types of references are simple lists that don't link back to a document's text, such as a glossary. Word lacks tools specific to create these types of references.

Table of Contents

If you want to be one of the cool kids and pretend that you're part of the publishing industry, you refer to the table of contents as the *TOC*. Say "tea-oh-see." Don't say "tock," or you sound like a dork. Once you know this secret, you can proceed with using Word's Table of Contents tool to add a nicely formatted, accurate, and effortless TOC to your document.

TIP

>> The key to making a Table of Contents is to employ heading styles in your document. You can use Word's built-in heading styles, or you can create your own heading styles.

>> If you create your own heading styles, ensure that the style's Outline Level attribute is properly set; otherwise, the Table of Contents tool doesn't work.

Inserting a TOC

Hopefully, you're done writing. Even if you aren't (and you aren't), to set the document's table of contents, follow these steps:

1. **Place the insertion pointer at the top of a page where you want the table of contents to appear.**

The TOC is one of the first items in a manuscript, after the title and copyright pages. I recommend separating this part of your document from the rest by setting it into its own section or at least framing it with hard page breaks before and after.

2. **Type a page title for the table of contents.**

My favorite title is *Table of Contents,* though I'm sure you can think of something more exciting.

TIP

Do not use a heading style to format the table of contents title unless you want the TOC to reference itself. (Rumor has it that Christopher Nolan did so when writing "Inception.")

3. Position the insertion pointer on the next line, below the TOC title.

4. On the References tab, in the Table of Contents group, click the Table of Contents button.

The Table of Contents icon is shown in the margin. After clicking this button, you can choose a preset TOC from the gallery, but the dialog box offers you more control.

5. Choose Custom Table of Contents.

The Table of Contents dialog box appears, as shown in Figure 18-1. It offers two previews: one for printed documents and another for the web, which also counts for publishing eBooks.

Page number control

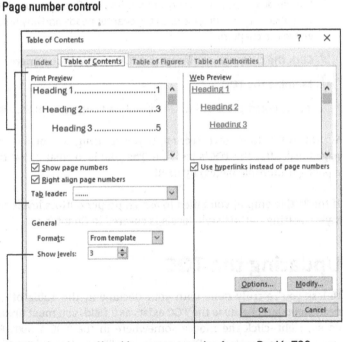

FIGURE 18-1:
Customizing
the TOC.

Heading level   Use this necessary option for an eBook's TOC

6. Configure the page numbers' appearance.

If you want page numbers in the TOC, place a check mark by the Show Page Numbers option.

To right-justify the page numbers, place a check mark by the Right Align Page Numbers option. If you choose this option, you can set a tab leader from the Tab Leader menu.

The preview in the top left area of the dialog box shows how the TOC appears based on the page numbering options you select (refer to Figure 18-1).

7. Set hyperlinks for web or eBook publishing.

If you plan to publish an eBook, place a check mark by the option Use Hyperlinks Instead of Page Numbers. eBooks don't use page numbers, but links come in handy.

You can remove the options for page numbers if you plan on publishing an eBook, but for eBooks that use the HTML (web page) format, that step isn't necessary in Word. See Chapter 22 for further details on eBook publishing.

8. Determine how deep you want the TOC to go.

The maximum number of levels you can choose depends on how you apply the Heading styles in your document. For my eBook manuscripts, I set the TOC to 2 levels. That setting includes the chapter heads and any first-level heads within the chapters.

9. Click the OK button to insert the TOC into your document.

10. Examine the TOC.

If you goofed, press Ctrl+Z (Undo) and start over again at Step 4.

REMEMBER

Set the TOC into its own section, if you're using sections. Otherwise, set a hard page break after the TOC's last line. The goal is to ensure that the TOC appears on a page (or multiple pages) by itself.

TIP

If the TOC is empty, you failed to assign proper outline levels to your document's styles. Setting outline style levels is covered in Chapter 4.

Updating the TOC

Unless you're truly done with your document, the Table of Contents will soon need an update. Because the TOC exists as a field, you must update its contents. To do so, right-click the mouse somewhere in the TOC's text. From the shortcut menu, choose the Update Field command. The TOC is refreshed.

WARNING

» Do not attempt to edit the TOC. You can try, but to properly present the table of contents, follow my advice for setting document heading styles and refresh the TOC field.

» See Chapter 21 for more information on document fields.

Footnotes and Endnotes

Footnotes and endnotes are similar concepts, references applied to your text. The difference is in where they appear: A footnote reference dwells at the bottom of the page; endnotes lurk at the end of a document. In both cases, a superscripted note number appears by the reference in the text.

>> Choose either footnotes or endnotes for your document. Don't use both.

>> The purpose of a footnote or endnote is to further explain something in the text, to reference a quote, or to offer other information that would otherwise be distracting.

>> It's better to use a footnote or endnote, as opposed to writing multiple parenthetical references in the same paragraph.

>> Word automatically formats and places footnotes and endnotes.

>> For both the footnote and endnote, Word handles the numbering for you, keeping all the notes sequential.

>> To see a footnote's or endnote's text, point the mouse at the superscripted number in the document's text. The note appears in a pop-up bubble.

Adding a footnote

Your document desperately needs a footnote, probably to reference where that whacky quote came from. Follow these steps:

1. Place the insertion pointer just after the word or phrase the footnote references.

You can also select the text you want referenced.

2. On the References tab, in the Footnotes group, click the Insert Footnote button.

The keyboard shortcut for the Insert Footnote command is Alt+Ctrl+F.

Instantly, Word superscripts a number by the text. The insertion pointer zooms to the bottom of the page, where a horizontal line separates the document's body text from the footnote(s). The same superscripted number appears, as shown in Figure 18-2.

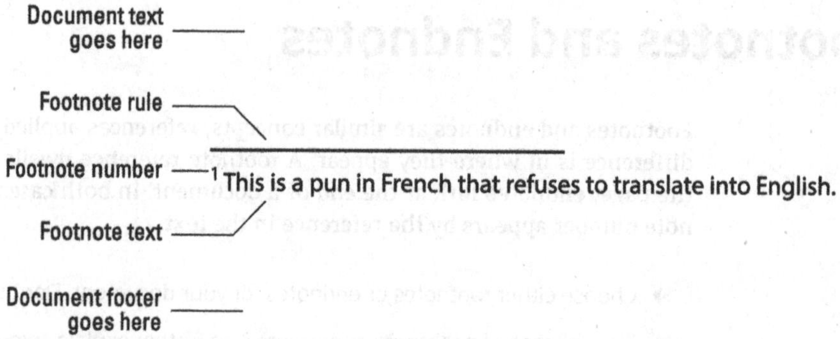

Document text
goes here

Footnote rule

Footnote number ——¹ This is a pun in French that refuses to translate into English.

Footnote text

FIGURE 18-2:
A footnote.

Document footer
goes here

3. **Type the footnote text.**

4. **Click the mouse back in your document and continue editing.**

You can press the Shift+F5 keyboard shortcut to return to the location you clicked in Step 1. This trick may not work when you've done extensive editing within the footnote.

TIP

These steps add a footnote anywhere in your document. You never need to worry about renumbering the notes; Word does it automatically.

» If you're using Word to create an eBook or a web page, use an endnote instead of a footnote. Web pages and eBooks don't feature pages. Therefore, footnotes are irrelevant.

» A document's word count usually doesn't include footnotes. Some scholars use this exception to exceed the number of words allowed in their manuscripts; they place excess verbiage into the footnotes. Try to avoid using that sneaky trick. Refer to Chapter 15 for information on Word's word count command.

TECHNICAL
STUFF

Creating an endnote

Endnotes work just like footnotes. Both are created in a similar manner, so if you're gifted with footnote talent, your endnote skills will closely follow. In fact, the same steps presented in the preceding section work to set a footnote. The difference is that in Step 2, choose the Insert Endnote button, icon shown in the margin.

» The endnote is placed after the last paragraph in the document, below a horizontal rule like the one shown for a footnote in Figure 18-2.

>> The keyboard shortcut to insert an endnote is Alt+Ctrl+D.

>> If you're using endnotes for citations, you can save time by writing *Ibid* for an endnote reference that's identical to the preceding reference. In fact, avoid putting too much text into an endnote. It's a reference, not an excuse to write a novella.

Working with notes

Footnotes and endnotes appear in the document window just as they print. If you need to review them, on the References tab in the Footnotes group, click the Next Footnote button (icon shown in the margin). Use the Next Footnote button's menu to view the previous footnote or to browse endnotes. Word relocates the insertion pointer to the spot where the note is placed.

If you desire to edit the note, double-click its superscripted reference in the text. Word shows the note, where you can edit the text as you would any text in Word.

Removing a note is done by deleting its superscripted reference: Select the teensy number and press the Delete key on the keyboard. The note is gone. Any remaining notes in the document are renumbered to account for the change.

Setting note options

To control various note options, such as the symbols used to flag a note, on the References tab, in the Footnotes group, click the dialog box launcher. You see the Footnote and Endnote dialog box, shown in Figure 18-3.

The most common thing you'll likely change in the dialog box are the symbols used to reference the notes. To change them, choose a new scheme from the Number Format menu. (Refer to Figure 18-3.)

To set a custom symbol, click the Symbol button. Use the Symbol dialog box to pluck out a special character to apply to the notes.

REMEMBER

Click the Apply button when you're done setting options in the Footnote and Endnote dialog box. If you click the Insert button, you're adding a new footnote or endnote, depending on which option is selected at the top of the dialog box.

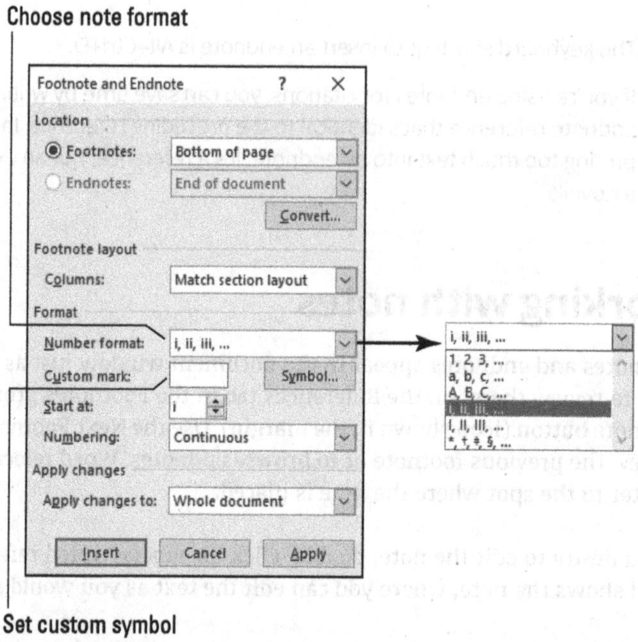

Choose note format

Footnote and Endnote   ?   ×

Location

◉ Footnotes: Bottom of page

○ Endnotes: End of document

                                    Convert...

Footnote layout

Columns: Match section layout

Format

Number format: i, ii, iii, ...

Custom mark: Symbol...

Start at: i

Numbering: Continuous

Apply changes

Apply changes to: Whole document

        Insert   Cancel   Apply

i, ii, iii, ...
1, 2, 3, ...
a, b, c, ...
A, B, C, ...
i, ii, iii, ...
I, II, III, ...
*, †, ‡, §, ...

FIGURE 18-3:
The Footnote
and Endnote
dialog box.

Set custom symbol

Converting between footnotes and endnotes

When you goof and you need an endnote when you have a footnote, or vice versa, follow these steps to convert between the two:

1. **Double-click the note's superscript.**

When you double-click the superscript, you're taken to the note itself.

2. **Right-click on the note.**

You can click anywhere on the note's text.

3. **Choose the command Convert to Endnote or Convert to Footnote.**

The note is converted.

I recommend that you repeat these steps for each note in your document. Though it's technically possible to mix footnotes and endnotes in Word, it's not something the reader expects.

Citations and the Bibliography

A *citation* is a reference to another published work. It appears within the body of the text, with the author's name and year enclosed in parentheses. For example, I once wrote that there is no logic in the computer industry (Gookin, 1989). The citation is what appears in parentheses. It also implies that additional information is available later in the document, appearing in an organized bibliography.

In Word, you create a citation by marking the related text, then providing information, the author's name and work's title. From these entries, Word automatically builds a bibliography. Plus, you can more easily create future citations from the ones you've already cited.

Creating citations

A citation starts by referencing the related text. Follow these steps:

1. **Click the mouse where you want the citation (reference) to appear in the text.**

2. **If you're adding a new citation, on the References tab, in the Citations & Bibliography group, click the Insert Citation button and choose Add New Source.**

   To insert an existing citation, one you've already added, choose it from the Insert Citation button. Otherwise, use the Create Source dialog box to continue.

3. **Fill in the text fields relevant to the citation.**

   Important are the Author, Title, Year, and possibly Publisher fields. If you need more fields, place a check mark by the option Show All Bibliography Fields.

4. **Click the OK button to create the source and insert the citation into the text.**

   The citation is inserted at the spot you clicked in Step 1.

The citation looks like text, but it's not! Word uses a content control to present the citation's text. When you click on the text, you see the control's features. See Chapter 23 for more details on working with content controls.

> » Determining how much information to include for the citation depends on the type of document. Some periodicals and journals require more information than others.

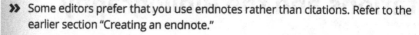

WARNING

» Some editors prefer that you use endnotes rather than citations. Refer to the earlier section "Creating an endnote."

» The Reference tab's Table of Authorities group sports a Mark Citation button. This button is not the same as the Insert Citation button, referenced in this section. The Mark Citation button is used for preparing legal documents. Refer to Chapter 12.

» To change a citation, click the content control and choose Edit Source from the menu. Any changes you make are reflected in all similar citations in your document as well as the bibliography.

Building the bibliography

The endgame for the citations in your document is a *bibliography*, which lists the full details for each source cited. Like most document references, the bibliography appears at the end of your manuscript, after the document's text and before the index. Word creates the bibliography based on the document's citations you've created, as described in the preceding section.

To insert the bibliography into your document, obey these steps:

1. **Start a new page for the bibliography.**

    I recommend setting the bibliography after a hard page break or within its own section.

 2. **On the References tab, in the Citations & Bibliography group, click the Bibliography button.**

3. **Choose a bibliography style from the menu.**

    A formatted bibliography, including a title, appears in your document. The bibliography's text lists, in alphabetical order, all citations you created.

If you prefer to create your own bibliography, type **Bibliography** on a line by itself after Step 1. Format that line as a top-level heading style so that it's included in the document's table of contents. Work Step 2, but for Step 4 choose the Insert Bibliography command. The citations are inserted, which you can then format to match the document's text.

REMEMBER

As with the citations, the bibliography is a content control. To update the bibliography, click the control and choose the Update Citations and Bibliography command.

Figure Captions

This book covers captions on figures in Chapter 7. The advice there works, but if you're creating a manuscript where a list of figures is required, I recommend that you use Word's captioning feature. It helps you to automatically build a list of figures and page numbers as a document reference.

To add one of Word's captions to an image, table or an equation, follow these steps:

1. **Click to select the object: picture, table, or equation.**

2. **On the References tab, in the Captions group, click the Insert Caption button.**

The Caption dialog box appears, as shown in Figure 18-4.

Whether the label is removed or replaced, the sequential number remains. You cannot delete the number, which is the whole point of using the Insert Caption command to sequentially number items in a document.

Choose preset label text

Label (supplied by Word)

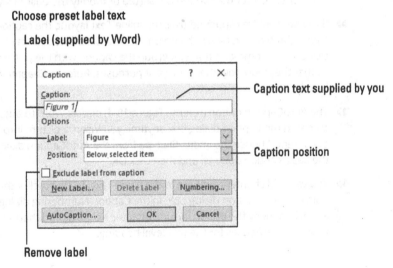

Caption text supplied by you

Caption position

FIGURE 18-4:
The Caption
dialog box.

Remove label

3. **Type the caption's text.**

The text is placed after the caption label.

4. **Set the caption's position, either above or below the item.**

The two options are chosen from the Position menu.

5. **Click OK to set the caption.**

After you've set a document's captions, you can smack the whole list of them into your document with a single command. That's the point of having Word set the captions, as opposed to creating them manually.

 To insert the list of captions, start on a blank page near the back of the document. Type a title. On the References tab, in the Captions group, click the Insert Table of Figures button. Set various options in the dialog box, which works like creating a TOC as covered earlier in this chapter. Click OK to insert the captions.

You may additionally want to end the list with a hard page break or section page break. Add that break to keep the list of captions separate from the document's other end matter.

REMEMBER

>> Like most automatic references in Word, the list of captions is a field. If you edit, add, or remove any captions, you need to update the field: Right-click in the list of captions and choose the command Update Field. See Chapter 21 for more information on fields.

>> Word uses its built-in Caption style to format the caption. You can select another style after the caption is inserted or modify the built-in style.

>> If the item you've captioned uses the Inline Text layout, the caption appears as a paragraph of text below the object. Otherwise, the caption is placed inside a text box. I recommend that you group the caption with the picture (or object) so that they work together for layout purposes. Refer to Chapter 7 for text box details.

>> The AutoCaption option (refer to Figure 18-4) directs Word to automatically summon the Caption dialog box anytime you insert a picture into your document. Choose the image file type from the AutoCaption dialog box, set the basic caption options, and then click OK.

>> You can add chapter numbers to the figure text. To do so, click the Numbering button in the Caption dialog box. In the Caption Numbering dialog box, place a check mark by the option Include Chapter Number, and then set which style your document uses for the title-level heading.

Cross-References

As you might expect by now, Word lets you insert cross-references into your document that automatically update as you edit text. So, "see page 6" becomes "see page 8" after you re-work your introduction.

Word's cross-references can point to a variety of different items in a document: heading, bookmark, figure, footnote, or table. Follow these directions to create a cross reference:

1. **Click the mouse where you want the cross-reference to appear.**

   The reference can appear as a page number or the text from a heading. Word sticks the reference into your text at the point where you click the mouse.

2. **On the References tab, in the Captions group, click the Cross-Reference button.**

   The Cross-Reference dialog box appears.

3. **Choose what you want to reference from the Reference Type menu.**

   For example, to reference a bookmark, choose Bookmark. To reference a specific document heading, choose Heading. To reference a figure, you must reference a set caption for the figure, as covered earlier in this chapter.

4. **Select the item to reference from the large list in the center of the dialog box.**

   Choose a specific heading, a bookmark, or whatever else appears in the list.

5. **Choose how to reference the item from the Insert Reference To menu.**

   For example, to reference a heading's text, choose Heading Text. To reference the page number where the heading is found, choose Page Number.

6. **If you're composing an eBook or a web page, place a check mark by the item Insert As Hyperlink.**

   Because eBooks lack pages, a page number cross-references make no sense.

REMEMBER

7. **Click the Insert button to place the cross-reference.**

   The cross-reference text appears at the insertion pointer's location (from Step 1).

8. **Close the Cross-Reference dialog box.**

   Or you can continue to insert cross-references.

Also see Chapter 19 for more information on hyperlinks in eBooks.

The Index

An index allows your reader to reference information by subject or key word. It's the way printed documents let you perform a topic or subject search, but it works only when the term you're looking for is referenced and that term is found in the context you desire.

» An index should not merely repeat the table of contents.

» You don't need an index for an eBook. eBook apps feature a Search command, which negates the need to add an index. Also, eBooks lack page numbers, so an index is useless anyway.

Marking entries for the index

The key to building a strong index is to tag words and phrases in your document that you figure someone may want to reference. For example, a cookbook may have an index that references various ingredients, styles of cooking, or food categories such as desserts.

To make an index entry, follow these steps:

1. Select the text to include in the index.

You need to select only a single word; double-click the word to select it. Select more than one word when you want all that text to appear in the index. Don't go nuts.

2. On the References tab, in the Index group, click the Mark Entry button.

The Mark Index Entry dialog box appears, similar to what's shown in Figure 18-5. This dialog box stays open so that you can continue to mark index entries without having to repeat this Step.

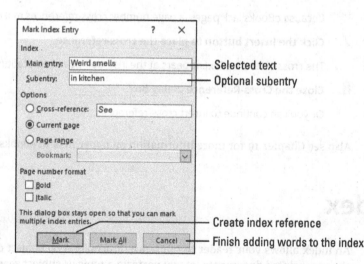

FIGURE 18-5:
The Mark Index Entry dialog box.

Selected text — Main entry: Weird smells
Optional subentry — Subentry: in kitchen

Create index reference — Mark
Finish adding words to the index — Cancel

3. **Click the Mark button.**

TECHNICAL
STUFF

When you mark an index entry, Word activates the Show/Hide command to reveal the document's secret formatting. In this instance, the index-marking field appears in the document next to the word you marked. It looks similar to this:

```
{ ·XE·"Weird·smells:in·kitchen"·}
```

Don't delete this reference! It flags the phrase "Weird smells" for inclusion in the document's index. Step 6 explains how to hide the field's guts.

4. **Continue working through your document, selecting text and clicking the Mark button or Mark All button in the Mark Index Entry dialog box.**

The dialog box stays open, and you can work on your document without closing it; slide it off the document window if its location bugs you.

TIP

The Mark All button marks all instances of text in your document. Be careful! You want the references to be relevant to the reader.

5. **When you're done marking entries, click the Close button in the Mark Index Entry dialog box.**

Word continues to show document markup and hidden characters. To hide them, you use the Show/Hide command, as shown in the next step.

6. **On the Home tab, in the Paragraph group, click the Show/Hide button.**

The ugly field guts are hidden.

You can stop and start the indexing process at any time while you work on your document. You don't need to hurry up and finish it all at once. In fact, I recommend creating the index after your first draft and then looking for index items again just before you finish the final draft.

TIP

>> You can edit the text in the Main Entry text box. If the word you select isn't precise, you can make it so. For example, if you selected the text *Swiffer type of mop,* you can edit it to read *Swiffer mop* in the Mark Entry text box.

>> To create a useful index, you need to view your manuscript topically. Consider terms or phrases that someone might want to search for in your text.

>> The Subentry text box in the Mark Index Entry dialog box helps readers locate more specific information related to a general main topic. For example, you can index the word *email* and then offer subentry text to include topics like sending, receiving, forwarding, attachments, and so on. Especially for common topics, consider adding subentries.

Inserting the index

After you feel that you've sufficiently marked plenty of index entries, you can insert the manuscript's index. Obey these directions:

1. Position the insertion pointer to the location where you want the index to appear.

The index is located at the end of a document. Of all a document's references, the index appears last, though I can find no rule to confirm this fact. Some publishers may add advertising material after the index, but not additional appendixes or references.

2. Insert a hard page break or a next-page section break.

You want the index to start on its own page.

3. Type a heading for the index.

The word *Index* seems appropriate. If your manuscript features a table of contents, set the text style to the top-level heading so that the index appears in the TOC.

4. Press the Enter key to insert the index text on a new line.

5. On the References tab, in the Index group, click the Insert Index button.

The Index dialog box appears, shown in Figure 18-6.

Index column format

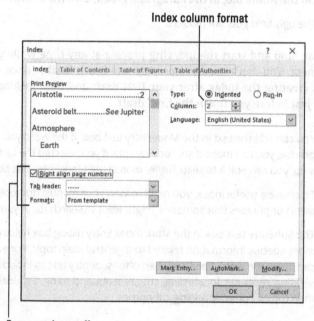

FIGURE 18-6:
The Index
dialog box.

Page number stuff

6. **If you want the page numbers to appear right-justified, place a check mark in the box by Right Align Page Numbers.**

   You can also select a tab leader style from the Tab Leader menu.

   If you don't right-align the page numbers, the numbers appear next to the index entry. Use the Print Preview window in the dialog box to gauge the differences.

7. **Set the number of columns for the index.**

   Because index entries are generally brief, Word presets two columns per page for the index. (Refer to Figure 18-6.) If you prefer one column, use the Columns gizmo to specify 1 instead of 2.

8. **Click the OK button to add the index to your document.**

9. **If any pages follow the index, add another hard page break after the last line in the index.**

The index reflects the items you marked in your document, each with its appropriate page number. Any subentries appear indented below the main entry.

TECHNICAL STUFF

Word adds a continuous section break above and below the index's text (the field). This type of section break is what allows the index to be formatted into multiple columns. A continuous section break, however, does not force the index to reside on its own page, only within its own section.

Updating the index

Similar to other Word references, the index is a field. It looks like static text, but it's not. Because it's a field, it's necessary to update the index after you edit your document. Doing so ensures that new page renumbering is reflected in the index. It's also necessary to update the index should you mark any new entries.

To update the document's index, right-click the mouse inside the index. Choose Update Field from the shortcut menu. The index is refreshed.

TECHNICAL STUFF

The index is a field. When you click the mouse inside of the field, the text grows a gray background. See Chapter 21 for more information on document fields.

IN THIS CHAPTER

» Authoring an eBook

» Making formatting considerations

» Inserting hyperlinks

» Coming up with a good title

» Prepping for publication

» Determining price and royalty rates

» Exploring marketing opportunities

Chapter **19**

eBook Publishing

t's all the rage these days: Skip over the arduous process of obtaining an agent and shopping a book to the various publishers. A pox on their houses! You can now self-publish your prose electronically and it costs you nothing. Millions of mobile device users can then buy your literary efforts, transforming you into an overnight success! That's the dream, anyway.

The eBook Process

Whether you want your book to be published traditionally or electronically, the process remains the same: Write!

I'm serious, writers devote a great portion of their day to sitting (or standing) and writing. Words! Words! Words! Don't be that person who brags about her novel to the gals at Thursday luncheon but lacks the dedication to finish it. You want to be a writer, write!

The content of your book is more important than the format, though you must be mindful of a few tidbits to take into consideration when publishing electronically. These items are based on an eBook's presentation, which is digital, not on paper.

>> Word is fully capable of producing your eBook, including references, pictures, or whatever you want in the book. You do not need a separate desktop publishing app to make an eBook.

>> Any Word document can be converted to an eBook. If you specifically set out to create an eBook, however, you can save yourself some time by heeding the advice listed in this section.

>> An eBook is not simply a PDF copy of your book. eBooks use a special document format that can be read only by eBook reader software.

Writing the manuscript

I recommend that you write your eBook as a single document in Word. You can write separate chapters if you like, as mentioned in Chapter 17. Eventually, you want all your eBook's text in a single Word document. This step is required for the final conversion into the eBook file.

To start a new chapter in your eBook document, or to bring any element to the top of a page, insert a page break. Use a hard page break: Ctrl+Enter. You can also use a Next Page section break, though because an eBook lacks any meaningful page formatting (see the next section), breaking up your text into sections isn't necessary.

>> Document elements separated by a hard page break include the cover page, front matter, chapters, and any back matter. See the nearby sidebar, "Front matter and back matter."

>> You can copyright your own work. Write the word *Copyright* followed by the copyright symbol and the date, as in ©2026. In Word, type **(C)** and those three characters are autocorrected into the copyright symbol.

>> You do not need to register your text with any official department or agency. Any individual can obtain a copyright. Please don't pay to have your own work copyrighted.

>> A *foreword* (not *forward*) is text appearing in the front matter and written by someone other than yourself. It serves as an introduction to the work, usually by a professional or another well-known person. Not every book needs a foreword.

>> A *preface* is written by the author. It serves as extra narrative for the book, to explain the topic or provide background. Like the foreword, a preface is optional.

FRONT MATTER AND BACK MATTER

The official publishing name for pages of text that appear at the start of a book is front matter. The front matter can include the book's title page, a copyright page, the table of contents (TOC), a foreword, a preface, and an introduction. Of these items, a title page is a must. The book's title and author should sit on a page by themselves at the start of your eBook. Most eBooks also include a copyright page, with information about the book, the publication date, and details about the publisher and author. Also include the eBook version number on this page.

Back matter is any information that follows the main body of the text. Examples include a glossary, appendixes, a bibliography, endnotes, and — in print books — an index. The final thing in any book can be marketing material, as described in this chapter.

>> The *introduction* is written by the author. It's more formal than a preface and typically found in technical and trade books.

>> Refer to Chapter 18 for information on adding the table of contents, glossary, bibliography, and index to your eBook.

Formatting your eBook document

REMEMBER

Perhaps the most important thing to remember when you write an eBook is that page size, page count, or anything having to do with page formatting is irrelevant: eBooks lack pages!

If you like, you can format the document as it might present itself on an eBook reader. This special page formatting doesn't translate to the eBook reader software, but it can help visually remind you of the text's final appearance.

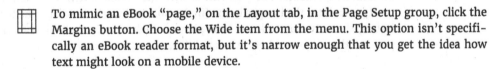

To mimic an eBook "page," on the Layout tab, in the Page Setup group, click the Margins button. Choose the Wide item from the menu. This option isn't specifically an eBook reader format, but it's narrow enough that you get the idea how text might look on a mobile device.

REMEMBER

Even when you adjust the margins, what you see in the document window only approximates what a reader sees. Remember that readers allow the user to reorient the device from vertical to horizontal, which reformats the eBook's text accordingly.

>> Don't bother with headers or footers in your manuscript. They won't show up in the final eBook.

>> Don't bother with page numbers.

>> Don't fuss over choosing a special font. Many eBook reader programs let the reader choose the typeface and font size.

>> Be careful when using special characters. Basic characters and symbols translate well into the eBook format, but some characters may appear as tiny squares (unknown characters). You might even see unpredictable characters, depending on what you're trying to do and how the eBook reader app interprets the text. The only way to know for certain is to use the eBook publisher's app preview software, as described later in this chapter.

>> Text color transfers to the eBook reader app, though specific colors may not. I would just avoid using special colors in your text, especially given that many e-reader apps show only grayscale.

>> Paragraph formatting still applies to an eBook — specifically, the spaces before and after a paragraph as well as left-right indents and first-line indents. Line spacing might translate to the final eBook, though some eBook apps let the user adjust line spacing.

TIP

>> Though eBooks don't feature page counts, your readers might want to know the word count; refer to Chapter 15. Another relevant eBook attribute is the final file size. This topic is covered later in this chapter.

Using pictures or graphics

Do you love to spice up your book with clever illustrations, photos, or even festive dingbats between the chapters? Don't. eBooks and graphics mix like oil and water.

The problem isn't with Word, which can deftly manipulate pictures and other nontextual elements. The problem is with the eBook software, which inconsistently translates the images in the final, published work. As with some formatting issues, the only way to know how pictures look in a final eBook document is to preview the document before you publish.

Some eBook publishers do allow exceptions for graphics-heavy manuscripts, such as children's books. These are often published as a form of PDF, which ensures that the images and text layout remain consistent. But for plain text, such as a novel, be wary of graphics.

>> Unlike printing on paper, in an eBook an image's dimensions in pixels plays a role in how large or small the image appears in an eBook reader app. Don't be surprised if one image is quite large and the next image — formatted the same in Word — appears tiny in an eBook.

>> If you can, try to be consistent with the image resolution as measured in pixels, horizontally and vertically. Pixel depth is also important; an image set to 72 pixels will appear smaller than an image set to 300 pixels.

>> Ensure that you know which file format the eBook publishing software uses before you create the images. Some eBook publishers may limit their documents to specific file types, such as JPEG and not PNG.

>> When formatting the images, I recommend you use the inline-with-text layout option. Keep the images on a line by themselves, centered from left to right. Any fancy layout options you attempt may not translate to the final document.

>> See Part 2 of this book for details on how to work with graphical objects in Word.

Creating hyperlinks

When you need to reference another part of your eBook, insert a hyperlink into your document. People who read eBooks are accustomed to tapping a link as opposed to flipping pages. It's natural. Follow these steps to stick a hyperlink into your eBook manuscript:

1. Select the text that you want to appear as a link.

2. On the Insert tab, in the Links group, click the Link button.

The Insert Hyperlink dialog box appears, as illustrated in Figure 19-1.

3. On the left side of the dialog box, on the Link To list, choose Place In This Document.

The center portion of the Insert Hyperlink dialog box changes, showing only linkable items in the document. These include bookmarks as well as text formatted in Word's heading styles. Of the two, I recommend setting bookmarks as the target for your eBook's hyperlinks.

4. Scroll through the list to find an item, a heading, or a bookmark to link to.

5. Click the OK button to create the link.

The text stays linked to the bookmark or heading in the document. Even if you modify the text, the link remains valid. Only when you delete the heading or bookmark does the link cease to function.

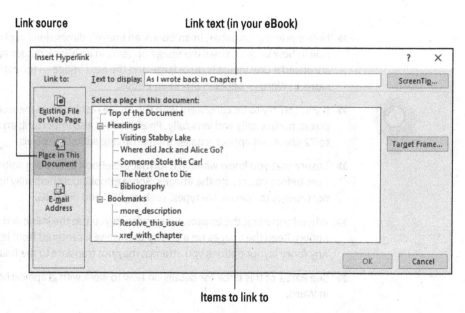

Link source   Link text (in your eBook)

FIGURE 19-1:
The Insert
Hyperlink
dialog box.

Items to link to

The link appears in the document as blue underlined text. In Word, Ctrl+click the link to follow it. When the document is published as an eBook, the user can click or tap the link to jump to another part of the text.

>> Refer to Chapter 17 for information on creating bookmarks.

>> Word can create automatic hyperlinks for its references, such as a table of contents. See the next section.

>> The keyboard shortcut for inserting a hyperlink is Ctrl+K. Follow Step 1 in the preceding step list, and then press Ctrl+K to summon the Insert Hyperlink dialog box.

>> Right-click on a hyperlink to change its target. Choose the Edit Hyperlink command, and then use the Edit Hyperlink dialog box to make any necessary modifications.

>> To erase a hyperlink, right-click on the blue underlined text. Choose the Remove Hyperlink command from the shortcut menu. This command doesn't delete the hyperlink text.

>> The Select a Place in This Document list (refer to Figure 19-1) shows headings and bookmarks. Only those headings formatted by using Word's built-in Heading styles appear in the list. If you've created your heading styles, they don't show up. This is a good reason why I recommend using bookmarks instead.

Adding document references

The number of references you place into your eBook depends on the topic. All eBook publishers, however, recommend that you place a table of contents in your document.

REMEMBER

Chapter 18 covers creating a table of contents. Refer there for specific directions on adding a TOC to your eBook. Remember to use hyperlinks in the TOC, not page numbers.

Don't bother with an index for your eBook. Readers use the Search command to look for text in an eBook. Also, the lack of page numbers in an eBook renders an index useless.

eBook Publishing Tips

In a way, an eBook publisher is more like a vanity press than a traditional publisher. The difference is marketing: A traditional publisher has a vested interest in selling your book. A vanity press doesn't care, because you're paying for everything. An eBook publisher provides the venue and markets its app or reading hardware, but it's still up to you to pull more weight as an author than you would when using a traditional book publisher.

Titling your tome

Crafting a proper title for a book is an art form. It's a lot tougher than you think. In fact, you might be surprised to discover that most authors don't title their own books. Even when they do, the publisher may devise a better title. And getting the title correct is highly important: The title is the first introduction to your book.

If an easy book-titling formula existed, I'd gladly pass it along. Yet even the big publishing houses struggle. To provide a suggestion, consider pulling text from your book — a quote or thought you find rather pithy. For example, *Outnumbered, Outsmarted, but Not Defeated* might be some text found in a book that the author would otherwise title *That Time Those Aliens Came to Earth and Nearly Killed Everyone*.

>> Pull a quote from poetry or another source if you lack inspiration. I can't imagine how many pieces of literature have been titled by taking quotes from Shakespeare's *Hamlet*.

>> Avoid starting your eBook's title with *How To* as it's not that creative. (Yes, I know about the musical *How to Succeed in Business Without Really Trying*, which is why I wrote *avoid* instead of *don't*.)

>> You cannot copyright your book's title. You might be able to trademark the title, which involves a legal process. Book series can be trademarked, or in the case of *For Dummies*®, a registered trademark is used.

REMEMBER

>> To help confuse you further, rules for naming books always have exceptions, such as Abbie Hoffman's *Steal This Book*. Remember, the goal is to get someone to notice your eBook — and pay for it.

Generating a cover

After you dream up the perfect title, another important-yet-difficult job is to apply that title to a festive book cover. Traditional publishers pay graphics artists way too little money to dream up professional covers. Even when the publishers chicken out and buy stock photos, a lot of thought goes into the selection — or at least one would hope.

If you want the best cover for your eTome, hire a professional graphics designer to create one. A designer is far better at the task than you would be. Otherwise, keep the cover simple and attractive.

>> eBook publishers require that you upload a graphics file for the cover. This image is separate from the document. Don't insert the image inside the manuscript's text, unless you really want to.

>> Check with the publisher to confirm the graphics file format. You can use whatever means available to create the image, but it must be uploaded in a specific format, such as JPEG.

WARNING

>> Most images on the Internet are copyrighted — even if the image doesn't say that it's copyrighted or have the © symbol, you still need permission to use it. *Fair use* doesn't apply to an eBook you plan on selling. Only when an image is flagged as being in the public domain can you use it.

>> A good source for public domain images is the government. NASA images are all public domain, though using such a photo may not help you design a cover for your 17th century romance novel.

REMEMBER

>> An AI tool, such as Copilot, can generate an image for you. Try typing "Create a cover image for this document."

Finding a publisher

Plenty of eBook publishers rim the online galaxy. That's good news! The only bad news is that many of them mandate exclusivity. So, my advice is to pick one publisher and stick with it.

Any quick search of the Internet provides you with a list of eBook publishers. Of the lot, I believe that Amazon Kindle Direct Publishing (KDP) is the best choice. Kindle offers a wide exposure, and Amazon is a Goliath of the online retail world.

Each eBook publisher has its own procedures for submitting your manuscript. The directions are found on the eBook publisher's web page, and they're written with the best intentions. Still, the process can be intimidating. Don't worry if you screw up: You're given plenty of opportunities to preview the book and even to unpublish it.

WARNING

» Amazon KDP requires exclusivity for a period of time, depending on which services you subscribe to. After that time, it's possible to submit your eBook to another publisher. Check with the terms of your Amazon publishing agreement before you do so.

» You do not need to pay a third party to prep and publish the book. Though some services might be worth it, offering marketing advice and such, most are completely unnecessary.

» One of the beauties of eBook publishing is that it's very easy to submit a new edition of your book. If readers find mistakes, you can fix them and upload a better eBook to replace the one currently online.

» Check with the eBook publisher to see in which formats it wants the material submitted. Word is capable of saving in a variety of formats, one of which is most likely what the publisher wants. Refer to Chapter 10 for information on saving a Word document in a special file format.

WHAT'S AN ISBN?

The International Standard Book Number is a unique code, 13 digits long, assigned to books based on the title, format, publisher, and country. An ISBN is optional for an eBook, which is assigned a sales number or SKU (Stock Keeping Unit or "skew") by the eBook publisher.

If you plan to publish a lot of eBooks, you can obtain ISBN numbers, though it's not necessary. In the United States, ISBNs are obtained from R. R. Bowker (www.bowker.com). A registration fee is involved, and the ISBN numbers cost money.

Previewing the final eBook

Before you click the big Publish button and offer your efforts to digital libraries across the land, I strongly recommend that you download a preview of your eBook. All eBook publishers offer this feature: On the web page where you describe and submit your document, an option is available to preview or even download the final product.

To view the eBook preview, you need eBook reader software. You can use a preview program, such as the Kindle Previewer for Amazon KDP. Use this software to see how your book looks in digital form.

A preview program gives you the book's big picture. Ensure that the chapter breaks look okay. Check the layout and graphics, if you dared do anything fancy. You're not proofreading at this point, though it doesn't hurt.

If you see anything awry, fix it in the original Word document. Then follow the steps to convert and upload the eBook manuscript. This course of action is perfectly okay; not until you click the Publish button is the book available for purchase. Even then, the book may require approval by the publisher.

Setting the price

No one is an expert at determining what a book should cost. A book is worth what someone will pay for it, and no one can tell you what that price can be.

Generally speaking, an eBook is priced lower than its real-world copy. A $39 hardcover mystery novel may have an electronic cousin that retails for $14. How this price is calculated is probably witchcraft. I just don't know.

Your best guess is to look at your competition to see what the prices are. This comparison gives you an idea. The goal isn't to get rich by selling one book, but rather to make a steady stream of money by selling many books at a reasonable price.

Related to the price, of course, is what you get paid. For each eBook sold, you receive a portion of the price or *royalty*. The eBook publisher offers various royalty rates, depending on which services are available and on other items, such as your book's size. Foreign royalty rates are different from domestic.

WARNING

>> Beware of pricing a book too low! Consumers often believe that a low price implies low quality.

>> In most cases, taxes on foreign sales are paid by the publisher. In the United States, you are responsible for reporting your royalties as income on your taxes.

Marketing your eBook

I'm sure that eBook publishing has met with a lot of success for many authors, but take with a grain of salt the stories of people who've made a fortune. Few people stroll out of the eBook casino winning big with one pull at the lucky slot machine. Most successful eBook authors arrived at their position because of one word: marketing.

Welcome to the final phase of eBook publishing, the one where pretty much every author fails. That failure makes sense: Authors write, marketers market. Some authors are great at marketing (and lousy at writing, but that's another story), but most don't give it another thought.

Give marketing another thought.

You must push and sell your book. The publisher might have tools available to assist you, or services you can subscribe to. The onus is on you, however, to make the effort and let people know about your book. You can advertise, make the circuit attending self-publishing conferences, speak at libraries, and just do the whole PR routine.

TIP

>> One of the first pieces of marketing regarding your eBook, whether you know it or not, is the title. Refer to the earlier section "Titling your tome."

>> Always end your eBook manuscript with a list of your other titles — especially links to them. Place that page near the end of your eBook. Set the page title style so that it appears in the table of contents.

5

Document Automation

IN THIS CHAPTER

» **Understanding automatic text**

» **Correcting typos automatically**

» **Creating a new AutoCorrect entry**

» **Controlling AutoCorrect's changes**

» **Using AutoFormat**

» **Disabling AutoFormat features**

» **Adding an AutoText building block**

Chapter **20**

AutoCorrect, AutoText, and AutoFormat

Word tries its best to help you with the writing task. When you goof, mistakes are corrected. When it looks like you meant to type a special character, Word inserts the proper character for you. Formatted lists and paragraphs can also appear automatically. Some of these features save a lot of time, and some you may find get in your way. Together, these tools form what I call the Autos.

Know Your Autos

As you can infer from the chapter's title, Microsoft Word hosts several features that use the name Auto. They're all automatic, they serve comparable functions, and they have annoyingly similar names. Here's the Big Picture:

AutoText: Once a feature in Word prior to 2016, it's now called a Building Block. AutoText allowed snippets of text to be inserted instantly.

AutoComplete: Another old Word feature, it has been replaced by AutoCorrect.

AutoCorrect: This function corrects common typos and capitalizations.

AutoText Building Blocks: This function lets you insert preset chunks of text. It's the descendant of the old AutoText feature.

AutoFormat: This feature lets you format your document in one operation. It's a holdover from earlier versions of Word. The AutoFormat command isn't even found on the Ribbon. I list it here because it's easily confused with the AutoFormat As You Type command.

AutoFormat As You Type: This function deals with formatting text, applying similar paragraph styles (bullets, numbers, and so on), and converting individual characters to their proper equivalents (such as ½ for 1/2).

Don't let yourself become confused over the sloppy way the Auto commands are organized, how they seem to overlap, and which are no longer available. If you've used Word for any length of time, you might find this confusion oddly comfortable. As a consolation, most of these commands are headquartered in the same dialog box, as illustrated in Figure 20-1.

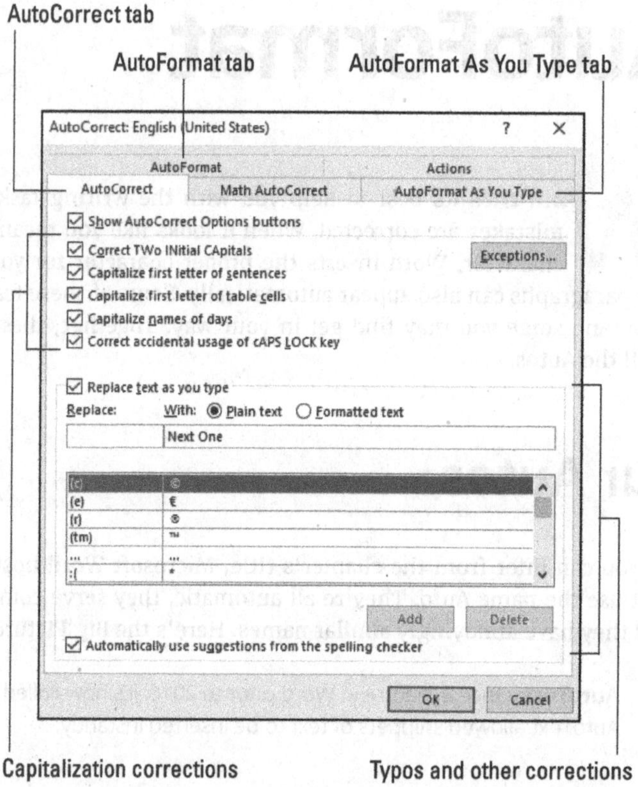

AutoCorrect tab

AutoFormat tab   AutoFormat As You Type tab

FIGURE 20-1:
Auto Central
in Word.

Capitalization corrections   Typos and other corrections

To summon the AutoCorrect dialog box, shown in Figure 20-1, follow these steps:

1. **Click the File tab.**

2. **Choose Options.**

   The Word Options dialog box appears.

3. **Choose Proofing from the left side of the Word Options dialog box.**

4. **On the right side of the dialog box, click the AutoCorrect Options button.**

   Behold the AutoCorrect dialog box.

 The remainder of this chapter covers specific items in the AutoCorrect dialog box. As a shortcut, look for the AutoFormat Options or AutoCorrect Options icon in your text. You can quickly access specific AutoFormat or AutoCorrect settings from this icon.

» The Math AutoCorrect tab provides an extension to the AutoCorrect entries — specifically, to conjure mathematical symbols. If you understand symbols such as ∩ and ≅, click the tab to review its repertoire.

» Options on the Actions tab are normally disabled. They provide extra commands on Word's right-click shortcut menu, on the Additional Actions submenu. For example, you can right-click on a date and choose Additional Actions ⇨ Schedule a Meeting.

**TECHNICAL
STUFF**

» The biggest question most people ask is why are two AutoFormat tabs available in the AutoComplete dialog box? The AutoFormat tab refers to manually formatting your document for a command that no one uses. The AutoFormat As You Type command is more useful.

AutoCorrect the Boo-Boos

Word's AutoCorrect feature supplements the spell check proofing tool. Basically, AutoCorrect lets you avoid the shame of having to proof certain words in your text. When AutoCorrect is active, common typos and capitalization errors are corrected automatically.

Working with AutoCorrect capitalization settings

It's not that you don't know how or when to capitalize words. No, the problem is that sneaky Shift key. When you're too late or too early with that key, or you dawdle too long, you create capitalization typos. The word may be flagged as misspelled, though it's just the uppercase/lowercase letters that are different.

The common capitalization errors appear in the center of the AutoCorrect dialog box, AutoCorrect tab (refer to Figure 20-1). These five settings cover the most common Shift key boo-boos.

To turn one or more of the capitalization settings on or off, visit the AutoCorrect dialog box as described in the preceding section. On the AutoCorrect tab, remove or add check marks by the options you want to deactivate or activate, respectively.

For example, if you don't want the first letter of a sentence capitalized in your poetry, remove the check mark by the option Capitalize First Letter of Sentences.

Click the Exceptions button in the dialog box to direct AutoCorrect *not* to capitalize certain words. For example, AutoCorrect doesn't interpret the period after a common abbreviation as the end of a sentence. That's because those abbreviations are listed in the AutoCorrect Exceptions dialog box, shown in Figure 20-2.

Type a word to add   Add the word

FIGURE 20-2:
Exceptions to
AutoCorrect's
capitalization
rules.   Abbreviations

You can add your own abbreviations to the list: Type the text into the box (refer to Figure 20-2) and click the Add button.

The INitial CAps tab lets you set exceptions for proper words that require more than one initial capital letter. Click the tab to see one example: IDs, short for identifications.

The Other Corrections tab allows you to type any old jumble of lowercase and capital letters and add each word to a list. AutoCorrect then ignores those words. My advice is to create this list as you work on your document. If the capitalization IdaHO is required in your text, add that exact word as an exception in the Auto-Correct Exceptions dialog box.

Replacing typos

Perhaps AutoCorrect's most useful feature (after fixing capitalization errors) is replacing common typos with correct versions. These corrections include converting common text abbreviations into their appropriate symbols, such as (C) into the copyright symbol, ©.

Typos and symbols are listed in the AutoCorrect dialog box, AutoCorrect tab as illustrated in Figure 20-1. When you type one of the items on the left side of the list, Word automatically inserts the proper text on the right — providing that the Replace Text As You Type command is active.

To ensure that the AutoCorrect replacement feature is active, or to add another word to correct, obey these steps:

1. **Summon the AutoCorrect dialog box as described in the earlier section Know Your Autos.**

2. **Ensure that the AutoCorrect tab is forward.**

3. **Ensure that there's a check mark by the option Replace Text As You Type.**

   When the check mark is present, the feature is active.

4. **In the Replace text box, type the word you frequently mistype.**

   For example, **braek**.

5. **In the With box, type the word to replace the mistyped word.**

   Such as **break**.

6. **Click the Add button.**

7. **Click OK to close the AutoCorrect dialog box, and then OK to close the Word Options dialog box.**

You can repeat Steps 4 through 6 to add all your favorite typos. Whenever the word you specify in Step 4 is typed, the word you enter for Step 5 replaces it automatically.

Undoing an AutoCorrect change

Every time AutoCorrect fixes capitalization, inserts a proper symbol, or corrects a typo, a small symbol appears in the document's text. You may not see it, so point the mouse at any word that AutoCorrect has changed. Upon success, a small, blue rectangle appears in the text, as illustrated in Figure 20-3.

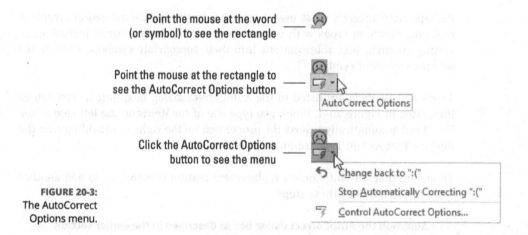

Point the mouse at the word (or symbol) to see the rectangle

Point the mouse at the rectangle to see the AutoCorrect Options button

AutoCorrect Options

Click the AutoCorrect Options button to see the menu

Change back to ":("
Stop Automatically Correcting ":("
Control AutoCorrect Options...

FIGURE 20-3:
The AutoCorrect Options menu.

Point the mouse at the rectangle to see the AutoCorrect Options button, also shown in Figure 20-3. Click the button to reveal a menu, which allows you to do one of three things:

Undo: Choose the Change Back To command to revert the change. You see the original word or characters listed in the menu, such as :(, shown in Figure 20-3.

Stop correcting: Choose the Stop Automatically Correcting command to remove the word or symbol from the AutoCorrect list. If you select this command, the selected item won't be corrected again, not in any document.

Visit the AutoCorrect dialog box: Choose the last command on the menu to visit the AutoCorrect dialog box, and the AutoCorrect tab.

TIP

If you find yourself becoming annoyed with all the automatic corrections, disable the AutoCorrect Replace As You Type feature. Heed these directions:

1. Click the File tab and choose Options.

2. Choose Proofing, and then click the AutoCorrect Options button.

3. In the AutoCorrect dialog box, on the AutoCorrect tab, remove the check mark by the item Replace As You Type.

4. Click OK to close the AutoCorrect dialog box.

5. Click OK to close the Word Options dialog box.

If you merely want to disable the AutoCorrect Options button (refer to Figure 20-3), follow Steps 1 and 2, but in Step 3 remove the check mark by the option Show AutoCorrect Options Buttons.

>> The rectangle (refer to the top of Figure 20-3) appears only when you point the mouse at a corrected word. It sticks with the altered word until you close the document. When you open the document again, all AutoCorrect terms are fixed and cannot be reverted.

>> The AutoCorrect Options button is nearly identical to the AutoFormat Options button. See the later section "Undoing an AutoFormat change."

AutoFormat As You Type

Word's AutoFormat feature automatically applies character formats and paragraph styles to your text. It works similarly to AutoCorrect in that AutoFormat makes its changes on the fly. But of the two features, AutoFormat causes users more woe. It tends to make assumptions you may not agree with. That's okay! You can cheerfully disable this feature.

Reviewing the AutoFormat options

The AutoFormat function hosts a suite of routines, some of which might fall under the category of AutoCorrect, but geniuses at Microsoft placed them under Auto-Format instead. The AutoFormat routines include:

Replace As You Type: This feature converts some characters and text sequences into other characters, such as -- (two hyphens) into an — (em dash), or 1/2 into ½. Word also creates hyperlinks for web page addresses and network paths.

Apply As You Type: This feature converts text into formatted elements, including bulleted lists, numbered lists, tables, and so on. This is the AutoFormat feature most people find annoying.

Automatically As You Type: This feature copies special paragraph formatting to subsequent paragraphs, such as when you set paragraph indents or create a hanging indent list.

A summary of specific options for these features appears at the end of this section.

The AutoCorrect dialog box, on the AutoFormat As You Type tab, lists all the specifics for each of these categories, as illustrated in Figure 20-4.

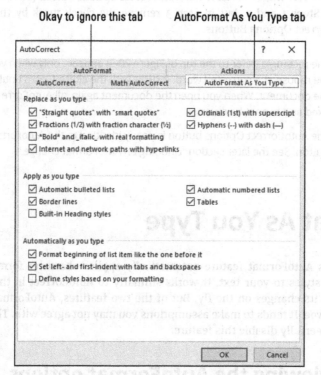

FIGURE 20-4:
The AutoFormat features.

To display the AutoCorrect dialog box, and the AutoFormat As You Type tab, follow these steps:

1. Click the File tab and choose Options.

2. Choose Proofing on the left side of the Word Options dialog box.

3. On the right side of the dialog box, click the AutoCorrect Options button.

4. **Click the AutoFormat As You Type tab.**

Don't click the AutoFormat tab. It shows similar items, but they apply to the all-at-once AutoFormat command.

The actions listed in the dialog box affect text as you type. If something annoys you, which is frequently the case, you can undo the action or disable the feature. See the next section.

>> Smart quotes are curved, "like this," as opposed to "like this." The apostrophe and single-quote characters are also affected by the Smart Quotes option.

>> Not all fractions are affected by the Fractions setting. Only specific fractions feature single characters, such as ½ and ¾. Other fractions you can create manually: Superscript the nominator and subscript the denominator.

>> The dash (—) is known as an em dash. Its width is the same as the letter M in whichever font you're using. The keyboard shortcut for this character is Alt+Ctrl+- (hyphen).

>> An automatic bulleted list is created whenever you start a line with an asterisk and a tab. Press the Enter key at the end of the paragraph to apply the bulleted list format.

>> To create an automatic numbered list, start the paragraph with a number and a tab.

>> To create automatic borderlines, type three hyphens on a line and press the Enter key.

>> As an example of the Format Beginning of List feature, if you apply bold formatting to a word set aside in a hanging indented list, subsequent paragraphs automatically apply the bold format to the first word.

>> The Set Left- and First-Indent with Tabs and Backspaces feature converts a tab at the start of a paragraph into a first-line indent format. This format is applied to all subsequent paragraphs.

Undoing an AutoFormat change

The AutoFormat command can be subtle, such as when straight quotes are converted to curly quotes, or it can be overt, such as when an automatic numbered list is created for you.

For AutoFormat's Replace As You Type features, undoing a conversion works similarly to undoing an AutoCorrect change: See the earlier section "Undoing an AutoCorrect change." Also refer to Figure 23-3, which illustrates how the process works. The commands on the menu are subtly different, yet their actions are similar.

For more major text adjustments, you see the AutoFormat Options button, illustrated in Figure 20-5.

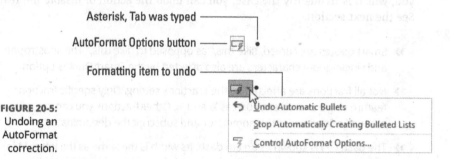

Asterisk, Tab was typed

AutoFormat Options button

Formatting item to undo

Undo Automatic Bullets

Stop Automatically Creating Bulleted Lists

Control AutoFormat Options...

FIGURE 20-5:
Undoing an
AutoFormat
correction.

In Figure 20-5, I typed an asterisk and then a tab to create a bulleted list. Word's AutoFormat As You Type feature converted the asterisk into a bullet character (big dot) and formatted the paragraph with a hanging indent. To undo this formatting, immediately follow these steps:

1. **Click the AutoFormat Options button.**

You must be quick with the click. If you continue to type or wait, the AutoFormat Options button (illustrated in Figure 20-5) vanishes.

2. **Choose the Undo command.**

The Undo command name is followed by whatever formatting was applied, such as Automatic Bullets shown in Figure 20-5.

You can also just press Esc after AutoFormat offends you, but you must be quick.

TIP

If you detest automatic paragraph numbering, choose the option Stop Automatically Creating Numbered Lists. This command directly dispenses with the feature.

Instant Typing with AutoText Building Blocks

Once upon a time, Word featured some Auto- tools that were summarily dismissed back around 2016. Two of these tools were rather popular with advanced Word users: AutoText and AutoComplete. In an effort to keep everyone confused, the AutoComplete tool was reinstated as something called an AutoText building block, which also kinda works like AutoText. It's a useful typing feature, but not one that's apparent or obvious.

Creating an AutoText building block

The AutoText building block is a typing assistant. You create building blocks for text you frequently type, such as your name, address, apologies, and so on. After you type the first few letters of an existing building block, Word pops up the Auto-Text building block bubble, as shown in Figure 20-6. Press the Enter key to have the text inserted automatically into your document.

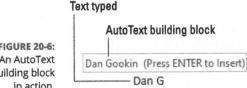

Text typed

AutoText building block

Dan Gookin (Press ENTER to Insert)
Dan G

Unlike the old AutoComplete function, the AutoText building block repertoire doesn't come stocked with common phrases. If you want to use this feature, you must get busy creating your own entries. Follow these directions:

1. **Type the text you want to stick into an AutoText building block.**

   For example, your name, street name, business, or any text you regularly type.

2. **Select the text.**

   If you want the building block to include the Enter keystroke at the end of a line, ensure that it's selected. If not, just select up to the last letter of the word you want in the building block.

3. **On the Insert tab, in the Text group, click the Quick Parts button.**

4. **Choose AutoText ⇨ Save Selection to AutoText Gallery.**

   The Create New Building Block dialog box appears. The options set are what you need to add the text selected in Step 2 as a building block. If you're using a specific template, however, ensure that you choose Normal.dotm from the Save In menu to ensure that the next building block is available to all documents in Word.

5. **Click OK.**

   The selected text is added to the list of building blocks.

To try out your invention, start a new line of text in a document and type the first few letters or words that you set as an AutoText building block. When you see the bubble appear (refer to Figure 20-6), press the Enter key to insert the text.

TIP

>> Word's predictive text feature pretty much eliminates any advantage that an AutoText building block once had. Only rarely — such as with my own name — have I needed to create a building block as opposed to relying upon Word's predictive text feature.

>> The keyboard shortcut for a building block is to press the F3 key. This keyboard shortcut works even when you've typed only a few characters.

>> You can select multiple lines of text as a building block. For example, your return address.

WARNING

>> Keep the building block names unique, as well as the starting text for a building block. For example, if you create two building blocks that start with the same text, neither ever appears when you type text.

Reviewing your building blocks

The building blocks you create are saved with a template file. If you don't choose a specific template, they're saved in the Normal.dotm template and made available to all your Word documents.

To review the building blocks that you've created, as well as other automatic document elements, you must summon the Building Blocks Organizer dialog box: On the Insert tab, in the Text group, click the Quick Parts button and choose Building Blocks Organizer.

AutoText building blocks appear at the top of the list. Other document elements are found in the list as well, which includes most of Word's built-in galleries.

You cannot edit your AutoText building blocks, but you can remove them: Click to select a building block in the Building Blocks Organizer dialog box, and then click the Delete button. You can then re-create the building block as discussed in the preceding section.

Close the Building Blocks Organizer dialog box when you're done poking around.

IN THIS CHAPTER

» **Understanding fields**

» **Adding fields to your text**

» **Refreshing field contents**

» **Editing a field**

» **Using page number fields**

» **Exploring date-and-time fields**

» **Creating document info fields**

» **Using a field to repeat text**

Chapter **21**

Document Fields

ext written in a word processor isn't the same as text "written in stone," but it's similar. After you type a line or paragraph, the text is fixed. To change its contents, you must edit the line. To use a nerd term, the text is *static*.

But Word also features *dynamic* text, or text that changes based on conditions in your document. This text is provided by inserting fields, or special text elements that change given various conditions. You can use fields to automate your document and keep information fresh as you edit and add text.

Field Philosophy

Even when you're unfamiliar with fields, you may have used them without knowing. For example, fields are used in the mail merge operation. They're found in Word's preset headers and footers. Many of Word's document reference features, such as a table of content, appear as fields. Even so, few mortal Word users bother with fields. As evidence, I offer that the Field command button isn't the most obvious thing to find on the Ribbon.

Inserting a field

All of Word's fields are accessed from the Field dialog box. To summon this dialog box, and insert a field into your document, follow these generic steps:

1. Position the insertion point at the spot in your document where you want the field's text to appear.

The field is inserted like any other text. It can go inside the body of the document, into a header or footer, into a text box, or anywhere. Its contents appear as text along with other text, but the contents can change.

2. On the Insert tab, in the Text group, click the Quick Parts command button and choose Field from the menu.

The Field dialog box appears, as shown in Figure 21-1. It's a bit overwhelming, but it works from left to right.

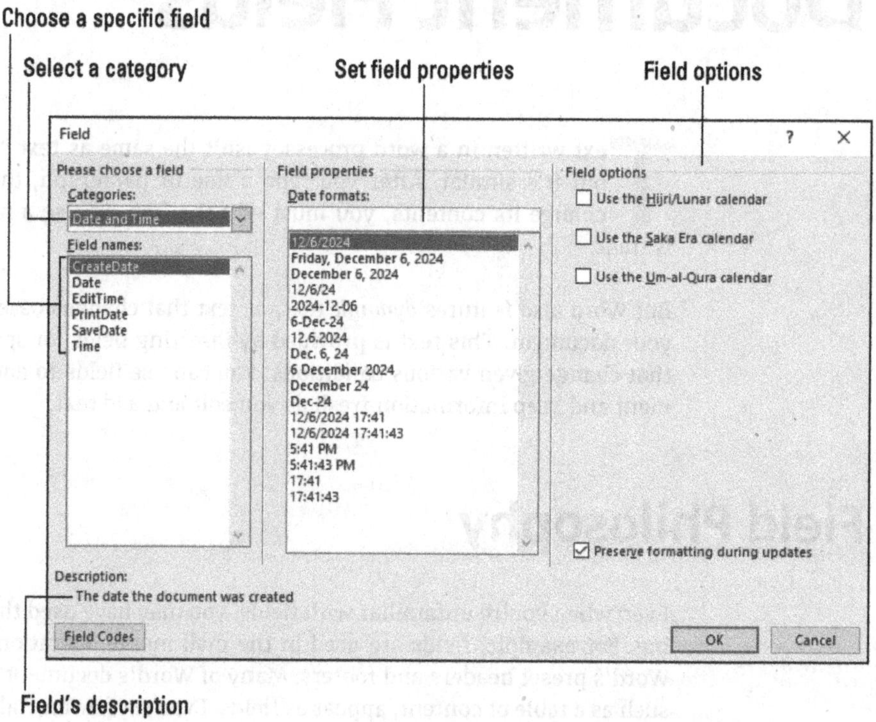

Choose a specific field

Select a category   Set field properties   Field options

FIGURE 21-1:
The Field
dialog box.   Field's description

3. **Choose the field.**

   Choose a category from the Categories list. Then select a specific field from the Field Names list.

   Use the Description text to help understand what information or content the specific field represents.

4. **Select the field properties.**

   Field properties don't appear for every field. In Figure 21-1, the date format is shown as a field property.

5. **Set field options.**

   As with field properties, not every field sports options.

6. **Click OK to insert the field into your document.**

   The field's text appears.

When a field is selected, its text background becomes gray. This highlight confirms that the text is a field. Although you can try to edit the field's contents, they are set dynamically and will be reset after your failed editing attempt.

To remove a field, select it and then press the Delete or Backspace key twice. This extra key press reminds you that you're removing a field and not static text.

Working with fields behind the scenes

Word's fields have two sides: a shiny, pretty side and a dark underside. Mostly you see the pretty side, which is the dynamic text the field generates — for example, the date field shown at the top of Figure 21-2.

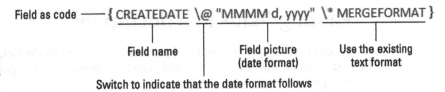

Field as text —— March 18, 2016

Field as code —— { CREATEDATE \@ "MMMM d, yyyy" * MERGEFORMAT }

Field name

Field picture (date format)

Use the existing text format

Switch to indicate that the date format follows

FIGURE 21-2: Two faces to a field.

The ugly side has value in that you can access the field's innards. In Figure 21-2, you see the field's internal workings. These commands tell Word what to display as the field's text and how this information is to be presented.

To switch between the field text and field codes, right-click the field and choose the command Toggle Field Codes. The field changes to shows its ugly guts (refer to the bottom of Figure 21-2) or to text, the opposite of its current state.

>> When visible, field codes appear between curly brackets. All fields start with a code name, written in all caps. The name is followed by an optional switch, which is the backslash and another character, such as \@, shown in Figure 21-2. An optional field property appears in double quotes. Any further options appear after the field property, before the final curly bracket.

>> Yes, you can edit the field's secret internal codes — but don't. I recommend using the Field dialog box instead, as described in the preceding section. Right-click the field and choose the command Edit Field as a shortcut.

Updating a field

Fields are up-to-date when they're created. As you work with your document, the field's content becomes stale. For example, a reference to page 4 might jiggle around to page 3, but the field still shows the number 4. To address this issue, fields must be updated.

To manually update a field, right-click on the field text and choose the Update Field command. The field is generated anew, reflecting current document conditions.

>> Some of Word's fields update when you close and reopen the document, but most don't. See the next section for tips on locating fields to update them.

>> To ensure that fields update before you print a document, click the File tab and choose the Options command to display the Word Options dialog box. Choose Print. In the Display category, ensure that a check mark is set by the option Update Fields Before Printing.

Finding fields in a document

Fields look like text — until they're selected. To reveal all the fields in your document, press the Alt+F9 keyboard shortcut. Press Alt+F9 again to show the fields as text.

To hunt down fields without squinting your eyes, follow these steps:

1. Press the Alt+F9 keyboard shortcut.

All fields in your document are revealed.

2. Press Ctrl+F to summon the Navigation pane, with the Results tab forward.

3. Type ^d.

That's the caret character followed by a lowercase *D*. Don't type a period or press the Enter key.

Instantly, all fields in your document are highlighted.

4. Use the Previous and Next buttons (up and down chevrons) in the Navigation pane to browse the fields in your document.

Unlike other times the Find command is used, text previews for fields may not appear in the Navigation pane.

To stop searching, you can close the Navigation pane. Press Alt+F9 again to transform all the document's fields back into text.

TIP

» And now . . . the shortcut: To skip between fields in a document, press the F11 key. You're taken from one field to the next each time you press F11.

» Want to cycle from bottom to top in the document? Press Shift+F11.

Field Cookbook

Many of Word's commands stick a field in the document without you having to mess with the Field dialog box as described earlier in this chapter. For example, on the Insert tab, in the Header & Footer group, you find the Page Number command. It's a shortcut to the various page number fields, all preformatted and preset for you. On this same tab, in the Text group, is the Date & Time button, which is a shortcut to insert a specific date or time field.

The problem with the buttons on the Ribbon is that they don't provide much in the way of customization. Therefore, I present this Field Cookbook. It's chock full of field recipes you can use in your document to automate specific tasks and keep information fresh.

Inserting page number fields

Page number references frequently find themselves in a document's header or footer. These fields can also go into any part of a document. So if you want to write "This is page 316" on page 316, you can do so.

REMEMBER

>> If you're writing an eBook, use hyperlinks instead of page number references. See Chapter 19.

>> Also see Chapter 2 for more information on fields that go into document headers and footers.

The current page number

The quick way to add the current page number to your document is to use the Page Number command button on the Insert tab. For more control, set a field. Follow these steps:

1. **Position the insertion pointer to the spot where you want the page number to appear.**

It can be in the text, in a header or footer — anywhere text is allowed.

2. **On the Insert tab, in the Text group, choose Quick Parts ⇨ Field.**

The Field dialog box appears.

3. **In the Fields dialog box, choose Numbering from the Categories list.**

4. **Choose Page from the Field Names list.**

5. **Choose a page numbering format from the Format list.**

Choose numbering style, such as Roman Numerals for an introduction, or letters, or just plain numbers.

6. **Click OK.**

The page number appears in your document's text where you set the insertion pointer in Step 1.

REMEMBER

The page number field reflects the current page number when the field was first inserted. If the wrong number appears, update the field as described in the earlier section, "Updating a field."

Total page numbers

Your document's total page count is considered a document information field, not a numbering field.

1. **Position the insertion pointer at the spot where you want the document's total page count to appear.**

2. **On the Insert tab, in the Text group, click the Quick Parts button and choose Field from the menu.**

   The Field dialog box appears.

3. **Choose Document Information from the Category menu.**

4. **Select the NumPages field.**

5. **Choose the page number format.**

6. **Click OK to insert the field.**

The total page number figure frequently follows the current page number in a footer. For example: 8/20 for page 8 in a 20-page document.

Page numbers of other document elements

When you need to refer to another item in the document, such as a figure or quote, you can insert a page number reference to the item. The secret is to set a bookmark and then use the PageRef field to obtain the item's page number. Follow these steps:

1. **Bookmark the item you want to reference.**

   Refer to Chapter 17 for details on creating bookmarks.

2. **Click the insertion pointer where you want the page number reference to appear.**

3. **On the Insert tab, in the Text group, click Quick Parts and then choose Field.**

4. **Choose the Links and References category.**

5. **Select the PageRef field.**

6. **Choose the bookmark name you set in Step 1.**

7. **Click OK to insert the field.**

The field references the bookmark's page number no matter where that item ends up in the final document.

Using date-and-time fields

Word's date-and-time fields reference not only the current date and time but also dates and times related to your document. For example, you can insert today's date or a date field that updates to reflect the current date. My favorite date field is the print date. And of all Word's fields, the date-and-time fields are perhaps the easiest to edit directly.

>> The keyboard shortcut to insert the current date into your document is Alt+Shift+D.

>> The keyboard shortcut to insert the current time into your document is Alt+Shift+T.

>> They current date and current time keyboard shortcuts insert content controls, which work like fields, but they appear differently when you reveal their codes or click to select them. Still, they remain a handy way to get the date or time into a document. See Chapter 23 for more information on content controls.

TECHNICAL STUFF

>> If you want the user to choose a document date, use the Date Picker content control. See Chapter 23.

A custom date or time field

When the date and time keyboard shortcuts fail you, and you want more customization, insert a specific date and time field in your document. Heed these directions:

1. **Position the insertion pointer where you want the date or time (or both) field to appear.**

2. **On the Insert tab, in the Text group, choose Quick Parts ➪ Field.**

3. **From the Categories menu, choose Date and Time.**

   A series of options appear. Both Date and Time have the same formats, though the Date option features additional options.

4. **Choose Date or Time from the Field Names list.**

5. **Pluck out a format from the Field Properties area of the Field dialog box.**

   The variety of formats available demonstrates how this option is better than using other date/time shortcuts in Word.

6. **Click OK.**

The date or time (or both) field you insert is a field reflecting the current date/time in the format chosen in Step 5. This field reflects only the current date or time it was inserted. You can update the field (refer to the earlier section, "Updating a field"), but the field itself doesn't update after it's initially inserted.

The document print date

The PrintDate field is updated only when the document is printed. It's the field I use at the top of my letter template to ensure that the date on a letter always matches the date on which I print (and, hopefully, send) my correspondence.

To insert a PrintDate field, follow the steps from the preceding section, but in Step 4 choose the PrintDate field name.

Don't freak if the field looks like this: *XXX 0,0000*. This cryptic text reflects Word's confusion when the document hasn't yet been printed. Printing the document updates the field automatically. In fact, the next time you open the document, the previous print date appears. Print the document again, Word updates the field with the date the document was printed.

Adding document info fields

A *document info* field says something about the document itself, its name, the author's name, and similar information. In fact, just about every aspect of a document can be stuffed into a field.

The document's author name

You may not remember, but Word (or Office) asked your name when you first installed the program. It knows your full name and initials. You can summon that information in a field so that a heading or another tag in the document can read *Author: Dan Gookin* (or whatever your name is).

1. **Position the insertion pointer where you want the document's author name to appear.**

2. **On the Insert tab, in the Text group, click the Quick Parts button and choose Field.**

3. **From the Categories menu, choose User Information.**

4. **Select the UserName field.**

   You can choose a format, though the (none) format just sticks the name into the document as-is.

5. **Click OK.**

To review or reset your username in Word, open the Word Options dialog box: Click the File tab and choose Options. In the Word Options dialog box, in the General category, the User Name text box contains the author name associated with Word.

The document's filename

Your readers may not be thrilled to know the document's filename, but putting a filename in a header is something done often in professional and business environments. Follow these steps:

1. Click to place the insertion pointer where you want the document's filename to appear.

2. On the Insert tab, in the Text group, choose Quick Parts ➪ Field.

The Field dialog box appears.

3. From the Category menu, choose Document Information.

4. Select the FileName field.

5. Choose the text format from the Field Properties area of the dialog box.

6. If you want to include the full pathname, place a check mark by the Add Path to Filename option.

7. Click OK.

When editing a header or footer, you can insert a filename from the Header & Footer tab: In the Insert group, on the Document Info menu, choose the FileName command. This field is inserted into the header, though only the filename is shown. This limitation shows why I prefer to use the Field dialog box to insert a field directly.

>> To insert the document's file size, choose FileSize in Step 4. Choose a number format, and then specify whether the total should appear in kilobytes or megabytes.

>> Refer to Chapter 2 for more information on headers and footers.

Document editing information

When you need to justify your literary efforts, you can insert a field to show how long you've been working on a document.

1. **Summon the Field dialog box.**

   On the Insert tab, in the Text group, choose Quick Parts ⇨ Field.

2. **Select the Time and Date category.**

3. **Choose the EditTime field.**

4. **Ensure that you choose either (none) or 1, 2, 3 as the number format.**

   Any other format prevents the field from being rendered properly.

5. **Click OK.**

The EditTime field is expressed in minutes. So, if you've been working on the document for two hours, the value 120 appears.

The EditTime field represents the number of minutes a document is open on the screen. It doesn't indicate whether you were interacting with the document in any way. (Don't tell the boss.)

TECHNICAL STUFF

Echoing text in a field

One bit of magic you can pull with a field is the ability to echo text from one part of a document to another. So, if you have a pithy quote in your term paper that you keep referencing, you need not search and then copy and paste when the quote changes. Instead, update all the reference fields.

To use a field to echo a chunk of text, obey these directions:

1. **Select the chunk of text to echo.**

   Select all the text — whatever it is that you want repeated throughout your document. Keep in mind that the chunk of text you reference is the source. Edit this text and all the copycat fields update to reflect the changes.

   The next set of steps bookmark the text.

2. **On the Insert tab, in the Links group, click the Bookmark button.**

   The Bookmark dialog box appears.

3. **Type a bookmark name and then click the Add button.**

   Bookmark names cannot contain spaces.

4. **Position the insertion pointer where you want the text echo to appear.**

   This is the spot where you'll insert the reference field.

REMEMBER

5. **Still on the Insert tab, in the Text group, click the Quick Parts button and choose Field.**

The Field dialog box appears.

6. **From the Categories menu, choose Links and References.**

7. **From the Field Names list, choose Ref.**

8. **Choose the bookmark name (from Step 3) in the Field Properties list.**

9. **Click OK to insert the field.**

The text is echoed in your document.

The magic of the Ref field is that when you modify the original text, all the echoes are changed as well — but only after you update the fields. Refer to the earlier section "Finding fields in a document," which is the first step to updating. When you locate a Ref field, right-click it and choose Update Field to refresh its contents.

Refer to Chapter 17 for more information on setting bookmarks in Word.

IN THIS CHAPTER

» **Revealing the Developer tab**

» **Building a new macro**

» **Testing the macro**

» **Removing macros**

» **Creating macro shortcuts**

» **Saving a macro in a document**

» **Dealing with macro security**

Chapter **22**

The Big Macro Picture

A macro is a shortcut. It provides a way to do many routine tasks with a quick, single action. In Word, you can create a macro to automate a repetitive task, create a new command, or build a custom document. Macros can also offer full programming power to Word, though you don't need to be a programmer to get the most from Word's macros.

» Macros are task-oriented. In Word, macros perform a specific task or a sequence of tasks.

» Generally speaking, any time you find yourself repeating the same sequence of commands in Word, you can create a macro to automate the process.

» *Macro* is short for *macroinstruction.* That roughly translates as "a single directive that does multiple things." *Macro* is from the Greek word μακρο, for *long* or *large.*

TECHNICAL STUFF

» Word has featured a macro capability almost since its original version. The Macro command began as a simple keystroke/command recording and playback tool. With Word 97, Microsoft introduced Visual Basic for Applications (VBA). This programming language is still used in Word today.

Behold the Developer Tab

 The View tab sports a Macros group, in which you find the Macros button. You can use this button to build macros and do all sorts of wondrous things, but instead I recommend that you unveil the normally hidden Developer tab. Follow these steps:

1. Right-click anywhere on the Ribbon.

2. Choose the Customize Ribbon command.

The Word Options dialog box appears, with the Customize Ribbon portion shown automatically. On the right side of the dialog box appears a list of main tabs that can appear on the Ribbon.

3. Place a check mark by Developer.

The check mark ensures that the Developer tab is visible.

4. Click the OK button.

The Developer tab appears just to the left of the Help tab on the Ribbon.

The Developer tab contains commands for automating Word documents. It hosts several groups to assist in this process. The Code group is where you'll find the Macro commands, many more than appear on the View tab. Keep the Developer tab open while you read this chapter.

>> To hide the Developer tab, repeat the steps in this section, but in Step 3 remove the check mark.

>> I keep the Developer tab open all the time, not just for macros but also to access document protection and template commands.

>> See Chapter 25 for information on building your own custom tab on the Ribbon.

WARNING

>> The tabs shown in the Word Options dialog box appear on the Ribbon automatically when needed. For example, the Design and Layout tabs appear whenever a table is selected. The Format tab appears whenever a drawing object is selected. You don't need to mess with the check marks by these tabs to show or hide their contents.

Word Macro 101

Macros are immensely useful in that they help automate tedious tasks. They can be intimidating because of the VBA programming language, which isn't the friendliest thing to understand. Even the notion of a Developer tab implies a level of knowledge and sophistication to the process.

Ignore all that!

Instead, concentrate on the roots of a typical Word macro, which is the ability to record keystrokes and command choices and just about anything else you normally do in Word.

Understanding macros

At its simplest level, a *macro* is a series of commands or actions in Word, stacked together so that they run one after the other. Macros can become more complex, of course, but I offer that most useful macros are simple.

The process of creating a macro works like this:

1. **Know what you want the macro to do.**

    Look for repetitive tasks, processes you repeat often, or something you do where Word lacks a specific command. For example, you routinely must format the first three words of a paragraph in bold text. You must do this for many paragraphs in the document. This kind of repetitive task is what a macro can make easier.

2. **Start recording the macro.**

    You give the macro a name and select other options before recording starts.

3. **Perform the desired actions.**

    When recording starts, all your keystrokes, command choices, and other actions are memorized by Word and stored in the macro.

4. **Stop recording.**

    The macro is saved and made available to run again.

How you run the macro depends on how you assigned it when the macro was created: All macros can be run directly, as covered in the later section "Running a macro." For more direct access, you can assign the macro to a command button on the Ribbon or to a keyboard shortcut. Later sections in this chapter discuss the details.

>> Macros can be saved in the current document, in the Normal template, or in a specific template. You determine the location when the macro is created.

>> Most of the time, I recommend saving the macro in the Normal template, which is the best and simplest option.

Recording a macro

If you've never created a macro, a good way to start is to create a simple keystroke macro. This type of macro records some keyboard commands for quick playback when the macro is run.

As an example, the following steps create a macro that adds the bold text attribute to the next three words after the insertion pointer:

1. **Ensure that you are editing a document that contains text and that the document has been saved.**

   You need some text to practice on to create any text-modification macro. If you need some throwaway text to use, on a new line, type **=rand()** and press the Enter key.

2. **Position the insertion pointer in the document.**

   You can't assume anything when you create a macro, but for this example, set the insertion pointer at the start of a paragraph.

3. **Click the Developer tab.**

   Refer to the earlier section "Behold the Developer Tab" if you don't see it.

 4. **In the Code group, click the Record Macro button.**

   The Record Macro dialog box appears, as illustrated in Figure 22-1. At minimum, you need to name the macro. The other features of the dialog box are discussed elsewhere in this chapter.

5. **Type the macro's name.**

   Macro names cannot contain spaces; use the underscore character instead, as shown in Figure 22-1. When you forget this rule, Word barks at you — but only after Step 6.

   You can immediately assign the macro to a command button or keyboard shortcut in the Record Macro dialog box. Examples are provided later in this chapter.

   The Save Macro In menu selects where Word stores the macro's code. You can save in the current document, in a specific template, or in the Normal template. When you choose the Normal template, the macro is available to all Word documents, as shown in Figure 22-1.

Macro shortcut options

No spaces in the macro name

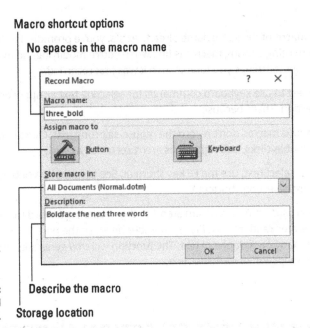

FIGURE 22-1:
The Record
Macro dialog box.

Describe the macro

Storage location

6. **Click the OK button to start recording the macro.**

   Word records your actions. The mouse pointer changes to show the cassette tape icon (which is a throwback to the 1990s) to remind you.

   The changed mouse pointer is pretty much your visual clue that a macro is recording, though you might also see the Macro Recording item on the status bar. It appears as an empty square, the Stop icon. Refer to Chapter 15 for information about the status bar.

   TIP

7. **Type the keystrokes or click the commands to save in the macro.**

   In the example of making three words boldface, type the following:

   a. Press the F8 key to enter Selection mode.

   b. Press Ctrl+→ three times to select three words.

   c. Press Ctrl+B to make the text bold.

8. **On the Developer tab, in the Code group, click the Stop Recording button.**

   The macro is saved.

The next thing to do is to test the macro. See the next section.

>> It's important to know where the insertion pointer needs to be when you record a macro and when you run the macro. If you're creating a macro only for yourself, the position isn't an issue. Just keep in mind where the insertion pointer needs to be; otherwise, the macro may not do what you want.

>> If a macro of the same name already exists, you're prompted to overwrite it. Overwriting existing macros is fine when you're modifying the macro to account for things you forgot when it was first recorded.

>> It's best to use keyboard commands for selecting text as opposed to mouse-selection. That's because:

REMEMBER

• Word macros don't record the mouse selecting text. Clicks in the text, double-clicks, and right-clicks aren't recorded as well.

• To select text, use the F8 key shortcut. See the nearby sidebar, "The F8 key text-selection shortcut."

TECHNICAL STUFF

>> The =rand() command (from Step 1 in this section) is a Word function that generates random text. Place a number between the parentheses to generate that many paragraphs of text. The function =lorem() generates the traditional "Lorem ipsum" placeholder text.

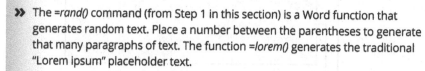

TIP

THE F8 KEY TEXT-SELECTION SHORTCUT

Of the many forgettable-yet-useful function keys that Word uses is F8. It's the Extend Selection key, which activates keyboard text selection.

Press the F8 key once to enter extend selection mode. At this point, use any of the cursor keys to select text in any direction. You can also type a letter to select text up to the next instance of that letter.

Press the F8 key twice to select the current word.

Press the F8 key thrice to select the current sentence.

Press the F8 key four times (frice?) to select the current paragraph.

Press the F8 key five times to select all text in the document. The Ctrl+A keyboard shortcut also selects all the text.

Press the Esc key to cancel the F8 key's text selection, or manipulate the block to exit extend selection mode.

Running a macro

The power of a macro lies in its capability to issue multiple commands at once. To make this power useful, macros are traditionally assigned to keyboard shortcuts or a command button. Even so, all macros can be run from the Macros dialog box. To run a macro in this manner, heed these directions:

1. If necessary, position the insertion pointer so that the macro can proceed.

Some sophisticated macros may set the insertion pointer automatically. For simple macros, you may have to click the mouse at a specific spot in the text, such as the start of a paragraph for the *three_bold* macro created in the preceding section.

2. On the Developer tab, in the Code group, click the Macros button.

The Macros dialog box appears, as shown in Figure 22-2. It lists all available macros, including those in the Normal template as well as any found in the current document or associated with the current document's template.

Available macros

Selected macro

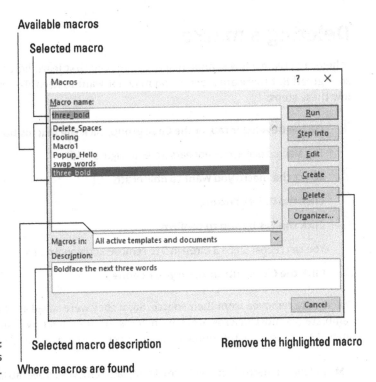

FIGURE 22-2: The Macros dialog box.

Selected macro description

Remove the highlighted macro

Where macros are found

3. **Select a macro to run.**

For example, the *three_bold* macro.

4. **Click the Run button.**

The dialog box vanishes. Word passes control to the macro, which does whatever magic it's supposed to do.

Most macros work quickly. In fact, it's difficult to tell that anything is going on, other than you witness the results of the macro's actions. Even so, you can't do anything with your document while the macro runs.

After the macro runs, you can continue working with the document: Write, save, edit, format, or do whatever.

>> A macro stops automatically after its final instruction.

>> If a macro runs amok, press Ctrl+Break to stop it. (Break and Pause share the same key on most keyboards, located above the cursor control keys.)

Deleting a macro

It helps to create a few sample macros when you first learn how they work. Doing so is great! But these are macros you may not want to keep. To remove them, follow these steps:

1. **On the Developer tab, in the Code group, click the Macros button.**

The Macros dialog box appears (refer to Figure 22-2).

2. **Select the macro you want to obliterate.**

3. **Click the Delete button.**

4. **Click the Yes button to confirm.**

You can repeat Steps 3 through 5 to remove additional macros.

5. **Click the Close button when you're done.**

Macros are removed from their source. So, if they were saved as part of the Normal template (as most macros are), the macros are no longer available in any document. Otherwise, macros found in a single document are removed from that source.

>> Deleting a macro from the Normal template removes its availability from all documents in Word.

REMEMBER

>> A deleted macro may still sport a dead command button or an invalid keyboard shortcut. See the next section for information on macro shortcuts. See Chapter 25 for information on removing dead command buttons and invalid keyboard shortcuts.

Quick Macro Access

All macros available to the current document are listed in the Macros dialog box. If you used this dialog box to run macros as covered earlier in this chapter, you may have noticed something: The process is slow. Two options are available to make accessing a macro more convenient. The first is to assign the macro to a Quick Access toolbar button. The second is to assign the macro to a keyboard shortcut.

Assigning a macro to a Quick Access toolbar button

A convenient way to access your macros is to place them as buttons on the Quick Access toolbar, found in the upper left corner of the Word program window. In Figure 22-3 you see a macro button on the toolbar. You can add this button as you build the macro or assign it after the macro is created.

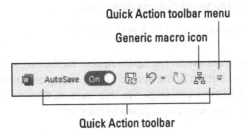

FIGURE 22-3:
Macro icons as
Quick Access
toolbar buttons.

Quick Action toolbar menu

Generic macro icon

Quick Action toolbar

If you've already created a macro, follow these steps to assign it to a Quick Access toolbar button:

1. **Click the menu button to the right of the Quick Access toolbar and choose More Commands.**

    The Word Options dialog box appears, with the Quick Access Toolbar screen displayed.

2. **From the Choose Commands From menu, select Macros.**

   A list of all macros available to the current document appears.

3. **Select the macro you want to add to the toolbar and click the Add button.**

   The macro is copied to the list of items currently on the Quick Access toolbar, shown on the right side of the dialog box.

   Use the up or down buttons to move the command, changing its order on the toolbar.

TIP

   At this point, the macro is set on the Quick Access toolbar, but you might want to spiff it up with a new name and possibly a new icon.

4. **With the macro selected on the right side of the dialog box, click the Modify button.**

   The Modify Button dialog box appears, showing a host of icons.

5. **Choose a new, better icon for the macro.**

   Your choices are rather limited, but I'm certain you can find something more interesting than the generic Macro icon (shown in the margin).

6. **Type a shortcut name for the macro.**

   The macro's full, technical name appears in the Display Name box. Type a better name to appear in a pop-up bubble when you point the mouse at the macro's button on the Quick Access toolbar.

7. **Click the OK button to lock in the new icon and name.**

8. **Click OK to close the Word Options dialog box.**

   The icon is accessible from the Quick Action toolbar.

To assign a macro as a button on the Quick Access toolbar when the macro is created, click the Hammer button in the Record Macro dialog box (refer to Figure 22-1). Then follow along with Steps 3 through 7 in this section, though in Step 3 the macro you're creating is the only one that appears in the list.

>> When you modify the Quick Access toolbar, you're making that change for all your documents.

REMEMBER

>> If you delete a macro, any buttons you've assigned remain on the Quick Access toolbar. To remove the orphaned buttons, right-click on the button and choose the command to remove it from the toolbar.

WARNING

>> See Chapter 24 for information on the Quick Access toolbar.

>> When the Quick Access toolbar becomes too crowded, consider creating a custom tab on the Ribbon. This topic is also covered in Chapter 24.

Creating a macro keyboard shortcut

For macros I use frequently, especially those that manipulate text, I prefer to assign the macro to a keyboard shortcut. This assignment can be made when the macro is created or after creating the macro. To assign a keyboard shortcut to a macro, obey these directions:

1. **Right-click on the Ribbon and choose the command Customize the Ribbon.**

   No, you're not customizing the Ribbon. You must access the part of the Word Options dialog box from which you can create keyboard shortcuts.

2. **Click the Customize button.**

   The Customize Keyboard dialog box appears, as illustrated in Figure 22-4.

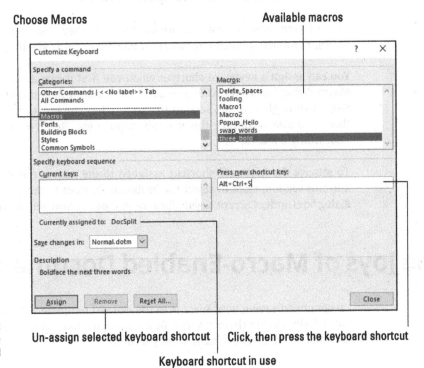

Choose Macros   Available macros

FIGURE 22-4:
The Customize
Keyboard
dialog box.

Un-assign selected keyboard shortcut | Click, then press the keyboard shortcut

Keyboard shortcut in use

3. **From the Categories list, choose Macros.**

   The Macros category is located near the bottom of the list. When you select it, you see the list of available macros appear on the right side of the dialog box. (Refer to Figure 22-4.)

4. **Click the mouse in the Press New Shortcut Key box.**

5. **Press the shortcut-key combination.**

TIP

Many of the Alt+Ctrl+letter as well as Shift+Alt+letter key combinations are available to assign to macros. Try these first.

If a keyboard shortcut is in use, such as Alt+Ctrl+S, shown in Figure 22-4, select another key combination. I recommend that you don't alter any of Word's existing keyboard shortcuts.

When a keyboard shortcut isn't used by Word, you see the text [unassigned] appear in the Customize Keyboard dialog box.

6. **Click the Assign button to lock in your choice.**

7. **Click the Close button to dismiss the Customize Keyboard dialog box.**

8. **Click OK to banish the Word Options dialog box.**

Try out your new keyboard shortcut: Press the key combination you typed in Step 5. The macro runs, doing whatever marvelous thing you programmed it to do.

You can assign a keyboard shortcut when you first create a macro: In the Record Macro dialog box (refer to Figure 22-1), click the Keyboard button. Proceed with Steps 3 through 7 in this section to assign a key combination to the macro, and then continue recording the macro's commands. Refer to the earlier section "Recording a macro."

To remove the keyboard shortcut assigned to the macro, follow Steps 1 through 4 in this section. Click to select the keyboard shortcut in the Customize Keyboard dialog box (under Current Keys). Click the Remove button. Finish with Steps 7 and 8.

The Joys of Macro-Enabled Documents

I recommend saving your macros in the Normal template. This location is where Word desires to put them anyway. By doing so, the macros are available to all your documents, which is probably what you want.

When you need a macro to be specific to a single document, you must assign the macro to that document. This process involves creating a macro-enabled document, which is a special file type that's different from the standard Word document. You can also create macro-enabled templates, which provide a set of unique macros to the macro-enabled documents those templates create.

Saving macros with the current document

To save a macro to a specific document you must ensure that the document is saved in a specific format. This process begins when you create the macro: In the Record Macro dialog box, use the Store Macro In menu to choose the current document. (Refer to Figure 22-1.)

After the macro is created (or even before), you must save the document as a macro-enabled file type. Word uses the proper format for you — unless you press the F12 key to access the Save As dialog box. In this instance, from the Save As Type menu, choose the format Word Macro-Enabled Document (*.docm).

When a document has already been saved as a standard Word document (*.docx), and you and you try to save the document with its macro created, a warning appears. You're informed that the document contains a "VBA project" (Visual Basic for Applications), which means if you desire to keep the macro-enabled document, you just use the Save As command and choose the proper file type.

To re-save an already-saved document as a macro-enabled document, press the F12 key. In the Save As dialog box, use the Save As Type menu to choose the format Word Macro-Enabled Document (*.docm). Work the rest of the dialog box to set a location and name for the file. Then click the Save button to save the macro-enabled document.

WARNING

>> When you open a macro-enabled document, a warning appears just below the Ribbon in the document window. Click the Enable Content button to allow macros to run.

>> The macros you create are available only in the macro-enabled document. Macros in the Normal template continue to be available.

TECHNICAL STUFF

>> The Normal template, which Word uses for all new documents and which contains all Word's default styles and settings, is actually a macro-enabled template. The full filename is Normal.dotm. This template's macro powers don't extend to any new documents you create. Only a macro-enabled template has such capabilities. See the next section.

Creating a macro-enabled template

When special macros are needed beyond a single document, you can create a macro-enabled template. This template extends its macros to any document created based on the template. But you must ensure that you properly save the template in the proper macro-enabled template format. Heed these directions:

1. **Create the template as you would any template in Word.**

Add styles, preset text, and any other options required by the documents that the template will create. See Chapter 4 for more information on templates.

2. **Create or add the macros you want included with the template.**

As you create the macros, choose the current document as the macro's location. See the preceding section.

3. **Save the template as a macro-enabled template.**

Use the file type menu to choose Word Macro-Enabled Template (*.dotm).

All documents created based upon the macro-enabled template can access the template's macros. These macros are in addition to any macros held in the Normal template.

WARNING

Macros available in documents based on a macro-enabled template aren't stored within the document. For example, if you copy such a document to another computer, the macros won't be available. To retain the macros within the document, it must be saved as a macro-enabled document. Refer to the preceding section.

IN THIS CHAPTER

» **Understanding content controls**

» **Adding a content control**

» **Customizing a content control**

» **Creating fill-in-the-blanks items**

» **Adding an image content control**

» **Working with the Date Picker**

» **Building a Combo Box content control**

Chapter **23**

Dynamic Templates with Content Controls

A *template* is a marvelous tool for rapid and consistent document creation. You can stuff into the template preset text, styles, graphics, and anything else that makes it easier to start your writing duties. To further bolster a template's power, you can add content controls.

A *content control* is a tiny box in which only a specific tidbit of information may reside. It allows you to help the user make specific choices with regard to a document's content. For example, you can create a fill-in-the-blanks field for a document title or have a preset image location where users can fetch their own graphics file. The content controls help the user create the document in the way you want it to look.

> » Some content controls can be quite complex, involving programming and other seriously advanced aspects of Word. This chapter covers only the more common and basic common content controls.

> » You can also use fields to automate document and template content. Refer to Chapter 21.

The World of Content Controls

To work with content controls, you must summon Word's Developer tab. Heed these steps:

1. **Right-click the Ribbon and choose Customize Ribbon.**

The Word Options dialog box appears. Word's commands appear on the left side of the dialog box, with tabs on the Ribbon represented on the right.

2. **On the right side of the dialog box, place a check mark by Developer.**

The check mark ensures that the Developer tab is visible.

3. **Click the OK button.**

The Developer tab appears on the nexd to the Help tab on the Ribbon. Content controls are found in the Controls group.

Content controls can reside in any document, but they're most useful in document templates. The goal is to focus user attention on specific items that must be set in a proper manner, such as the document's title, an image, or any of the other wonderful things a content control can bring to a document.

Inserting a content control

Most content controls deal with text, though a wide variety are available. As an element in your document, the content control works like any tidbit of text or inline graphics. As such, before you add a content control, you need to know where it sits on the page.

For example, a Rich Text content control serves as a text placeholder. It works like a fill-in-the-blanks gizmo. Follow these steps to insert a Rich Text content control into a document, which follows the general steps for adding any content control:

1. **Position the insertion pointer where you want the content control to reside.**

2. **Click the Developer tab.**

Refer to the preceding section for details on conjuring forth the Developer tab.

Aa **3.** **In the Controls group, click the Rich Text content control.**

The icon is shown in the margin. After you click, the Rich Text content control appears in your document at the insertion pointer's location. It's selected, as shown on the left in Figure 23-1.

Handle

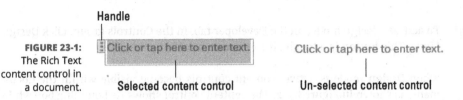

FIGURE 23-1:
The Rich Text
content control in
a document.

Selected content control   Un-selected content control

The content control's text suggests that the user click or tap and then type something new. You can change the shading color (on the left in Figure 23-1) and format the text with the surrounding text. Though you cannot change the prompt from the default wording, *Click or tap here to enter text,* you can type text such as *Type the document title here* into the content control as a prompt.

Content controls are also found on the Insert tab. Those content controls insert document building blocks — specifically, information about the current document. Here's how to insert one of these document info content controls:

1. **On the Insert tab, in the Text group, click the Quick Parts button.**

2. **Choose Document Property and select an item from the submenu.**

   The item you select, such as Author, is inserted into the document as a content control.

Though a Document Property item is secretly a content control, I consider it to work more like a field than the other content controls discussed in this chapter. See Chapter 21 for information on fields.

>> Refer to the later section, "Setting up a fill-in-the-blanks item" for more details on the Rich Text content control.

>> To move the content control, click to select it; refer to the left side of Figure 23-1. Use the handle to drag the content control within your document's text.

>> The handle may change position when the content control has a title. It still looks the same (three vertical dots) and is located near the content control's upper left corner.

Changing the content control view

The standard way to view content controls is shown earlier, in Figure 23-1. This view shows the content control when the insertion pointer is inside, but transforms the content control into regular text otherwise. To better view content controls, and to see them at any time in your document, activate Design mode.

To activate design mode, on the Developer tab, in the Controls group, click Design Mode. This button is a toggle; it's either on or off.

When Design mode is active, content controls become visible within the document, as shown in Figure 23-2. The content control shows its bounding box while selected (on the left in Figure 23-2), but when the insertion pointer is elsewhere in the document, the content control sports tabs to the right and left (shown on the right in Figure 23-2).

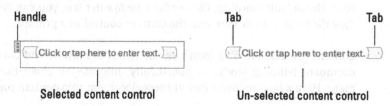

FIGURE 23-2:
A content control
in Design mode.

To deactivate Design mode, click the Design Mode button again.

Setting a content control's properties

Word permits you to modify some content control attributes, changing the way it appears in a document. Of the things you can mess with, adding a title to a content control is about the most productive. To add or change a content control's title, follow these steps:

1. Click to select the content control.

The content control's bounding box appears as well as its handle, shown on the left in both Figures 23-1 and 23-2.

2. On the Developer tab, in the Controls group, click the Properties button.

If you don't follow Step 1, a long, detailed Properties window appears. Close this window and start over with Step 1.

If you follow Step 1, the content control's Properties dialog box appears, as shown in Figure 23-3. Items in the Content Control Properties dialog box affect only the selected content control.

3. Click the Title box and type a title for the content control.

The title appears next to the handle when the content control is selected. It helps to identify the control, and perhaps helps explain its purpose.

4. Click the OK button when you're done setting the content control's properties.

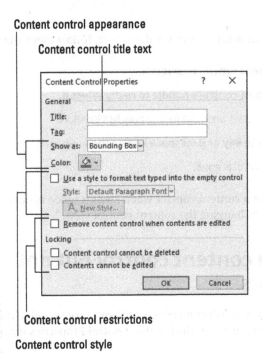

Content control appearance

Content control title text

FIGURE 23-3:
The Content
Control
Properties
dialog box.

Content control restrictions

Content control style

The Show As drop-down menu (refer to Figure 23-3) allows you to set the content control's appearance, either as a bounding box, shown on the left in Figure 23-1, or a start/end tag, shown on the left in Figure 23-2, or without any tags.

The Style settings allow you to apply styles to the content control, though it can be formatted along with any text in your document.

The Content Control Cannot Be Deleted option allows the user to type text into the content control, but not to convert it into plain text or otherwise remove it.

See the later section "Converting a content control to text," for information on the Remove Content Control When Contents Are Edited option.

Deleting a content control

You can delete text in a content control just as you can delete text or graphics anywhere in a document. Deleting the content control's text, however, doesn't remove the content control.

To remove a content control from the document, follow these steps:

1. **Click the content control to select it.**

2. **Click the content control's handle to really select it.**

   Refer to Figures 23-1 and 23-2 for the handle's location.

3. **Press the Delete key or Backspace key on the keyboard.**

   The content control is gone.

TIP

It's easier to delete a content control when Design mode is deactivated. Refer to the earlier section "Changing the content control view."

Deleting a content control but not its contents

Content controls stay in a document unless they're converted to text or the option to remove the control is set in the Content Control Properties dialog box.

In the Content Control Properties dialog box, place a check mark by the option Remove Content Control When Contents Are Edited. Setting this option means that when a user types text or otherwise manipulates a content control, it's converted into document text. The content control is gone. Refer to the section "Setting a content control's properties" earlier in this document for more information.

The second way to convert a content control into text, or to remove an empty content control, is to right-click it and choose the command Remove Content Control. If the content control has been manipulated, it's converted to text. Otherwise, the content control is deleted.

Useful Content Controls

Content controls find their home in a template where they serve to help a user provide the proper information. A content control can indicate where to type text, which text to type, or serve a tool to input specific details, such as a date.

You've probably seen content controls in action if you've used any of Word's preset templates. It's relatively simple to add these features to your document templates. Just follow the examples provided in this section.

>> Content controls work best in a template.

>> Refer to Chapter 4 for more information on document templates.

Setting up a fill-in-the-blanks item

Perhaps the most common and useful content control is the Rich Text content control, what I call the fill-in-the-blanks thing. It's the content control you see most often in Word's sample templates. It's also the content control most users want to use in their own document templates.

To add a Rich Text content control to your document, follow these steps:

1. Position the insertion pointer.

The content control works like text. It can sit in a line, on a line by itself, or anywhere on the page. You can format the text or apply a style.

Aa **2. On the Developer tab, in the Controls group, click the Rich Text Content Control button.**

The content control appears in your document.

3. On the Developer tab, in the Controls group, click the Properties button.

The Content Control Properties dialog box appears.

4. Type a Title for the content control.

The Title appears above the content control when it's selected. This text helps a user to understand what to type, such as Your Name, Job Description, or Places Where You're Ticklish.

5. Place a check mark by the option Remove Content Control When Contents Are Edited.

This step is optional, though I prefer to convert the content control to text so that it doesn't distract me after I'm done with it.

6. Click OK.

The property changes are applied to the Rich Text content control.

You can continue creating the template, adding more text, setting up styles, or throwing in a few more content controls.

>> The Rich Text content control works best for text items required in the final document.

REMEMBER

» The "rich text" part means that the text inside the control can be formatted by character, word, or some random chunk.

» You cannot edit the placeholder text.

» I use the Rich Text content control in my chapter document templates. The chapter number is a content control. It's also set to convert to text after I type the chapter number.

Adding a multiline text field

For entering multiple lines of text, use a Plain Text content control. The name may seem to imply that this content control doesn't allow the text to be formatted, but that's incorrect. The text can be formatted as a single block. Even so, the primary bonus from using the Plain Text content control is that the user can set its properties to allow for multiline input.

Follow these steps to add a Plain Text content control for multiline input:

1. Set the insertion pointer to the location where you want to place the Plain Text content control.

2. On the Developer tab, in the Controls group, click the Plain Text Content Control button.

3. In the Controls group, click the Properties button.

4. Type a title.

The title text helps the user to understand what needs to go into the content control.

5. Place a check mark by the option Allow Carriage Returns (Multiple Paragraphs).

6. Click OK.

With the multiple paragraphs setting active, users can type as much text into the content control as they like. You cannot, however, apply formatting to any specific part of the text; it all carries a single text format.

To exit the control, click elsewhere in the document or press the → after typing the last item in the content control.

Inserting an image

The Picture content control expands the realm of content control possibilities. You use the control to preset an image's position, format, and layout. The content control allows the user to choose a photo from the PC's library or the Internet, which inherits the content control's formatting.

To insert a Picture content control, follow these steps:

1. **Position the insertion pointer to the picture's eventual location.**

If you're using advanced layout options, don't worry: You can apply them after inserting the content control.

 2. **On the Developer tab, in the Controls group, click the Picture Content Control button.**

The Picture content control appears as shown in Figure 23-4. Like any image, it sports handles for manipulation, but as a content control it features a title and command buttons, as illustrated in the figure.

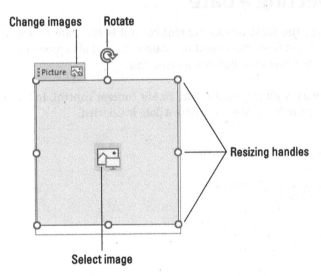

FIGURE 23-4:
The Picture
content control.

3. **Position and format the Picture content control's layout.**

Picture layout options are covered in Chapter 5. Also refer to Chapter 7 for additional picture formatting options.

To use the Picture content control, click on the button in the center. A dialog box appears, listing sources for placing an image: from a file on your PC, stock images, online images, and icons.

TIP

>> The content control shows the title text Picture in Figure 23-4. To change this title, refer to the earlier section "Setting a content control's properties."

>> Just as you can type preset text into a text content control, you can preset a picture; choose a picture for the content control before you close the document or template. When you set a picture, ensure that you change the content control's title to read, "Click the icon to the right to set a new picture," or something similar.

>> The Change Images button (refer to Figure 23-4) lets the user replace the content control's original image with something else. This icon doesn't work if the option Contents Cannot Be Edited is set in the content control's Properties dialog box.

Selecting a date

Perhaps the most unique content control is the Date Picker. It's a text content control, but it restricts input to a date format. It also provides a handy menu from which the user can choose a specific date.

Figure 23-5 illustrates the Date Picker content control. In the figure, the content control's menu is shown, where a date is selected.

Menu button

FIGURE 23-5:
The Date Picker content control.

 To insert the Date Picker content control, click its icon, shown in the margin. The content control is inserted at the insertion pointer's position.

The date format is selected in the Date Picture Content Control's Properties dialog box. Even if the user types in another date format, the resulting date is displayed in the format set in the Properties dialog box.

Building a drop-down list

Two content controls let you create menus or lists in a document. From these lists the user can choose specific items, which then become the content control's text. The two content controls are the Combo Box and Drop-Down List. Both content controls serve a similar function and look nearly identical. The main difference is that you can edit and format text in a Combo Box. The Drop-Down List content control shows text that cannot be changed.

To insert a Combo Box content control into your document, obey these directions:

1. **Position the insertion pointer where you want the combo box to appear.**

2. **On the Developer tab, in the Controls group, click the Combo Box content control.**

In the document, a combo box (or drop-down list) looks like any content control. Its text says, "Choose an item." When you click the menu button, shown in Figure 23-6, a list of choices appears.

The choices shown in Figure 23-6 don't appear until you add them, which is the next step.

FIGURE 23-6:
A Combo Box
content control.

3. **In the Controls group, click the Properties button.**

The Combo Box Properties dialog box looks different from the standard Content Control Properties dialog box. In Figure 23-7, you see the version of the dialog box that sets items in the Combo Box drop-down list.

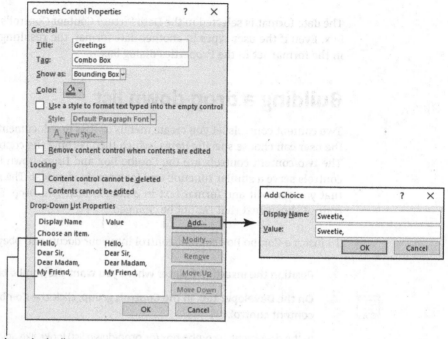

FIGURE 23-7:
Adding combo
box entries.

Items in the list

4. **Click the Add button to set a new item in the list.**

5. **In the Add Choice dialog box, type a Display Name.**

   The Value field echoes the text typed in the Display Name field.

6. **Click OK to add the item.**

7. **Repeat Steps 5 through 7 to add more items.**

8. **Click the OK button to create the list.**

The user selects the combo box's menu to choose an item, one that you selected. This text is placed into the document.

REMEMBER

If you want the content control to disappear, you must select the item Remove Content Control When Contents Are Edited in the Content Control Properties dialog box.

Creating a Drop-Down List content control works similarly to the steps described in this section. Choose the Drop-Down List icon (shown in the margin) in Step 3. The Drop-Down List content control works just like the Combo Box content control, but the user cannot edit text inside the content control.

6

The Part of Tens

Chapter 24

Ten Ways to Customize Word

Customizing Word can be a blessing or a curse. The blessing part deals with changing the program's behavior and appearance to match what you prefer. The curse comes from a departure from the traditional and well-documented ways that Word looks and acts. As long as you can keep in mind that your custom settings will make your copy of Word different, you're good to go.

TECHNICAL STUFF

Changes to Word's options and all customization settings are saved as part of the Normal template. Other changes may be saved elsewhere, depending on what you're modifying.

Showing Special Characters

Word hides some special characters in a document, items that you don't see but which affect your text. For example, when you press the Enter key to start a new paragraph, you add a New Paragraph character to the text. It doesn't show up — unless you tell Word to show it.

¶ All the secret characters appear when you use the Show/Hide command. But if you find that the command summons too many characters and you just want to see a few — such as the tab or Enter key press — you can select individual characters to appear all the time. Follow these steps:

1. **Click the File tab and choose Options.**

   The Word Options dialog box appears.

2. **Choose the Display category.**

   The list of special characters appears in the Always Show area, illustrated in Figure 24-1.

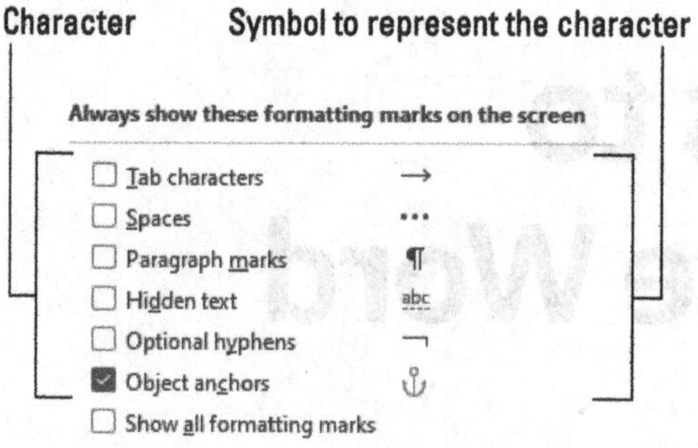

Character   Symbol to represent the character

Always show these formatting marks on the screen

- ☐ Tab characters   →
- ☐ Spaces   ...
- ☐ Paragraph marks   ¶
- ☐ Hidden text   abc
- ☐ Optional hyphens   ¬
- ☑ Object anchors   ⚓
- ☐ Show all formatting marks

FIGURE 24-1:
Special characters
to show in
a document.

3. **Place a check mark by the character you want to always see.**

   In Figure 24-1, you see that the Object Anchors character is selected. This character helps anchor (get it?) an image or another object to a paragraph of text. Refer to Chapter 5 for details on how it works.

4. **Click the OK button to lock in your choices and close the Word Options dialog box.**

The Show All Formatting Marks option (refer to Figure 24-1) activates all marks, similar to the Show/Hide command.

» When the paragraph mark is activated, heading styles in a document are prefixed with a square bullet.

» The Spaces option directs Word to show space characters as small dots. One dot appears for every space character in the document. It's very annoying.

» Hidden text is a text formatting attribute, like bold or italics, but hidden text doesn't appear in a document — unless you activate the Hidden Text option as described in this section. Even then, the hidden text doesn't print unless you set its option: Follow Steps 1 and 2 in this section, and in the Printing Options area, place a check mark by the Print Hidden Text setting. Of course, then what's the point of hiding the text in the first place?

» Use the Font dialog box to apply the hidden-text format. It's listed as an "effect."

Controlling Text Selection

Word believes that you desire to automatically select text by the word as you drag the mouse. This option allows for rapid text selection, but it might not be what you want. For example, I prefer to select text by the character, which can be tedious, but it's what I prefer.

To direct Word to select text by character instead of by word, obey these directions:

1. **Open the Word Options dialog box.**

   Click the File tab and choose Options.

2. **Select Advanced from the items listed on the left side of the dialog box.**

3. **Remove the check mark by the option When Selecting, Automatically Select Entire Word.**

4. **Click OK.**

One of my primary motivations in making this change is to better select text at the end of a paragraph. If you keep word selection active, selecting these words can be difficult. Also, I select text in the middle of a word to edit the word or change its ending.

Setting Text-Pasting Options

Word allows you to choose how text is pasted. You can access the Paste Options from the Home tab in the Clipboard group, or you can press the Ctrl key after pasting to view the different ways to paste. Here are some of your choices:

Keep Source Formatting (Default): The text retains its original format as set in its original source.

Merge Formatting: The text is reformatted to match the formatting before and after. If the text is a bulleted or numbered list, the bullets and numbering match the paragraphs before and after.

Keep Text Only: Only text is pasted, just the same as if you typed the text. Any existing text formats are applied. The keyboard shortcut for this setting is Ctrl+Shift+V.

You may have a preference for one of these options, which can be set in the Word Options dialog box. Follow these steps:

1. **Click the File tab and choose Options to visit the Word Options dialog box.**

2. **Choose the Advanced category.**

3. **Select your preferences in the Cut, Copy, And Paste area.**

This area is illustrated in Figure 24-2.

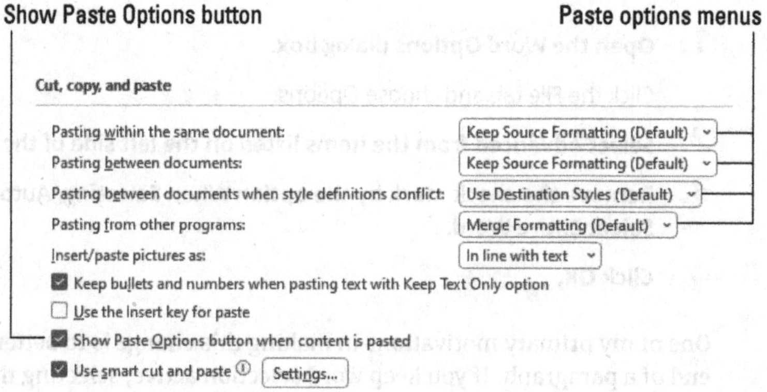

Show Paste Options button   **Paste options menus**

Cut, copy, and paste

Pasting within the same document:	Keep Source Formatting (Default) ⌄
Pasting between documents:	Keep Source Formatting (Default) ⌄
Pasting between documents when style definitions conflict:	Use Destination Styles (Default) ⌄
Pasting from other programs:	Merge Formatting (Default) ⌄
Insert/paste pictures as:	In line with text ⌄

☑ Keep bullets and numbers when pasting text with Keep Text Only option
☐ Use the Insert key for paste
☑ Show Paste Options button when content is pasted
☑ Use smart cut and paste ⓘ   [Settings...]

FIGURE 24-2:
Paste options and
other settings.

The menus to the right of the first four settings (refer to Figure 24-2) set the way Word pastes the text. By default, pasting text between Word documents retains the source formatting. The Pasting from Other Programs setting, however, is one you might want to reset to Keep Text Only.

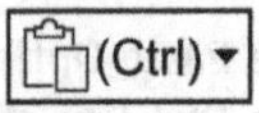

If you don't desire to see the Paste Options button appear after you paste text (shown in the margin), remove the check mark by the option Show Paste Options Button When Content Is Pasted.

Disabling Annoying Features

Despite Word's tiresome efforts to be helpful, I often find it getting in the way. Some options pop-up or appear, which can distract or vex. The good news is that many of these options can be disabled, stifling their intrusive behavior. The key is to summon the Word Options dialog box: From the File tab, choose Options. Peruse the following sections for details on how to disable many of these noisome features.

AutoCorrect and AutoFormat

Refer to Chapter 20 for details on disrupting the behavior of these Auto commands.

Click-and-Type

The Click-and-Type feature allows you to click anywhere on a blank page and start typing. Word formats the document instantly, providing whatever spacing commands are necessary to let you plop down text just anywhere.

The key to using Click-and-Type is to look for the weird mouse pointer, such as the one shown in the margin. Four of these weird pointers are available, indicating their format for the text typed after you click.

To disable this feature, in the Word Options dialog box, choose the Advanced Category. In the Editing Options area, remove the check mark by Enable Click and Type.

The Start Screen

If you prefer that Word open directly with a fresh, blank document ready for writing, you want to disable the Start Screen. In the Word Options dialog box, choose the General category. In the Start Up Options section, remove the check mark by the only item, Show The Start Screen When This Application Starts.

The Backstage

The Backstage is the full-screen presentation for the Save As and Open commands, which replaced the traditional Save As and Open dialog boxes. To disable it, in the Word Options dialog box, choose the Save category. Beneath the Save Documents heading, set a check mark by the option Don't Show The Backstage When Opening Or Saving Files With Keyboard Shortcuts.

The Mini Toolbar

The Mini Toolbar is that pop-up thing that appears whenever you select text or right-click on text. To banish it from your copy of Word, in the Word Options dialog box, choose the General category. Under the User Interface Options area, remove the check mark by the option Show Mini Toolbar on Selection.

Specifying the Default Document Folder

You may have a favorite folder for saving new documents, in which case it's a good idea to inform Word of your choice. Otherwise, Word has its own preferences.

To set the default local file location for saving new documents, obey these directions:

1. **Click the File tab and Choose Options.**

2. **Click the Save category.**

3. **In the Save Documents area, click the Default Local File Location box and type a folder's pathname.**

Or you can use the Browse button to browse for your favorite folder. Whatever you choose becomes the folder in which Word saves documents by default.

Word isn't stuck with whatever folder you choose in Step 3. You can always use the Save As dialog box to save a document in any folder. When you do, Word uses that folder as the current folder. But the default remains the Word's preference when you haven't chosen a folder.

Altering Word's Appearance

The Word window is your oyster. You can keep it as is, you can eat it whole, you can even pluck out the pearls. You just need to know what can be changed and how to change it.

Also see the later section, "Building a Custom Tab on the Ribbon."

Showing the ruler

I like the ruler. It appears above the document, measuring margins and indents and allowing you to set tab stops and do all sorts of fun stuff. But the ruler doesn't show up unless you bid it come. To do so, on the View tab, in the Show group, place a check mark by Ruler.

To banish the Ruler, repeat these steps, remove the check mark.

If you're fond of rulers, a vertical ruler is also available. It shows the page top and bottom margins, but doesn't let you control anything. To summon the vertical ruler, obey these steps:

1. **Click the File tab and choose Options.**

   The Word Options dialog box appears.

2. **Choose the Advanced category.**

3. **In the Display area, ensure that a check mark appears by the option Show Vertical Ruler in Print Layout View.**

   In the Display area you also find an option to set the measurement units for the rulers. In the United States, "inches" is the default because we are the most technologically advanced country on Earth.

TIP

4. **Click OK.**

The Vertical Ruler appears only in Print Layout view.

REMEMBER

Revealing the scrollbars

You may think nothing of having scrollbars in the document window, but you can control their visibility. Two settings in the Word Options dialog box determine whether the horizontal or vertical scrollbar appear in the document window.

To access the scrollbar settings, follow Steps 1 and 2 in the preceding section. In the Display area are two options for the scrollbars: Show Horizontal Scroll Bar and Show Vertical Scroll Bar. Add or remove the check marks to set either item.

I always write it as one word: scrollbar. What is Microsoft thinking?

TECHNICAL STUFF

Customizing the Quick Access Toolbar

I consider the Quick Access toolbar to be home for those commands I use frequently and those that I want to use but are absent from the Ribbon. It's highly configurable with a smorgasbord of options.

To control the Quick Access toolbar, click its menu button, then the downward-pointing chevron to the right of the buttons, as illustrated in Figure 24-3. Many of the controls that configure the toolbar are found on the menu presented when you click the button.

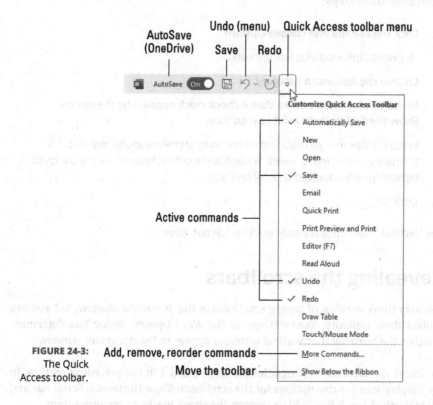

Here are some useful ways you can customize the Quick Access toolbar:

Relocate the Quick Access toolbar. From the Quick Access toolbar menu button, choose the option Show Below the Ribbon or Show Above the Ribbon to move the toolbar. The command name changes to reflect the toolbar's current position. I recommend putting the toolbar below the Ribbon when it grows more than half a dozen or so commands.

Add and remove commands. Use the Quick Access toolbar menu to choose common commands to add or remove from the toolbar. Choose a command to add. Commands with check marks next to them are already on the toolbar (refer to Figure 24-3). Choose one to remove it. Additional commands are found by choosing the More Commands option, then using the Word Options dialog box to add any Word command to the toolbar. You can also shove any Ribbon command to the

Quick Access toolbar by right-clicking the command button and choose the item, Add to Quick Access Toolbar.

Reset the toolbar. When you want a do-over, you can reset the Quick Access toolbar to its pristine condition, as it appeared when Word first installed and before you began messing around. From the Quick Access toolbar menu and choose More Commands. In the Word Options dialog box, click the Reset button menu and choose the command Reset Only Quick Access Toolbar. Click Yes to confirm.

Building a Custom Tab on the Ribbon

When you fill up the Quick Access toolbar, consider creating your own custom tab on the Ribbon. The task isn't that difficult to do, but like most customizations you're locking yourself into a feature set that's available only on your copy of Word.

To start, right-click on the Ribbon and choose the Customize the Ribbon command. The Word Options dialog box appears, shown in the Customize Ribbon area, as illustrated in Figure 24-4. You see a list of Word's commands in the left column and the Ribbon's current tabs on the right.

The list of tabs on the right side of the window (refer to Figure 24-4) shows all tabs available in Word. To add your own, custom tab, click the New Tab button. You see the new tab inserted, along with a new group, as illustrated in Figure 24-4.

To rename your tab, select it and click the Rename button. You can do the same for the group: Select the New Group (Custom) item and click the Rename button to give it a new group name. Group names should reflect the items in the group.

The tab is empty until you add commands and groups. To do so, follow these steps:

1. **Select a group on your custom tab.**

2. **Choose a category from the list of commands on the left side of the dialog box.**

   All of Word's commands are listed in the All Commands category.

3. **Select a command and click the Add button.**

   The command is placed into the group selected in the list on the right side of the dialog box.

4. **Repeat Steps 3 and 4 to populate the group with a clutch of commands.**

5. **Click OK to close the dialog box and survey the group you've created on a custom tab.**

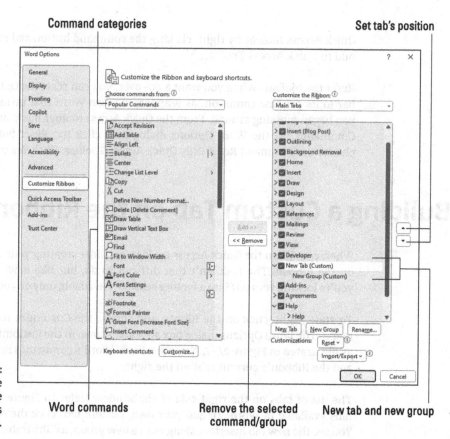

Command categories   Set tab's position

FIGURE 24-4:
Customizing the
Ribbon in the
Word Options
dialog box.

Word commands   Remove the selected   New tab and new group
                                     command/group

Use the up and down arrows to reposition a command within a group. If you change your mind, select a command in your new tab and click the Remove button (refer to Figure 24-2).

TIP

To help with organization, I recommend that you organize commands on your custom tab into groups of related commands. For example, you can have a group of favorite commands, commands you use but can't find on the Ribbon, macros, commands with funny names, or whatever groups you desire.

>> Your new tab appears in the position it's set in in the list of tabs on the right side of the Word Options dialog box. To change its location, select the tab and use the up and down arrows to set a new position. The tabs at the top of the list appear on the left side of the Ribbon.

>> The custom tab shows up as long as you set a check mark in its box.

>> Rather than remove a new tab, simply uncheck its box in the list. That way, the tab remains available, just hidden.

WARNING

» A limit exists for the number of groups on a tab. Word starts hiding commands when too many are available on the Ribbon and the window isn't wide enough to show them all.

» You cannot add, remove, or rename any command from one of Word's standard tabs. You can try, but Word gets huffy and displays an angry warning, thwarting your efforts.

Assigning a keyboard shortcut to a command

All the handy keyboard shortcuts are owned by various Word commands, popular or not. What remains are unhandy keyboard shortcuts, like Alt+Ctrl+Shift+9. But you can assign these unused keyboard shortcut to your favorite commands.

To create a custom keyboard shortcut, first find a command you use frequently, one for which a keyboard shortcut isn't available. For example, I prefer having the Ruler visible when I edit, but the View Ruler command lacks a keyboard shortcut. To assign a shortcut to the View Ruler command, or any other command in Word, heed these steps:

1. **Right-click the Ribbon and choose the command Customize the Ribbon.**

   The Word Options dialog box appears.

2. **Click the Customize button, found by the prompt Keyboard Shortcuts.**

   The Customize Keyboard dialog box appears, illustrated in Figure 24-5.

3. **Choose a category to help you hone down the command you want to assign to a keyboard shortcut.**

   You can select a specific category from the Categories list or select All Commands to view the hoard of Word's commands.

4. **Select the command from the Commands list.**

   When a command already features a keyboard shortcut, it appears in the Current Keys list. If so, you can assign a second keyboard shortcut, or just commit to memory the current shortcut.

5. **Click to select the Press New Shortcut Key text box.**

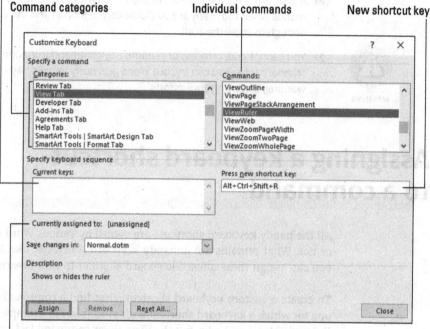

Existing shortcut keys

Command categories   Individual commands   New shortcut key

Customize Keyboard   ?   ×

Specify a command

Categories: Commands:

Review Tab   ViewOutline
View Tab   ViewPage
Developer Tab   ViewPageStackArrangement
Add-ins Tab   ViewRuler
Agreements Tab   ViewWeb
Help Tab   ViewZoomPageWidth
SmartArt Tools | SmartArt Design Tab   ViewZoomTwoPage
SmartArt Tools | Format Tab   ViewZoomWholePage

Specify keyboard sequence

Current keys: Press new shortcut key:

                                         Alt+Ctrl+Shift+R

Currently assigned to: [unassigned]

Save changes in: Normal.dotm

Description

Shows or hides the ruler

    Assign   Remove   Reset All...   Close

FIGURE 24-5:
The Customize
Keyboard
dialog box.   Keys already assigned

6. Type the shortcut key combination.

TIP

Use Ctrl+Shift, Alt+Shift, Alt+Ctrl, and Alt+Ctrl+Shift combinations for the
best results.

7. Confirm that the shortcut key combination isn't currently assigned.

Refer to the Currently Assigned To text in the dialog box to confirm, as
illustrated in Figure 24-5. If the text [unassigned] appears, the shortcut isn't
being used by any other command. If the shortcut you chose is used, go back
to Step 6 and try again.

8. Click the Assign button.

The shortcut isn't set until you click the Assign button.

9. Click the Close button to dismiss the Customize Keyboard dialog box.

10. Click OK to banish the Word Options dialog box.

The next thing you should do is test the new keyboard shortcut: Press the key combination to confirm that it works.

REMEMBER

WARNING

>> I recommend either using the keyboard shortcut right away or writing it down until you can commit it to memory.

>> It's okay to reassign a shortcut key. For example, if you never use the Alt+Ctrl+O keyboard shortcut to enter Outline view, feel free to reassign it.

>> When you reassign an existing keyboard shortcut, even a trivial shortcut like Alt+Ctrl+O, you are deviating your copy of Word from its documentation and Help information.

>> I strongly recommend never reassigning any of the plain Ctrl keyboard shortcuts, such as Ctrl+S to Save, Ctrl+C to copy, and so on.

>> Refer to Chapter 22 for information on assigning keyboard shortcuts to macros.

Setting a Symbol's Shortcut Key

You need not be limited to assigning a keyboard shortcut to a command. Unusual characters and special symbols can also sport shortcut keys. In fact, you may find that shortcut keys already exist for certain special symbols.

To affix a shortcut to a character or symbol, follow these directions:

1. **On the Insert tab, in the Symbols group, click the Symbol menu button.**

2. **Choose the More Symbols command.**

The Symbol dialog box appears. It lists a host of characters, symbols, and squiggles that you can stick into your document.

3. **Select a symbol to assign to a shortcut key.**

TIP

Some symbols may already sport a shortcut key. If so, you see it listed next to the Shortcut Key button, illustrated in Figure 24-6. Three types of shortcuts are available: a standard keyboard shortcut, an Alt+ keyboard shortcut, or the Alt+X shortcut.

Select font   Character categories

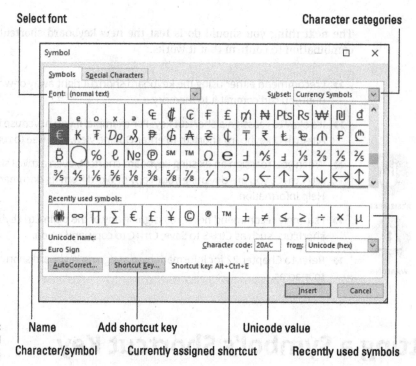

FIGURE 24-6:   Name   Add shortcut key   Unicode value
The Symbol
dialog box.   Character/symbol   Currently assigned shortcut   Recently used symbols

For example, the € symbol uses the Alt+Ctrl+E keyboard shortcut. Press
Alt+Ctrl+E to see the € symbol. Some characters feature an Alt keyboard shortcut.
For example, the × symbol has the keyboard shortcut Alt+0215. To generate
that symbol, press and hold the Alt key and type 0215 on the numeric keypad
(with Num Lock on). The character's Unicode value can also be used to input a
character. See the nearby sidebar "The Alt+X keyboard shortcuts" for details.

4. **Click the Shortcut Key button.**

5. **In the Customize Keyboard dialog box, click the Press New
   Shortcut Key box.**

6. **Press the shortcut key combination.**

7. **Confirm that the shortcut key isn't in use.**

   If the text [unassigned] appears by the Currently Assigned To prompt, you're
   good to go. Otherwise, choose another key combination; repeat Step 6.

8. **Click the Assign button.**

   The shortcut isn't set until you click the Assign button.

9. **Click the Close button to return to the Symbol dialog box.**

   Back in the Symbol dialog box, click the Insert button to insert the symbol,
   or close the dialog box and practice using your new keyboard shortcut.

THE ALT+X KEYBOARD SHORTCUTS

Just about every symbol available in the known universe can be inserted into your document. All you need to know is its Unicode value. The Unicode system is an international standard for representing characters on computers. Tens of thousands of symbols, from the basic Latin alphabet to special characters and symbols used by aliens from other galaxies, are assigned code values. The list is comprehensive, and Word uses those Unicode values as keyboard shortcuts.

As an example, the code for the 5/6 fraction character is listed as 215A, Alt+X. To insert that character, you type — right in your document — the code 215A and then press the Alt+X keyboard shortcut. Word converts the 4-digit code into the symbol: ⅚. Be aware that if the number starts with a zero, you must type the zero to properly input the code.

Unicode values are hexadecimal, using the base 16 counting system. This system consists of numbers 0 through 9 and letters A through F. You can browse the full list of Unicode characters online. The official site is unicode.org. A good online reference can be found at unicode-table.com.

Chapter **25**

Ten Ways to Solve Word Problems

ike any other computer programs, Word occasionally wanders into idyllic electronic pastures to pick digital daisies. Yes, it could be motivated to lose its mind because of something you did. More probable, however, is that Word locks up or crashes just like any software. The goal isn't to fix the blame, but rather to fix the problem.

To assist you with worrisome Word woe, the program comes packed with many handy features. Use them to help recover Word's sanity. If not that, then to recover what you can of your spoiled document. The goal is to get back to work typing out whatever useful thing you find necessary to write.

Your First Solution

The best weapon in your Word arsenal is the Undo command. Before you freak out, press Ctrl+Z to see whether you can bring back whatever you lost.

REMEMBER

» Word's Undo command remembers several layers of actions, so keep pressing Undo to reverse time and, hopefully, recover from the situation.

» Warnings appear when you use commands that cannot be undone, such as a search-and-replace operation in a long document. If you're warned, Undo can't fix the problem.

» If you undo too much, use the Redo command to re-create your steps. The Redo command is Ctrl+Y.

Lost Documents

The first place to look for the document is on the list of recently accessed files on the Open screen: Click the File tab and choose Open. Locate your document on the list of recently accessed files.

TIP

Below the file's name, you see its pathname, which is its location on your computer's storage system. These are the folders where the document is stored. To specifically open the document's folder, right-click and choose the command Open File Location, as illustrated in Figure 25-1.

File's location   File name   Right-click to choose this item

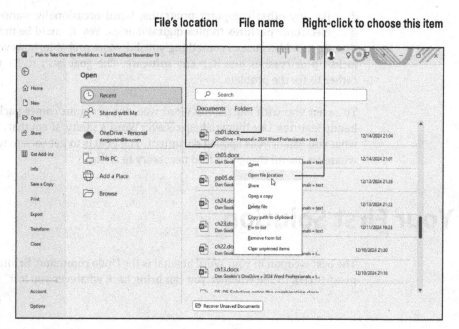

FIGURE 25-1: Locating a recently saved file.

If you still have trouble finding the file, open the document and save it again. This time, ensure that you save it in a location you won't forget.

TIP

>> Word prefers to use the Documents folder in your account's home folder in Windows. This location is the first place to look.

>> Working with folders and finding documents is part of Windows, not Word. Windows is the computer's operating system, and I strongly recommend that you become familiar with how it works and why it's considered separate software from Word.

>> You can also use the Windows Search command to locate a missing document. In Windows 10 and 11, press the Win+S key combination and type the filename into the search text box.

>> When the Windows Search command cannot locate the file, consider looking in the Windows Recycle Bin. Again, this is a Windows function and has nothing to do with Word.

TIP

>> After it's found, consider pinning the document so that it appears on the File tab directly: After finding and opening the file, choose Open from the File tab. Point the mouse at the file's entry and click the pushpin icon that appears.

REMEMBER

>> Word keeps unsaved documents because it knows you can forget to save something important. Use the Recover Unsaved Documents button (refer to Figure 25-1) to check for your lost document.

WARNING

>> If you saved the file directly to removable storage, such as a thumb drive, look for the file there as well. By the way: I do not recommend that you save anything from Word directly to a thumb drive. Save to your PC's primary storage first and then copy the file to a thumb drive.

Lines You Can't Remove

A common question I receive is, "How can I delete this line?" The reader isn't referring to a line of text, but rather a graphical element in the document.

The problem with removing a line is that many things in Word generate a line, which isn't often called a line: Some lines are text borders, some are text attributes, some are revision marks, some are rules, and some — believe it or not — are graphical lines.

The first step in eliminating a line is to select it. If you can click on the line and it becomes selected, it's a drawing object. Press the Delete key to remove it. Be aware that drawing objects can appear in a document's header or footer. You must open the header or footer to access and delete the wayward line.

The second step is to check the text format. Obey these directions:

1. **Select the text with a line in or around it.**

2. **Press Ctrl+D to summon the Font dialog box.**

3. **Ensure that the Underline Style menu shows "(none)" as the current selection.**

4. **If the text is underlined, choose "(none)" from the menu and click OK.**

    The underline style is removed.

A third step is to check the paragraph formatting to ensure that the line isn't a border style. Follow these steps:

1. **Select the text that features a line nearby.**

    The line can be above, below, to the right or left of, or even inside the text.

 2. **On the Home tab, in the Paragraph group, ensure that the Borders button isn't highlighted.**

    The Borders button is shown in the margin.

3. **If a border style is applied to the paragraph, click the Borders button and choose No Border from the menu.**

    If the line remains, it wasn't a border.

REMEMBER

Borders stick with a paragraph. If a stack of paragraphs feature the bottom border, only the last paragraph has a line below it.

Your fourth step is to ensure that revision marks are creating the lines concerning you. These lines may appear below the text or to the side of an edited paragraph. Refer to Chapter 11 for information on turning off revision marks, though they do serve a purpose and you should ask why the marks are present before you eliminate them.

The final step is to recognize that in Draft and Outline views a squat horizontal line marks the end of the document. You cannot remove this line.

Formatting Mysteries Revealed

Tabs are wonderful tools for creating tables, indenting text, and aligning headers and footers. All this action works best on a line by itself or the first line of text. When you use a tab inside a paragraph, or when multiple tabs are stacked next to each other, paragraph formatting can go nuts.

If you find paragraph text jostling and jiggling in an unwanted manner, go to the Home tab, and in the Paragraph group click the Show Hide button (shown in the margin). When activated, this command reveals otherwise invisible characters in the text. Tabs, for example, appear as tiny right-pointing arrows.

TIP

>> When tab stops are set properly, you never need to type more than a single tab in a row. In fact, what's probably messing up a paragraph's contents are double tabs. Use the Show Hide command to reveal tabs and remove the duplicates.

>> Odd formatting behavior also occurs when you double up on spaces. Especially when you use spaces to align text, the results look sloppy. Use tabs to line up text, not spaces. And just like tabs, your document should never have more than two spaces next to each other.

An Extra, Blank Page Prints

The document's done printing — or is it? At the end of the text you find a single blank page. What's up?

The process of typing words in a word processor causes excess spaces and paragraphs to accumulate like dirt in front of a plow. When spaces appear at the end of a paragraph, no one notices; the spaces don't print and no one is the wiser. When paragraphs (Enter key presses) accumulate at the end of a document, you get an extra, blank page.

To remove the extra blank page, follow these steps:

1. **Press Ctrl+End to move the insertion pointer to the end of your document.**

2. **Press the Backspace key.**

3. **Repeat Step 2 until you've backspaced over all the extra paragraphs and spaces at the end of your document.**

Eventually, you'll back up into the last bit of text on the true last page. This is when you stop pressing Backspace (obviously).

¶ If you still find a blank page at the end of your document, you probably have an extra hard page break or section break. Activate the Show/Hide command to confirm. If so, remove the page break by pressing the Delete key before it or the Backspace key after it.

The Document Needs a-Fixin'

If a document exhibits odd behavior, and you're certain that it's a Word document, you can try opening it for repair. Follow these steps:

1. **Press the Ctrl+F12 keyboard shortcut to summon the traditional Open dialog box.**

2. **Select the file you need to open and repair.**

3. **Click the menu by the Open button and choose Open and Repair.**

   See Figure 25-2 for the menu's location.

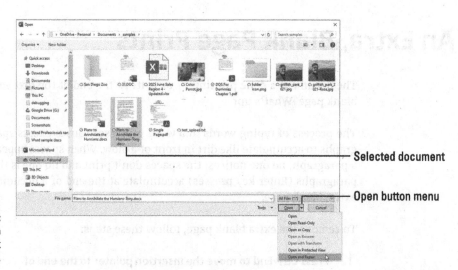

Selected document

Open button menu

FIGURE 25-2:
Opening a
document
for repair.

The document is opened, and Word attempts to fix any weirdness. The document's contents are placed into a new document window. This change is made so that you can save the repaired document under a new name, if you like, and keep the original.

After making any further fixes, save the repaired document.

>> To determine whether the problem is with a specific document or all of Word, try to open other documents and see whether the behavior is repeated. If the problem is with Word, see the section, "Word Startup Mode" later in this Chapter.

>> The document's weirdness may be related to its template. Try opening documents with another type of template to confirm whether the template is corrupted.

>> Also see Chapter 10 for information on extracting text from any file, which you can try as a last resort.

The Normal Template is Broken

Sometimes evil lurks in what's supposed to be Word's main repository of sanity: the Normal template file. To fix the Normal template, you must delete it (or rename it) and then Word automatically builds a new, proper Normal template.

If you rebuild the Normal template, you're removing some customizations you've added, macros you've created, or other settings you've modified. On the other hand, these changes may be causing your problem, so it's time for a fix.

To have Word re-create the Normal template, follow these steps:

1. **Quit Word.**

2. **Press Win+E to summon a File Explorer window.**

3. **Press the Ctrl+L keyboard shortcut to select the Address box.**

4. **Press the Delete key to clear the Address box.**

5. **Type the following line into the Address box:**

   `%USERPROFILE%\AppData\Roaming\Microsoft\Templates`

   As you start typing **AppData**, you see hints appear below your typing. These hints help to direct you and confirm that you're on the right track. Eventually, you see the Templates folder.

6. **Select the Normal.dotm file.**

   Only the first part of the file name, Normal, may appear.

7. **Press the F2 key, the Rename command.**

8. **Edit the name to Normal-old.dotm or Normal-old.**

   If you can see the dotm part of the name, don't change it.

9. **Press Enter to lock in the new name.**

   Keep the File Explorer window open.

10. **Restart Word.**

    You don't need to do anything in Word, though you may notice that any problems you have related to the old Normal template are gone.

This trick may not work, unfortunately, especially if the problem isn't in the Normal template. If so, you can restore the original Normal.dotm file: Quit Word, delete the new Normal.dotm file and then rename the backup file to Normal.dotm or Normal.

>> Word stores its templates in the folder referenced by the pathname you type in Step 5. This location holds true for the current version of Word. Earlier versions of Word stored the template files in a different location.

>> The %USERPROFILE% thing is a Windows environment variable. It represents your account's home folder on the computer's primary storage device.

Word Startup Mode

Sometimes the problem you're experiencing with Word has to do with an add-in or extra feature. These features extend Word's capabilities, but they might also lead to problems. To ensure that the problem isn't with those extensions, you can run Word in Startup mode.

To run Word in Startup mode, obey these directions:

1. **Ensure that Word is closed.**

   You can't enter Startup mode when Word is open.

2. **Press the Win+R keyboard shortcut.**

   The Run dialog box appears.

3. **Type** WINWORD /A **into the box.**

WINWORD is Word's secret program name.

4. **Click OK.**

Word starts normally at this point, minus any add-ins. If they were the source of woe, the problem should be gone. If not, try running Word in Safe Mode; see the next section.

Word's add-ins are controlled from the Word Options dialog box. From the File tab, choose the Options command. Click the Add-ins category. The right side of the window lists available add-ins, as illustrated in Figure 25-3. To remove one, choose its type from the Manage menu, then click the Go button. In the next dialog box that appears, remove the check mark by the add-in's item to disable it. You can also remove the add-in by selecting it and clicking the Remove button.

The full Add-in list   Add-in types

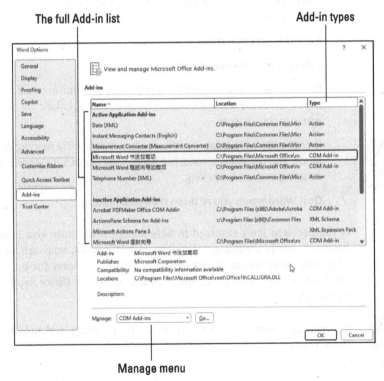

FIGURE 25-3:
Managing
Word's add-ins.

Manage menu

After an add-in has been disabled or removed, you can restart Word to see whether the issue is gone. If not, consider re-enabling the add-in or trying another approach.

Word Has a Safe Mode

Safe Mode works similarly to Startup mode. The difference is that Word starts without add-ins, modifications, or custom settings. What you get is the "raw" version of Word with no frills.

Follow these steps to start Word in Safe Mode:

1. **Ensure that Word is closed.**

2. **Press the Win+R keyboard shortcut.**

3. **Type** WINWORD /SAFE **into the Run dialog box.**

4. **Click OK.**

   Word starts, perhaps even filling the entire screen. The window title reads "Microsoft Word (Safe Mode)." A dialog box appears, explaining what you might do next.

5. **Click the Accept button, if prompted.**

6. **Attempt to replicate the problem in Word.**

   Do whatever you did before to see whether the issue arises. If so, the problem is with either the Normal template or an add-in; solutions are offered elsewhere in this chapter.

WARNING

   Do not attempt to create or edit any documents while running Word in Safe Mode. You can poke around, but keep in mind that Safe Mode is for trouble-shooting and not for writing.

7. **Quit Word when you're done troubleshooting.**

If the problem isn't resolved in Safe Mode, something else is at fault. You may have a PC hardware issue, a problem with Windows, malware, or any of a number of meddlesome issues. Check elsewhere in this chapter for information on troubleshooting document problems as well as using the Office Repair utility described in the next section.

TIP

You can also start Word in Safe Mode by pressing and holding the Ctrl key as Word starts.

The Office Repair Utility

Recognizing that "stuff" happens, Microsoft offers an Office Repair utility. Because Word is a part of the Office suite of programs, the Office Repair utility works to fix anything horrifically wrong with Word. Obey these steps:

1. **Close Word and any other Office programs.**

   You should do so now; otherwise, you're asked to do so again later.

2. **Right-click the Start button on the taskbar, and from the pop-up menu choose Installed Apps (Windows 11) or Apps and Features (Windows 10).**

   The Settings app starts.

3. **Scroll through the list of installed apps to find Microsoft 365 (Office).**

4. **In Windows 11, click the three dot (overflow) menu for the Microsoft 365 item and choose Modify; in Windows 10, click the Microsoft 365 (Office) item and choose the Advanced Options link.**

   The Settings app screen shows various items related to the Microsoft 365 installation. One of the headings is titled Reset, below which you find a button to Repair and a button for Reset.

5. **Click the Repair button.**

   The Office Repair utility attempts to figure out what's wrong. What happens next depends on whether anything is fixed. If something needs attention, obey the directions on the screen.

6. **Close the Settings app when you're done.**

If repairing doesn't work, repeat these steps and try the Reset option. This choice effectively reinstalls Microsoft Office *and* it resets all your settings. Your Word documents are unaffected.

Index

A

Accept button, 173
Accessibility Assistant pane, 218
Accessibility Checker, 217–219
Add a wrap point icon, 85
add an anchor icon, 98
Add Row gizmo, 49
add-ins, 374–375
Adjust List Indents dialog box, 30
Adobe Acrobat format, 152, 155–157
Align button menu, 100–101, 102
aligning
  cover page, 139–140
  graphics, 87–88
  objects on page for, 87–88
  shapes, 100–102
  text in table, 53–54
All Markup option, 171
Alt+X keyboard shortcut, 365
Amazon, 293
American Standard Code for Information Interchange (ASCII), 155
anchor points, 98
anti-virus program, 198
Apply As You Type feature, 306
Apply button, 273–274
arrangement
  aligning objects on page for, 87–88
  editing wrap points for, 83–85
  floating object in, 86–87
  inline option for, 82
  Inline Text, 278
  of picture, 120
  setting image's position in, 85–86
  setting options for, 80–81
  shape, 90
  Square option for, 82–83
  of text box, 120
  Through option for, 82–83
  Tight option for, 82–83
  Top and Bottom option for, 82–83
  wrapping text around object in, 82–83
artificial intelligence (AI), 207–213
Artistic Effects button, 115
ascender, 8
Aspect Ratio command, 112
Attach Template dialog box, 74
author
  document proofing for, 233–238
  document window for, 227–231
  Thesaurus for, 239
  tools for, 238–241
  translation tool for, 240
  word count for, 231–233
Auto Central, 300
AutoCaption option, 278
AutoComplete feature, 300
AutoCorrect dialog box, 301, 303, 306–307
AutoCorrect Exceptions dialog box, 302
AutoCorrect feature, 300, 301–305, 355
AutoCorrect Options button, 305
AutoCorrect Options icon, 301
AutoCorrect Options menu, 304
AutoCorrect Replace As You Type feature, 305
AutoCorrect tab, 300
AutoFit button, 51
AutoFormat As You Type feature, 300, 305–308
AutoFormat As You Type tab, 300, 306
AutoFormat feature, 13, 300, 355
AutoFormat tab, 300
automatic backup, 220–221
Automatically As You Type feature, 306
AutoRecover feature, 221
AutoText Building Blocks feature, 300, 308–310
AutoText feature, 299

B

back matter, 287
Back Up This Document warning, 195
background, 112–113, 191
background object, printing, 144
Backstage, 355
bars
Gradient Stops, 19
Mini Toolbar, 355–356
Quick Access toolbar, 254, 357–359
scrollbars, 357
status, 230–231
baseline, 8
Bézier curve handle, 98
bibliography, 276
Bibliography button, 276
block quote, 188–189
Body Text outline level, 65
book
collecting chapters into final document for, 260–261
one chapter per document of, 259–260
as one document, 258–259, 261–265
writing, 257–261
Bookmark button, 263, 321
Bookmark command, 261
bookmarking, 261–263, 279, 317
border
automatic, 307
for document, 145–146
for page, 145–146
paragraph, 370
for picture, 117–118
style, 370
in table, 55
for text box, 141
Borders and Shading command, 55
Borders and Shading dialog box, 145, 146
Borders button, 55, 370
bounding box, 83–85
Breaks button, 136
Building Blocks Organizer dialog box, 310
bulleted list, 307
buttons

Accept, 173
Apply, 273–274
Artistic Effects, 115
AutoCorrect Options, 305
AutoFit, 51
Bibliography, 276
Bookmark, 263, 321
Borders, 55, 370
Breaks, 136
Change Images, 345, 346
Chart, 130
Chart Elements, 131
Chart Filter, 131
Chart Styles, 131
Close, 138
Close Header and Footer, 35–36
Close Outline View, 246
Collapse, 253
Color, 115
Combo Box Content Control, 347
Compare, 174, 176
Corrections, 114
Crop, 111
Cross-Reference, 279
Date Picker Content Control, 346–347
Demote, 249
Demote to Body Text, 251
Design Mode, 339–340
Display for Review, 171–172
Distribute Columns, 52
Distribute Rows, 52
Document Stats, 217
Document Template, 73
Draw Table, 51
Editing, 170
Enable Content, 194
Enable Editing, 195
Eraser, 51
Expand, 253
Go to Footer, 36
Go to Header, 36
Header, 136, 146
Hyphenation, 27

Import/Export, 66
Insert, 273–274
Insert Caption, 277
Insert Citation, 275, 276
Insert Endnote, 272
Insert Footnote, 271
Insert Index, 282
Insert Table of Authorities, 186
Insert Table of Figures, 278
Layout Options, 79, 81, 86, 131, 141
Line Numbers, 182, 183
Link, 289
Macros, 324, 329, 330
Manage Styles, 66
Mark Citation, 185, 276
Mark Entry, 280
More, 56, 190
Move Down, 248
Move Up, 248
New Comment, 167
New Style, 64
Next, 41, 172
Next Citation, 185
Next Comment, 169
Next Footnote, 273
Numbering, 29, 32
Object, 123, 129, 260
Outline, 245
Page Borders, 145
Paste Options, 126
Picture Border, 117
Picture Content Control, 345–346
Picture Effects, 118
Plain Text Content Control, 344
Position, 92–93
Previous, 41
Previous Comment, 169
Promote, 249
Promote to Heading 1, 249
Properties, 340, 343, 344, 347
Quick Access toolbar, 331–334
Quick Parts, 233, 309, 312, 316, 317, 318, 319, 321, 322
Quick Print, 254

Record Macro, 326
Recover Unsaved Documents, 369
Reject, 173
Reset Picture, 116
Rich Text Content Control, 343–344
Shapes, 89–90
Share, 177
Shortcut Key, 363, 364
Show Comments, 169
Sort command, 58
Spelling & Grammar, 235
Split, 264
Split Table, 59
Stop Recording, 327
Symbol menu, 363
Table of Contents, 269
Track Changes, 170
View in One-Drive, 178
Watermark, 142
Word Count, 232
By gizmo, 14, 17

C

calculating, 124
cap height, 8
Cap Type menu, 21
capitalization, 302–303
Caption dialog box, 277
Caption Numbering dialog box, 278
Caption style, 278
captioning, 118–120, 277–278
Captions command, 118
cell, table, 46–47, 49–52
Change Back To command, 304
Change Images button, 345, 346
character spacing, 14–15
chart, 78, 130–132
Chart button, 130
Chart command, 130–132
Chart Elements button, 131
Chart Filter button, 131
Chart Styles button, 131
citation, 184–186, 273, 275–276

Click-and-Type feature, 355
Close button, 138
Close Header and Footer button, 35–36
Close Outline View button, 246
code, field as, 313–314
Code group, 324
collaboration
  ending, 179
  highlighting text for, 166
  inserting comment for, 167–168
  online, 176–179
  overview of, 165
  reviewing comments for, 168–169
  showing and hiding comments for, 169
  Track Changes feature for, 169–176
Collapse button, 253
color
  background, 191
  creating new, 97
  font, 191
  highlighting, 166
  of picture, 115
  for redaction, 190–191
  shape, 90, 95–97
  text, 288
  in Track Changes feature, 170
Color button, 115
column, table, 47, 48–49, 51–52
Combine command, 176
Combo Box Content Control button, 347
Combo Box Properties dialog box, 347–348
commands
  Aspect Ratio, 112
  assigning keyboard shortcut to, 361–363
  Bookmark, 261
  Borders and Shading, 55
  Captions, 118
  Change Back To, 304
  Chart, 130–132
  Combine, 176
  Compare, 175
  Crop to Shape, 112
  Customize the Ribbon, 359

Delete Cells, 49
Draw Table, 46, 51
Draw Text Box, 140
Edit Wrap Points, 84–85
Equation, 124
Export, 156
File Name, 146
Find, 229
Format Shape, 106
Full-Screen Mode, 228
Group, 102–103
Keep Source Formatting, 127, 353
Keep Text Only, 127, 354
Link & Keep Source Formatting, 127
Link & Use Destination Styles, 127
Merge Formatting, 354
Numbering, 28–29
Open File Location, 368
organizing, 360
Picture, 127
Quick Print, 253–254
Quick Tables, 46
=rand(), 328
Redo, 368
Scale, 13
Search, 369
  warning for, 368
commenting, 167–169
Compare button, 174, 176
Compare button menu, 176
Compare command, 175
Compare Documents dialog box, 174
Compatibility Checker dialog box, 154, 219–220
Compatibility Mode, 158
Compound Type menu, 21
connecting
  header, 40–41
  hyperlinks, 270, 279, 289–290
  Link button for, 289
  shape, 105
  text box, 104
  Word document and Excel worksheet, 126–127
  worksheet, 127–129

content control
  changing view of, 339–340
  defined, 337
  deleting, 341–342
  drop-down list as, 347–348
  fill-in-the-blanks item as, 343–344
  image as, 345–346
  inserting, 338–339
  multiline text field as, 344
  overview of, 338
  Rich Text, 338–339
  selecting a date as, 346–347
  setting properties of, 340–341
  useful, 342–348
Content Control Cannot Be Deleted option, 341
Content Control Properties dialog box, 341, 342
continuous section break, 283
Copies gizmo, 160, 161
Copilot, 2, 207–213, 292
Copilot icon, 208
Copilot pane, 208–209
copying, 109, 127–129
copyright laws, 109
copyrighting, 286
Corrections button, 114
Courier New typeface, 9
cover page, 135–142, 292
Create New Building Block dialog box, 309
Crop button, 111
Crop to Shape command, 112
cropping, 110–112
Cross-Reference button, 279
cross-references, 278–279
curve, editing, 98
Custom Dictionaries dialog box, 236–237
Customize Keyboard dialog box, 333, 362
Customize the Ribbon command, 359
customizing
  controlling text selection in, 353
  disabling annoying features in, 355–356
  keyboard shortcuts to commands in, 361–363
  overview of, 351
  Quick Access toolbar, 357–359

  Ribbon tabs, 359–361
  Ruler, 356–357
  scrollbars, 357
  setting text-pasting options in, 353–354
  shortcut key for symbol in, 363–364
  showing special characters in, 351–353
  specifying default document folder in, 356

D

Dash Type menu, 21
Date Picker Content Control button, 346–347
date-and-time field, 318–319
default document folder, 356
Define New Number Format dialog box, 33
Delete button menu, 48–49
Delete Cells command, 49
Demote button, 249
Demote to Body Text button, 251
descender, 8
Design Mode button, 339–340
Design tab, 11
desktop publishing (DTP) program, 107
Developer tab, 73, 324, 338
dialog boxes
  Adjust List Indents, 30
  Attach Template, 74
  AutoCorrect, 301, 303, 306–307
  AutoCorrect Exceptions, 302
  Borders and Shading, 145, 146
  Building Blocks Organizer, 310
  Caption, 277
  Caption Numbering, 278
  Combo Box Properties, 347–348
  Compare Documents, 174
  Compatibility Checker, 154, 219–220
  Content Control Properties, 341, 342
  Create New Building Block, 309
  Custom Dictionaries, 236–237
  Customize Keyboard, 333, 362
  Define New Number Format, 33
  Document Inspector, 214–215
  Field, 312
  File Conversion, 154, 159

dialog boxes *(continued)*
Footnote and Endnote, 273–274
Formatting, 64, 65
Formula, 59–60
General Options, 205
Index, 282–283
Insert Hyperlink, 290
Insert Picture, 108
Insert Table, 46
Layout, 93, 94, 95
Line Numbers, 183
Macros, 329
Manage Access, 179
Manage Styles, 66
Manual Hyphenation, 27–28
Mark Citation, 185
Mark Index Entry, 280, 281
Open, 67, 157, 202
Options, 324, 354, 360, 375
Organizer, 66
Page Number Format, 138
Page Setup, 148
Paragraph, 34–35
Printed Watermark, 143–144
Readability Statistics, 217
Record Macro, 327, 335
Save As, 153–154
Send Link or Share, 177
SmartArt Graphic, 122
Sort, 57
Style Pane Options, 62–63
Symbol, 364
Table of Authorities, 187
Table of Contents, 269
Table Properties, 52
Templates and Add-Ins, 73
Trusted Location, 197
Word Count, 232
dictionary, 236–237
Display for Review button, 171–172
Display for Review menu, 176
Distribute Columns button, 52
Distribute Rows button, 52

document
accepting or rejecting changes to, 172–173
accessibility of, 217–219
accessing properties of, 148–149
attaching template to, 74
building one long, 258–259, 261–265
choosing specific format of, 157–158
collecting chapters into, 260–261
comparing two versions of, 173–176
compatibility of, 219–220
cover pages for, 135–142
downloaded restriction for, 197–198
Excel worksheet in, 125–132
exporting, 153
as file, 151
filename extension of, 153, 154
filename placement of, 146–147
first draft of, 209–210
formats of, 152–153
gutter for, 147
highlighting, 166
inserting comment on, 167–168
inserting graphics into, 80–81, 159
inspection of, 214–220
locking, 171
lost, 222–223, 368–369
macro-enabled, 334–336
marking as final, 202–203
master, 260–261
mixing text and objects in, 79–80
multiple pages per sheet in, 162–163
non-text elements for, 78–79
as novel, 257–261
one chapter per, 259–260
page border for, 145–146
page numbering of, 37–38, 137–138, 316
password for, 203–205
as PDF, 152, 155–157
pinning, 369
print date of, 319
proofing, 233–238
protection for, 200–205
putting document into, 123

recovering text from, 158–159

recovery of, 220–223

repairing, 372–373

reviewing comments on, 168–169

saving, 153–155, 158, 369

searching for lost, 222–223

setting view of, 228–229

sharing, 177–178

storing, 151

summarizing, 213

for three-ring binding, 147–148

Track Changes feature for, 169–176

trust locations for, 196–197

updating template for, 72–73

viewing older version of, 221–222

watermark for, 142–144

word count of, 231–233, 272

Document Body style, 64

Document Compare tool, 173–176

document info field, 319–321

Document Inspector, 214–220

Document Inspector dialog box, 214–215

Document Property item, 339

document references

bibliography in, 276

citations and, 275–276

cross-, 278–279

in eBooks, 291

endnotes and, 271–274

figure captions and, 277–278

footnotes and, 271–274

index and, 279–283

overview of, 267–268

table of contents, 268–270

Document Stats button, 217

Document Template button, 73

document window, 227–231, 264, 265

downloaded documents restriction, 197–198

Draft view, 228

Draft with Copilot icon, 208, 211

Draw Table button, 51

Draw Table command, 46, 51

Draw Text Box command, 140

drawing, freeform shape, 91–92

drop-down list, as content control, 347–348

Drop-Down List icon, 348

E

eBook

adding document references in, 291

back matter for, 287

cover for, 292

finding publisher for, 293

foreword for, 286

formatting, 258, 286, 287–288

front matter for, 287

graphics for, 288–289, 292

hyperlinks for, 270, 279, 289–290

index for, 291

introduction for, 287

marketing, 295

pixels and, 289

preface for, 286

previewing final, 294

process for, 285–291

publishing tips for, 291–295

section break for, 286

setting price for, 294–295

special characters in, 288

table of contents in, 291

text color in, 288

word count for, 288

writing manuscript for, 286–287

Edit Wrap Points command, 84–85

editing, 170, 216–217, 233. *See also specific elements*

Editing button, 170

Editor pane, 216

Editor Score, 216–217

EditTime field, 321

effects

font, 10

Glow, 23–24

gradient, 19–21, 96

Grayscale, 115

picture, 115–116, 118

Reflection, 23–24

Shadow, 22–23

effects *(continued)*
shapes, 95–97
Soft Edges, 24
text, 17–24
The Elements of Style (Strunk and White), 234
em, defined, 11
em dash, 12–13, 307
em square, defined, 11
en dash, 12–13
Enable Content button, 194
Enable Editing button, 195
End Lines With menu, 154
endnotes, 272–273, 274
envelope template, 69–71. *See also* template
Equation command, 124
equations, summing, 124–125
Eraser button, 51
Excel worksheet, in document, 125–132
Expand button, 253
Export command, 156
exporting, 153
Extend Selection key (F8), 328

F

F8 (Extend Selection key), 328
fair use, 109, 292
features
Apply As You Type, 306
AutoComplete, 300
AutoCorrect, 300, 301–305, 355
AutoCorrect Replace As You Type, 305
AutoFormat, 13, 300, 355
AutoFormat As You Type, 300, 305–308
Automatically As You Type, 306
AutoRecover, 221
AutoText, 299
AutoText Building Blocks, 300, 308–310
Click-and-Type, 355
disabling, 355–356
Formatting Beginning of List, 307
Lock Tracking, 171
Recover Unsaved Documents, 222–223
Replace As You Type, 305

Set Left- and First-Indent with Tabs and Backspaces, 307
Track Changes, 170, 171–176
field
as code, 313–314
cookbook for, 315–322
date-and-time, 318–319
document info, 319–321
echoing text in, 321–322
EditTime, 321
finding, 314–315
inserting, 312–313
multiline text, 344
page number, 316
philosophy of, 311–315
Ref, 322
as text, 313–314
updating, 60, 270, 278, 283, 314, 316
UserName, 319
working with, behind the scenes, 313–314
Field dialog box, 312
figure captions, 277–278
File Block Settings, 199
File Conversion dialog box, 154, 159
file format
document, 152–153
legacy, 153
mysteries of, 371
opening strange, 157–159
unblocking, 198–200
Word Macro-Enabled Document, 335
File Name command, 146
filename
extension of, 153, 154
in footer, 320
in header, 320
placement of, 146–147
fill, text, changing, 19–21
fill-in-the-blanks item, as content control, 343–344
Find command, 229
first draft, 209–210
Fitzgerald, F. Scott, 258
Flesch Reading Ease scale, 217
font. *See also* text; typeface

ascender of, 8
attributes of, 9–11
AutoFormat feature for, 13
baseline of, 8
cap height of, 8
changing text scale of, 13–14
character spacing for, 14–15
color, 191
computer standards for, 12
consistency in, 9
defined, 7, 10
descender of, 8
describing text, 8–9
effects of, 10
height of, 14
hyphen in, 12–13
kerning of, 10, 15–16
knowledge of, 7–13
location of, 7–8
lowercase, 9
as majuscule, 9
as miniscule, 9
monospaced, 10
OpenType for, 12, 16
proportional, 10
sans serif, 9, 11, 65
selecting, 7–8
serif, 9, 11
size of, 10
slant of, 10
slope of, 10
text effects to, 17–24
tracking of, 10
TrueType for, 12
typeface of, 9
typography control for, 13–17
uppercase, 9
weight of, 10
width of, 10, 11
x-height of, 8
footer
creating odd and even, 41–42
document filename placement in, 146–147

filename in, 320
page numbers in, 37–39, 137–138
switching between header and, 36
Footer from Bottom gizmo, 39
Footnote and Endnote dialog box, 273–274
footnotes, 208, 271–272, 273, 274
foreign language translation, 240–241
foreword, 286
format, file
document, 152–153
legacy, 153
mysteries of, 371
opening strange, 157–159
unblocking, 198–200
Word Macro-Enabled Document, 335
Format Picture pane, 106, 114
Format Shape command, 106
Format Text Effects pane, 18–19, 22
formatting, eBook, 287–288
Formatting Beginning of List feature, 307
Formatting dialog box, 64, 65
formula, in table, 59–60
Formula dialog box, 59–60
Fractions setting, 307
framing, picture, 116–118
front matter, 287
Full-Screen Mode command, 228

G

General Options dialog box, 205
gizmos
By, 14, 17
Add Row, 49
Copies, 160, 161
Footer from Bottom, 39
Header Position From Top, 39
Left Indent, 31
Rotation, 95
Shape Height, 93
Shape Width, 93
Table Column Width, 52
Table Row Height, 52
Width, 21

Glow effect, 23–24. *See also* effects
Go to Footer button, 36
Go to Header button, 36
Google, 234
gradient, 19–21, 96
Gradient Fill, 19–21
Gradient Stops bar, 19
Grammar pane, 235–236
grammar-checking, 233–238
GrandView, 244
graphic. *See also* image; object
    aligning, 87–88
    for eBooks, 288–289, 292
    editing wrap points for, 83–85
    floating in front of or behind text, 86–87
    inserting, 80–81, 159
    layout choices for, 80–88
    In Line option for, 82
    mixing text with, 79–80
    setting position of, 85–86
    text and, 77–80
    transparency of, 87
    types of, 78
    wrapping text around, 82–83
Grayscale effect, 115. *See also* effects
Great Feature Wars, 77–78
The Great Gatsby (Fitzgerald), 258
gridlines, in table, 55
Group command, 102–103
guidelines, 141
gutter, 147

H

Hamlet (Shakespeare), 291
hanging indent, 30
header
    building, 35–36
    creating odd and even, 41–42
    filename in, 146–147, 320
    as linked, 40–41
    page numbers in, 37–39, 137–138
    placing objects in, 39

removing, 42
    resetting position of, 39–40
    sections of, 147
    switching between footer and, 36
    in tables, 53, 58
    typing text in, 36–37
    working with, in sections, 40–41
Header button, 136, 146
Header & Footer tab, 36, 39, 41–42, 136–137, 320
Header Position From Top gizmo, 39
heading style outline level, 64–65
Headings tab, 229
Helvetica Neue typeface, 9
hidden text, 352–353
highlighting, text, 166
Hoffman, Abbie, 292
Hyperlink warning, 194
hyperlinks, 270, 279, 289–290
hyphenation, 12–13, 25–28
Hyphenation button, 27

I

Ibid, 273
icons
    Add a wrap point, 85
    add an anchor, 98
    AutoCorrect Options, 301
    Copilot, 208
    Draft with Copilot, 208, 211
    Drop-Down List, 348
    Launcher, 52, 62, 94, 139, 147, 163, 230, 273
    macro, 332
    Move a wrap point, 85
    move an anchor, 98
    New Window, 265
    Numbering, 31
    Pencil, 91
    Plus, 90
    Print Layout, 228
    Quick Print, 254
    Read Mode, 228
    Remove a wrap point, 85

Remove an anchor, 98
Rich Text Content Control, 338–339
Send, 167
Swap, 174
Translate, 240
Web Layout, 228
image. *See also* graphic; object
  adding, from computer, 108–109
  adjusting color of, 115
  adjustments to, 110–116
  AI, 212
  alt text and, 218
  border for, 117–118
  captioning, 118–120, 277–278
  as content control, 345–346
  from Copilot, 208, 292
  copying, 109
  copyright laws and, 109
  cropping, 110–112
  defined, 78
  dragging, 109
  for eBooks, 288–289, 292
  effects to, 115–116, 118
  as fair use, 109, 292
  framing, 116–118
  framing in shape, 105–106
  making corrections to, 114
  as Online Pictures, 109
  overview of, 107
  pasting, 109
  preview of, 115
  public domain, 292
  removing background from, 112–113
  replacing, 110
  restoring, 116
  setting position of, 85–86
  as Stock Images, 108
  as watermark, 143–144
  worksheet as, 126
Import/Export button, 66
In Line option, for layout, 82
indent, left-right block, 188–189

indent, numbering, 30–31
index, 279–283, 291
Index dialog box, 282–283
INitial CAps tab, 303
Inline Text layout, 278
Insert button, 273–274
Insert Caption button, 277
Insert Citation button, 275, 276
Insert Endnote button, 272
Insert Footnote button, 271
Insert Hyperlink dialog box, 290
Insert Index button, 282
Insert Picture dialog box, 108
Insert tab, 78, 339
Insert Table dialog box, 46
Insert Table of Authorities button, 186
Insert Table of Figures button, 278
inserting
  comment, 167–168
  content control, 338–339
  field, 312–313
  graphic, 80–81, 159
  graphics, 80–81, 159
  index, 282–283
  object, 80–81
  page number fields, 316
  shape, 90–91
insertion pointer, 327
internal dictionary, 236–237
International Standard Book Number (ISBN), 293
introduction, 287
invitations, for online collaboration, 176–178

J

Join Type menu, 21

K

Keep Source Formatting command, 127, 353
Keep Text Only command, 127, 354
kerning, 10, 15–16

keyboard shortcut
  Alt+X, 365
  assigning to command, 361–363
  for macro, 333–334
  testing, 363
  Unicode system for, 365
Kindle Direct Publishing (KDP), 293
Kindle Previewer, 294

L

Launcher icon, 52, 62, 94, 139, 147, 163, 230, 273
lawyers
  left-right block indent for, 188–189
  line numbers on page for, 182–184
  marking citations for, 184–186
  redacting text for, 189–191
  Show/Hide command and, 186
  table of authorities for, 184–188
layout
  aligning objects on page for, 87–88
  choices for text in, 80–88
  editing wrap points for, 83–85
  floating object in, 86–87
  inline option for, 82
  Inline Text, 278
  of picture, 120
  setting image's position in, 85–86
  setting options for, 80–81
  shape, 90
  Square option for, 82–83
  of text box, 120
  Through option for, 82–83
  Tight option for, 82–83
  Top and Bottom option for, 82–83
  wrapping text around object in, 82–83
Layout dialog box, 93, 94, 95
Layout Options button, 79, 81, 86, 131, 141
Left Indent gizmo, 31
left-right block indent, 188–189
left-right pointer, 51
legacy formats, 153
legal profession
  left-right block indent for, 188–189

line numbers on page for, 182–184
  marking citations for, 184–186
  redacting text for, 189–191
  Show/Hide command and, 186
  table of authorities for, 184–188
ligature, 15–16
Line Numbers button, 182, 183
Line Numbers dialog box, 183
line style, for shapes, 95–97
Line tab, 34
lines, 182–184, 369–370
Link button, 289
Link & Keep Source Formatting command, 127
Link & Use Destination Styles command, 127
linking
  header, 40–41
  hyperlinks, 270, 279, 289–290
  Link button for, 289
  shape, 105
  text box, 104
  Word document and Excel worksheet, 126–127
  worksheet, 127–129
lists, numbered
  adjusting numbering indents in, 30–31
  automatic, 307
  creating custom paragraph, 33–34
  numbering paragraphs in, 28–30
  restarting numbered paragraphs in, 32
  skipping paragraph numbers in, 31–32
  starting at specific value, 32
local network storage, 197
Lock Aspect Ratio option, 94
Lock Tracking feature, 171
=lorem() function, 328

M

macro
  creating, 325
  defined, 323
  deleting, 330–331
  Developer tab and, 324
  Extend Selection key (F8) for, 328
  function of, 323

icon for, 332

insertion pointer for, 327

keyboard shortcut for, 333–334

macro-enabled documents benefits in, 334–336

macro-enabled template in, 335–336

overwriting, 328

Quick Access toolbar buttons for, 331–334

recording, 326–328

running, 329–330

saving, 326

shortcut-key combination for, 334

testing, 327

understanding, 325–326

macro security, 198

Macros button, 324, 329, 330

Macros dialog box, 329

magazine article, 258

Manage Access dialog box, 179

Manage Styles button, 66

Manage Styles dialog box, 66

Manual Hyphenation dialog box, 27–28

manuscript, 257–259

margin, 147, 189

Margins area, 147

Mark Citation button, 185, 276

Mark Citation dialog box, 185

Mark Entry button, 280

Mark Index Entry dialog box, 280, 281

marketing, eBook, 295

master document, creating, 260–261

Math AutoCorrect tab, 301

Melissa (virus), 193, 198

menus

Align button, 100–101, 102

AutoCorrect Options, 304

Cap Type, 21

Compare button, 176

Compound Type, 21

Dash Type, 21

Delete button, 48–49

Display for Review, 176

End Lines With, 154

Join Type, 21

Number Format, 273–274

Numbering, 29

Outline Level, 250

Paste Options, 126–127

Show As drop-down, 341

Show Level, 245–246

Status bar, 231

Symbol, 363

Table, 46

Merge Formatting command, 354

Microsoft Print, 156

Mini Toolbar, 355–356

minus sign character, 26

monospaced typeface, 10. *See also* typeface

More button, 56, 190

Move a wrap point icon, 85

move an anchor icon, 98

Move Down button, 248

Move Up button, 248

multiline text field, as content control, 344

N

narrative, adding, in outline, 251–252

Narrative (text) topic handle, 245

Navigation pane, 229, 254–255

New Comment button, 167

New Style button, 64

New Window icon, 265

Next button, 41, 172

Next Citation button, 185

Next Comment button, 169

Next Footnote button, 273

Next Page section break, 286

No Markup option, 172

Nolan, Christopher, 268

non-text elements, 78–79, 80–88

Normal template, 335, 373–374

Notepad program, 155

novel

collecting chapters into final document for, 260–261

one chapter per document of, 259–260

as one document, 258–259, 261–265

writing, 257–261

novella, 257

Number Format menu, 273–274
numbered lists
  adjusting numbering indents in, 30–31
  automatic, 307
  creating custom paragraph, 33–34
  numbering paragraphs in, 28–30
  restarting numbered paragraphs in, 32
  skipping paragraph numbers in, 31–32
  starting at specific value, 32
numbering, of lines, 182–184
numbering, page, 37–38, 137–138, 269–270, 316
Numbering button, 29, 32
Numbering command, 28–29
Numbering icon, 31
Numbering menu, 29
NumPages field, 38

O

object. *See also* graphic; image; shape
  aligning, 87–88
  defined, 78–79
  editing wrap points for, 83–85
  floating in front of or behind text, 86–87
  inserting, 80–81
  layout choices for, 80–88
  In Line option for, 82
  mixing text with, 79–80
  printing background, 144
  setting position of, 85–86
  SmartArt, 122–123
  transparency of, 87
  wrapping text around, 82–83
Object button, 123, 129, 260
Office Repair utility, 377
OneDrive, 178, 195, 221–222
OneDrive Message warning, 194
online collaboration, 176–179. *See also* collaboration
Online Pictures, 109
Open dialog box, 67, 157, 202
Open File Location command, 368
Open Styles pane, 229
OpenDocument format, 152, 154
OpenType, 12, 16

Options dialog box, 324, 354, 360, 375
Organizer dialog box, 66
Original option, 172
Other Corrections tab, 303
outline
  adding narrative in, 251–252
  collapsing and expanding outline topics in, 252–253
  construction of, 246–252
  demoting or promoting a topic in, 248–250
  heading styles for, 246
  moving topics in, 247–248, 250–251
  narrative in, 251–252
  Navigation pane for, 254–255
  Outlining tab for, 245–246, 250
  overview of, 243–244
  presentation, 252–255
  printing, 253–254
  shortcuts for, 255
  subtopics in, 249
  text, 21–22
  text selection in, 251
  topics in, 249
  top-level topics for, 246–247
  view, 244–246
Outline button, 245
Outline Level menu, 250
Outline view, 228
outline-level, style, 64–65
Outlining tab, 245–246, 250

P

page
  aligning objects on, 87–88
  blank, 371
  border for, 145–146
  centering, 139–140
  cover, 135–142
  distributing shape across, 101–102
  footers for, 35–43
  headers for, 35–43
  hyphenation in, 25–28
  line numbers on, 182–184
  mixing elements on, 79–80

numbering for, 37–39, 137–138, 269–270, 316

position setting of, 86

widow and orphan control for, 34–35

Page Borders button, 145

Page Breaks tab, 34

Page Number Format dialog box, 138

page numbering, 37–38, 137–138, 269–270, 316

Page Setup dialog box, 148

Pages tab, 230

panes

Accessibility Assistant, 218

adding, 229–230

Copilot, 208–209

Editor, 216

Format Picture, 106, 114

Format Text Effects, 18–19, 22

Grammar, 235–236

Navigation, 229, 254–255

Open Styles, 229

Restrict Editing, 201, 202

Reviewing, 170, 172

Selection, 99–100

Spelling, 235–236

Styles, 62, 63, 64, 229

Thesaurus, 239

paragraph

adjusting numbering indents in, 30–31

borders, 370

creating custom numbers for, 33–34

eBook, 288

handles, 245

hanging indent for, 30

hyphenating in, 25–28

indenting, 188–189

left-right block indent in, 188–189

line numbers in, 184

Normal, 251

numbering, 28–30

numbering at specific value, 32

restarting numbered, 32

skipping numbers in, 31–32

Paragraph dialog box, 34–35

passim, 188

password, for document, 203–205

Paste Options button, 126

Paste Options menu, 126–127

pasting, 90, 109, 127–129, 353–354

path, defined, 98

PDF, 152, 155–157, 158, 288

Pencil icon, 91

personal envelope, 69–71

personalizing

controlling text selection in, 353

disabling annoying features in, 355–356

keyboard shortcuts to commands in, 361–363

overview of, 351

Quick Access toolbar, 357–359

Ribbon tabs, 359–361

Ruler, 356–357

scrollbars, 357

setting text-pasting options in, 353–354

shortcut key for symbol in, 363–364

showing special characters in, 351–353

specifying default document folder in, 356

picture. See also graphic; object

adding, from computer, 108–109

adjusting color of, 115

adjustments to, 110–116

AI, 212

alt text and, 218

border for, 117–118

captioning, 118–120, 277–278

as content control, 345–346

from Copilot, 208, 292

copying, 109

copyright laws and, 109

cropping, 110–112

defined, 78

dragging, 109

for eBooks, 288–289, 292

effects to, 115–116, 118

as fair use, 109, 292

framing, 116–118

framing in shape, 105–106

making corrections to, 114

as Online Pictures, 109

picture *(continued)*
  overview of, 107
  pasting, 109
  preview of, 115
  public domain, 292
  removing background from, 112–113
  replacing, 110
  restoring, 116
  setting position of, 85–86
  as Stock Images, 108
  as watermark, 143–144
  worksheet as, 126
Picture Border button, 117
Picture command, 127
Picture Content Control button, 345–346
Picture Effects button, 118
Picture Format tab, 108–109
pixels, for eBooks, 289
Plain Text Content Control button, 344
plain text format, 152, 154, 155
Plus icon, 90
point size, 13
Policy Tip warning, 194, 195
Position button, 92–93
preface, 286
presentation, outline, 252–255
Previous button, 41
Previous Comment button, 169
Print Layout icon, 228
Print screen, 161
PrintDate field, 319
Printed Watermark dialog box, 143–144
printing
  background objects, 144
  blank page, 371–372
  collated, 160
  duplex, 160–162
  multiple copies, 160
  multiple pages per sheet, 162–163
  outline, 253–254
  overview of, 160
  to PDF, 156, 157
  for three-ring binding, 147–148
  tips for, 151
    two-sided, 160–162
    uncollated, 160
Privacy Option warning, 194
professional footer
  creating odd and even, 41–42
  document filename placement in, 146–147
  filename in, 320
  page numbers in, 37–39, 137–138
  switching between header and, 36
professional header
  building, 35–36
  creating odd and even, 41–42
  filename in, 146–147, 320
  as linked, 40–41
  page numbers in, 37–39, 137–138
  placing objects in, 39
  removing, 42
  resetting position of, 39–40
  sections of, 147
  switching between footer and, 36
  in tables, 53, 58
  typing text in, 36–37
  working with, in sections, 40–41
Promote button, 249
Promote to Heading 1 button, 249
proofing, document, 233–238
properties, document, 148–149
Properties button, 340, 343, 344, 347
proportional typeface, 10. *See also* typeface
Protected View warning, 194, 195, 197–198
protection
  anti-virus program for, 198
  for document, 200–205
  document password for, 203–205
  downloaded documents restriction for, 197–198
  macro, 198
  marking document as final for, 202–203
  read-only protection for, 202–203
  safe list for, 196–197
  setting text-editing restrictions for, 200–202
  Trust Center for, 195–200
  unblocking file types in, 198–200
  warnings, 193–195
prototype document, creating, 68

public domain images, 292
publisher, finding, 293
publishing, eBooks, 291–295

Q

Quick Access toolbar, 254, 357–359
Quick Access toolbar button, 331–334
Quick Parts button, 233, 309, 312, 316, 317, 318, 319, 321, 322
Quick Print button, 254
Quick Print command, 253–254
Quick Print icon, 254
Quick Tables command, 46

R

=rand() command, 328
Read Mode icon, 228
Readability Statistics dialog box, 217
read-only protection, 202–203
Record Macro button, 326
Record Macro dialog box, 327, 335
Recover Text from Any File option, 159
Recover Unsaved Documents button, 369
Recover Unsaved Documents feature, 222–223
recovery, document, 220–223
Recycle Bin, 223, 369
Redaction style, 189–191
Redo command, 368
Ref field, 322
Reference tab, 276
references, document
  bibliography in, 276
  citations and, 275–276
  cross-, 278–279
  in eBooks, 291
  endnotes and, 271–274
  figure captions and, 277–278
  footnotes and, 271–274
  index and, 279–283
  overview of, 267–268
  table of contents, 268–270
Reflection effect, 23–24. *See also* effects

Reject button, 173
removable storage, 369
Remove a wrap point icon, 85
Remove an anchor icon, 98
Remove Content Control When Contents Are Edited option, 342
repairing, document, 372–373
Replace As You Type feature, 305
Reset Picture button, 116
resizing, shape, 93–94
Restrict Editing pane, 201, 202
Results tab, 230
Reviewing pane, 170, 172
rewriting, 211–212
Ribbon
  custom tab on, 359–361
  limitations of, 315
  Quick Access toolbar on, 357–359
  showing or hiding, 228
  tabs on, 324
Rich Text Content Control button, 343–344
Rich Text Content Control icon, 338–339
Rich Text Format, 152, 155
rotating, shape, 94–95
Rotation gizmo, 95
row, table, 47, 48–49, 51–52
royalty, 294
Ruler, 30, 356–357

S

safe list, 196–197
Safe Mode, 376
sans serif, 9, 11, 65
Save As dialog box, 153–154
saving
  documents, 153–155, 158, 369
  macro, 326, 335
  to OneDrive, 221–222
scale, text, 13–14. *See also* text
Scale command, 13
Scribble tool, 91
scripted typeface, 12. *See also* typeface
scrollbars, 357

section break, 283, 286

security
  anti-virus program for, 198
  document password for, 203–205
  document protection for, 200–205
  downloaded documents restriction for, 197–198
  macro, 198
  marking document as final for, 202–203
  read-only protection for, 202–203
  safe list for, 196–197
  setting text-editing restrictions for, 200–202
  Trust Center for, 195–200
  unblocking file types in, 198–200
  warnings, 193–195
Security Alert warning, 194
Selection pane, 99–100
Send icon, 167
Send Link or Share dialog box, 177
serif, 9, 11
Set Left- and First-Indent with Tabs and Backspaces
    feature, 307
Shadow effect, 22–23. See also effects
Shakespeare, William, 291
shape
  aligning, 100–102
  arranging, 99–100
  Bézier curve handle of, 98
  changing shape of, 97–98
  colors for, 95–97
  defined, 78
  distributing, 101–102
  drawing freeform, 91–92
  editing curve of, 98
  effects for, 95–97
  framing picture in, 105–106
  freeform, 91–92
  grouping multiple, 102–103
  inserting, 90–91
  line styles for, 95–97
  linking, 105
  modifying, 90
  multiple, 99–103
  overview of, 89–90
  path of, 98

  position of, 92–93
  resizing, 93–94
  rotating, 94–95
  stack of, 99–100
  swapping, 97
  text inside, 103–105
  undefining, 98
  unlinking, 105
Shape Format tab, 90, 95
Shape Height gizmo, 93
Shape Styles Group, 95–96
Shape Width gizmo, 93
Shapes button, 89–90
Share button, 177
sharing
  ending, 179
  highlighting text for, 166
  inserting comment for, 167–168
  online, 176–179
  overview of, 165
  reviewing comments for, 168–169
  showing and hiding comments for, 169
  Track Changes feature for, 169–176
sharing, document, 177–178
shortcut, keyboard
  Alt+X, 365
  assigning to command, 361–363
  for macro, 333–334
  testing, 363
  Unicode system for, 365
Shortcut Key button, 363, 364
shortcut-key combination, 334, 363–364. See also
    keyboard shortcut
Show All Formatting Marks option, 352
Show As drop-down menu, 341
Show Comments button, 169
Show Level menu, 245–246
Show/Hide command, 186, 281, 352, 371, 372
Simple Markup option, 171
The Simpsons (television show), 125
slant, typeface, 10. See also typeface
smart quotes, 307
SmartArt, 78, 122–123
SmartArt Graphic dialog box, 122

Soft Edges effect, 24. *See also* effects
Solid Fill, 19
Sort command button, 58
Sort dialog box, 57
special characters, 288, 351–353
spell-checking, 233–238
Spelling & Grammar button, 235
Spelling item, 217
Spelling pane, 235–236
Split button, 264
Split Table button, 59
Square option, for layout, 82–83
Start Screen, 355
Startup mode, 374–375
status bar, 230–231
Status bar menu, 231
Steal This Book (Hoffman), 292
Stock Images, 108
Stock Keeping Unit (SKU), 293
Stop Automatically Correcting command, 304
Stop Recording button, 327
style
  border, 370
  Caption, 278
  frame, 116–117
  heading, 64–65, 246
  management of, 61–67
  modifying, 63
  outline level of, 64–65
  Redaction, 189–191
  selecting instances of, 63–64
  for shapes, 95–97
  stealing from another document, 66–67
  in templates, 66
Style Pane Options dialog box, 62–63
Style settings, 341
Styles pane, 62, 63, 64, 229
Subscript command, 16–17
superscript, 271
Superscript command, 16–17
Swap icon, 174
symbol, shortcut key for, 363–364

Symbol command, 124
Symbol dialog box, 364
Symbol menu button, 363

T

tabbed list, to table, 46
table
  adjusting row and column size in, 51–52
  aligning text in, 53–54
  assembling, 45–46
  cells in, 46–47
  column in, 47, 48–49
  editing, 46–52
  formats to, 55–56
  formulas in, 59–60
  function of, 45
  gridlines in, 55
  header row for, 53, 58
  math in, 59–60
  merging and splitting cells in, 49–51
  preset, 46
  row in, 47, 48–49
  selecting items within, 47–48
  setting size of, 51
  setting text direction in, 54–55
  sorting, 56–58
  splitting between two pages, 58–59
  style of, 55–56
  from tabbed list, 46
  working with text in, 46–47
Table Column Width gizmo, 52
Table Design tab, 55, 56
Table Layout tab, 52, 53–54, 57, 59
Table menu, 46
table of authorities, 184–188, 276
Table of Authorities dialog box, 187
table of contents, 268–270, 291
Table of Contents button, 269
Table of Contents dialog box, 269
Table Properties dialog box, 52
Table Row Height gizmo, 52

Table Styles gallery, 56
tabs
  AutoCorrect, 300
  AutoFormat, 300
  AutoFormat As You Type, 300, 306
  Design, 11
  Developer, 73, 324, 338
  Header & Footer, 36, 39, 41–42, 136–137, 320
  Headings, 229
  INitial CAps, 303
  Insert, 78, 339
  Line, 34
  Math AutoCorrect, 301
  Other Corrections, 303
  Outlining, 245–246, 250
  Page Breaks, 34
  Pages, 230
  Picture Format, 108–109
  Reference, 276
  Results, 230
  Ribbon, 359–361
  Shape Format, 90, 95
  stops, 37
  Table Design, 55, 56
  Table Layout, 52, 53–54, 57, 59
  View, 324
template
  corruption of, 373
  custom, 68
  defined, 337
  envelope, 69–71
  function of, 67–68
  macro-enabled, 335–336
  modifying, 71–72
  Normal, 335, 373–374
  reassigning, 74
  styles in, 66
  text in, 71
  updating, 72–73
Templates and Add-Ins dialog box, 73
text. See also font; typeface
  adjusting position of, 16–17
  aligning in table, 53–54

bookmarking, 261–263
changing fill of, 19–21
changing scale of, 13–14
character spacing for, 14–15
color, 288
controlling selection of, 353
direction of, in table, 54–55
dynamic, 311
echoing, in field, 321–322
editing restrictions for, 200–202
effects of, 17–24
field as, 313–314
fill of, 19–21
floating object in front of or behind, 86–87
Glow effect for, 23–24
graphics and, 77–80
hidden, 352–353
highlighting, 166
inside shape, 103–105
kerning of, 15–16
layout choices for, 80–88
ligatures of, 15–16
line on, 370
multiline field, 344
object mixing with, 79–80
outline for, 21–22
position of, 16–17
redacting, 189–191
Reflection effect for, 23–24
restrictions for, 200–202
rewriting, 211–212
scale of, 13–14
section break for, 286
selection of, in outline, 251
shadow for, 22–23
as SmartArt, 78, 122–123
static, 311
superscript, 271
in table, 46–47, 53–55
in templates, 71
for titles, 140–141
varieties of, 121–122
working with, in table, 46–47

text box
  for captioning pictures, 119–120
  creating inside shape, 103–104
  defined, 78
  linking, 104
  management of, 142
  resizing and positioning, 141
  for titles, 140–142
Text Box command, 103–104
Text Highlight Color command, 166
Thesaurus pane, 239
three-ring binding, printing for, 147–148
Through option, for layout, 82–83
Tight option, for layout, 82–83
Times New Roman typeface, 9
title, 140–142, 291–292
tools
  for author, 238–241
  Document Compare, 173–176
  Scribble, 91
  translation, 240
  Zoom, 92
Top and Bottom option, for layout, 82–83
Topic with subtopics handle, 245
Topic without subtopics handle, 245
top-level heading style, 65
top-level topics, in outline, 246–247
Track Changes button, 170
Track Changes feature, 170, 171–176
tracking, 10
Translate command, 240
Translate icon, 240
transparency, 87
TrueType, 12
Trust Center, 195–200
Trusted Location dialog box, 197
typeface. See also font; text
  character spacing for, 14–15
  choosing, 11–12
  Courier New, 9
  defined, 7, 9, 10
  effects of, 10
  height of, 14

Helvetica Neue, 9
  monospaced, 10
  proportional, 10
  scripted, 12
  selecting, 11
  size of, 10
  slant of, 10
  slope of, 10
  typography control for, 13–17
  weight of, 10, 11
  width of, 10
typos, replacing, 303–304

U

unbreakable hyphen, 28
Undo command, 116, 367–368
Ungroup command, 103
Unicode system, 365
Update Citations and Bibliography command, 276
Update Field command, 60, 270, 278, 283
updating
  bibliography, 276
  citations, 276
  fields, 60, 270, 278, 283, 314, 316
  index, 283
  template, 72–73
Use Destination Styles command, 127
UserName field, 319

V

View in One-Drive button, 178
View tab, 324
virus, 193, 198
Visual Basic for Applications (VBA), 323

W

warning, 193–195, 368
watermark, 142–144
Watermark button, 142
Web Layout icon, 228
web page format, 152

websites
  Acrobat Reader, 157
  Cheat Sheet, 4
  R. R. Bowker, 293
  Wabooli, 3
  YouTube/@dangookin, 4
weight, typeface, 10, 11. *See also* typeface
widow and orphan control, 34–35
width, typeface, 10. *See also* typeface
Width gizmo, 21
window, opening second, 265
Windows, 369
Word appearance, 356–357
word count, 231–233, 272, 288
Word Count button, 232
Word Count dialog box, 232
Word document format, 152, 154, 155, 158
WordPerfect format, 152, 158

wrap point, 83–85
writer
  document proofing for, 233–238
  document window for, 227–231
  Thesaurus for, 239
  tools for, 238–241
  translation tool for, 240
  word count for, 231–233

X

x-height, 8
XML format, 152
XPS document format, 156

Z

Zoom tool, 92

About the Author

Dan Gookin has been writing about computers since the reign of Charles II. He combines his love of writing with his gizmo fascination to create books that are informative, entertaining, and not boring. Having written over 170 titles with 12 million copies in print translated into over 30 languages on several planets, Dan can attest that his method of crafting technology tomes seems to work.

Perhaps his most famous title is the original *DOS For Dummies*, published in 1991. It became the world's fastest-selling computer book, at one time moving more copies per week than *The New York Times* number-one bestseller (though, as a reference, it could not be listed on the Times' Best Sellers list). That book spawned the entire line of *For Dummies* books, which remains a publishing phenomenon to this day.

Dan's least famous title is *Compute's Problem Solving with Sidekick Plus* (Compute! Books, 1989).

Dan's most popular titles include *PCs and Laptops For Dummies*, *Troubleshooting and Maintaining PCs All-In-One For Dummies*, and *C Programming For Dummies*. His website is www.wambooli.com, which was once ranked 104,578,296th most popular website on the Internet.

Dan holds a degree in Communications/Visual Arts from the University of California, San Diego. He lives in the Pacific Northwest with his wife, children, animals, and various robots. He enjoys being sesquipedalian and inaniloquent.

Publisher's Acknowledgments

Executive Editor: Steven Hayes

Project Editor: Christopher Morris

Copy Editor: Christopher Morris

Technical Editor: Guy Hart-Davis

Managing Editor: Murari Mukandan

Production Editor: Tamilmani Varadharaj

Cover Image: © Morsa Images/Getty Images